Sports *Phil Andrews*
Journalism
A Practical Guide

⑤SAGE Publications
London ● Thousand Oaks ● New Delhi

First published 2005

Apart from any fair dealing for the purposes of research or private
study, or criticism or review, as permitted under the Copyright,
Designs and Patents Act, 1988, this publication may be
reproduced, stored or transmitted in any form, or by any means,
only with the prior permission in writing of the publishers, or in
the case of reprographic reproduction, in accordance with the
terms of licences issued by the Copyright Licensing Agency.
Inquiries concerning reproduction outside those terms should be
sent to the publishers.

SAGE Publications Ltd
1 Oliver's Yard
55 City Road
London EC1Y 1SP

SAGE Publications Inc.
2455 Teller Road
Thousand Oaks, California 91320

SAGE Publications India Pvt Ltd
B-42, Panchsheel Enclave
Post Box 4109
New Delhi 110 017

British Library Cataloguing in Publication data

A catalogue record for this book is available
from the British Library

ISBN 1 4129 0270 3
ISBN 1 4129 0271 1 (pbk)

Library of Congress Control Number: 2004099433

BK
$99.95

Typeset by C&M Digitals (P) Ltd., Chennai, India
Printed and bound in Great Britain by Athenaeum Press, Gateshead

57355716

Contents

The best job in the world?

It's the best job in the world, isn't it? Travelling the globe, watching the big sporting events free from the best seats in the stadium, mingling with star players and athletes, seeing your byline in the newspapers or broadcasting to millions on radio or television, and being paid a lot of money for the privilege. That's the way many people see a sports writer's job. The reality can be rather different. Hard and demanding work to tight deadlines, long and unsocial hours (most of them worked in the evenings or at weekends), a lot of time spent in research and preparation, acquiring the same depth of knowledge about the sports you cover as the most fanatical of your readers or listeners, earning the trust of a wide range of contacts among players, coaches and administrators, and the skill to write accurately and entertainingly at great speed and often under difficult conditions.

Nevertheless, there is no shortage of people willing to put up with all that for the undoubted rewards and satisfactions sports journalism brings. Jobs in the media, and in sports journalism in particular, are more avidly sought after than almost any other. Fortunately, the opportunities are expanding, too – though there will never be enough seats in press boxes to accommodate every aspiring sports journalist.

Sport is the fastest-growing sector in the British media, and the same applies in most other English-speaking countries. Not long ago, the exploits of muddied oafs and flannelled fools were confined to two or three pages at the back of newspapers, and to weekend afternoons on radio and television. Today, sports men and women are among the best-known and best-paid people on the planet. The world wants to read and hear about them and the ranks of those who are paid to satisfy that demand are expanding accordingly. Sports people now feel the glare of the media spotlight more powerfully than almost anyone else in society. It's not unusual to find a hundred journalists covering a single match in English soccer's Premier League, and the jobs of national team managers are second in importance, in media terms, only to those of the head of state.

Sports coverage is vitally important to the health and prosperity of the print and broadcast media. The British newspaper market is the most competitive in the world, and increasingly, that competition takes place on the sports pages. From two or three pages at the back of the paper a few years ago, many national daily and Sunday newspapers have now expanded their sports coverage to daily, separate sections of up to 28 broadsheet pages – more space than they devote to general news or the arts.

In broadcasting, sport has spawned new radio stations in both the public and commercial sectors – BBC 5Live and Talksport. It's also in the vanguard of the battle for television ratings. The rights to cover important sporting events are fiercely contested between both terrestrial and satellite and cable channels. The success of Sky TV as a satellite broadcaster has not been built on the first television run of feature films, as originally intended, but around its acquisition of the rights to cover major sporting events live. As a consequence, the demands of the broadcasters have reshaped the sporting calendar, fragmenting the traditional Saturday afternoon hegemony in soccer, encouraging day/night cricket matches and converting rugby league from a winter into a summer sport.

The growth of the internet has generated a huge variety of websites devoted to sport, operated by media organisations, sports clubs and organisations, and fans. This new technology also means job opportunities for sports journalists because it offers an extra source of income to the media by providing sports updates and reports on the web or by mobile phone. In addition to their websites, the biggest clubs now also have their own television channels, a trend that is likely to expand as more sports organisations wake up to the commercial possibilities.

It's not difficult to see why sport is so attractive to the media. They have the same number of pages and the same amount of airtime to fill no matter what is happening (or not happening) in the world, but hard news is an unpredictable commodity. What's more, stories generated by governments and politicians are often found boring by many people and, as the political parties huddle together in the middle ground for popular support, have lost their power to generate controversy and debate.

Sport is the exact opposite. It is predictable in the sense that the media know months in advance when the big events are going to happen, it has its own in-built excitement and drama, and a cast of stars. Hollywood should be so lucky.

The international sporting calendar goes from World Cups to Olympic Games to Test matches to Super Bowls to Grand Nationals and Boat Races without cease. Sport could have been invented for an industry selling a daily dose of sensation.

It could also have been devised as a ready-made source of material for those who enjoy writing. That is just as important an element in successful sports writing as enjoying sport. 'Sports writer', as the term suggests, is made up of two words – 'sports' and 'writer' – and to succeed you will need to be enthusiastic about both. It's not enough merely to enjoy football or athletics or racing: you must be able to convey your knowledge and enthusiasm to others in a lively and entertaining way, and to be willing to devote as much time to practising your writing skills as the sports people about whom you are writing spend practising theirs.

Sports journalism is a specialist form of writing, and it is broken down into narrower specialisms. The major sports, such as soccer, cricket, rugby, racing, golf, tennis and athletics, are usually covered by specialists in these fields. Why? Because fans know their sports and their teams inside out, and unless sports journalists want to look foolish and ill-informed, they need to be equally knowledgeable. Keeping abreast of the daily developments in a major sport is a full-time job. Only a few journalists are able to pick and choose the sports and events they cover. These are usually the brightest, wittiest or most incisive writers – columnists or feature writers with a roving brief to provide 'colour' pieces about the key moments in the world of sport.

But sports writing consists of more than just covering the big events. The media have space to fill, no matter what is going on, and they do so by whetting the appetites of their consumers with pieces building up to events, profiling the participants, and analysing performances, as well as with a steady flow of background news and features. And sport often bursts out of the sports pages when the activities of high-profile people hit the front pages or the top of the news bulletins, or cross over into other specialist areas such as fashion, business or medicine.

To cover sport successfully, you need to know the requirements of the medium for which you are working, and you need to understand the audience who will be consuming your work. Serious and popular newspapers and specialist sports magazines have unique styles, and sport is covered differently by print journalists and broadcasters. Radio demands a different set of skills from those of television, while internet journalism is a whole new ballgame. This book will help you to acquire those skills. The craft of the sports journalist *can* be learned. Indeed, beginners have a head start over those seeking to acquire almost any other skill. Many of us consume the work of professional sports journalists every day, and will have absorbed some of their skills unconsciously. What's more, the tools of the trade are cheap and readily to hand: pen and paper and access to radio, television and newspapers are all that is required.

The following chapters break down the job of the sports journalist into its component parts, and look at every aspect of the skills required in detail. They also offer exercises designed to help you internalise those skills and hone them to professional standards.

The book ends with advice on how to get started in a very competitive field. That is something which often demands great perseverance and a long apprenticeship. But if you're prepared for all this, sports journalism *can* be the best job in the world.

Context setting: media environments

Summary Chapter Contents

The media's influence on sport
Sport's influence on the media
Organisation and practice of sports departments and sports journalists
Media markets and audience awareness
Sport's cultural significance

Learning Objectives

- To understand the organisation and needs of the media
- To recognise the importance of sports journalism to the media's commercial success
- To identify the constraints within which media organisations operate in the sports market
- To understand what determines the sports agenda of news organisations in different markets
- To recognise how media audiences determine content and style

The media has an important and growing role in the culture of developed countries. As leisure time has expanded and access to radio and television has become almost universal, not only in the home but also in cars and in pubs and clubs, so the demand for material with which to fill the burgeoning number of media outlets has grown. The expansion of leisure has also led to an upsurge in public interest in sport, and a corresponding growth in the commercial success of major sports clubs and organisations. Manchester United, Real Madrid and the New York Yankees are no longer simply sports clubs but global brands.

If media organisations are to remain successful in an extremely competitive market, they must reflect such movements in our culture and in the interests of their consumers. Indeed, the media not only reflect the culture in which they operate and the interests of their readers and viewers, they also help to form that culture and those interests.

The media's influence on sport

Much of the recent growth of interest in sport has been driven by the media, in particular satellite television, which has bought the rights to major sporting events and promoted them vigorously as one of the most effective ways of selling subscriptions to its services. To compete, terrestrial television (and radio) channels have had to follow suit. This has driven up the cost of media rights and vastly increased the income of sports clubs, governing bodies and professional sports men and women. It has been the major factor in turning many sports clubs into big businesses.

But the money television has put into sport has also given it the power to shape sports to its own ends. Beginning with the introduction by the Australian media mogul Kerry Packer of floodlit international cricket in the 1970s, television went on to fuel the massive growth of interest in soccer worldwide and the expansion of competitions like the European Champions League. It has even turned the traditions of some sports on their heads. Rugby League, a winter game in England for more than a century, has now become a summer sport, for the benefit of the broadcasters. Television has turned sport into a commodity and a sales tool.

Sport's influence on the media

Media organisations have grown and adapted accordingly. New radio stations and television channels have been set up devoted specifically to sport. They have developed radical new programmes such as sports phone-ins and rolling results services to attract and maintain viewers and listeners. There has been a similar growth in specialist and lifestyle publications aimed at specific sections of the media audience, such as young men. They have carved out niche markets, either by covering sport in general or by devoting themselves to individual sports.

Newspapers throughout the developed world are devoting more and more space to sport. This is partly in response to the general upsurge of interest in sport, which is common to all socio-economic classes, and partly because newspapers recognise the influence of television on people's lives, and try to reflect it in there own coverage. The fact that multinational media organisations like Rupert Murdoch's International Media Group own both satellite television networks and newspapers has undoubtedly influenced the promotion of televised sport in those newspapers. And even those newspaper groups which do not have a stake in television have been forced to pay greater attention to televised sport because their readers subscribe to satellite television channels and have come to expect that service.

With the arrival of the internet, a number of websites devoted to sport were set up by organisations who sought to support them through advertising and by selling online services. As with other online ventures, many of these proved to be unsustainable, and the bursting of the dot.com bubble was followed by a period of consolidation. Many of these sites are now in the ownership of online betting companies, who use the sports content of the sites as bait to attract customers.

The best and most successful websites are those operated by established media organisations such as the BBC, and by sports clubs and organisations which use the web as a marketing tool.

The sports department

Sport is so important to media organisations that all but the smallest operate sports departments as part of their editorial teams, staffed by specialist sports journalists. In the newspaper sector, at both national and regional level, sport is one of the three traditional departments – news and features being the other two – which make up the editorial team.

The sports department is allocated its own section, either free-standing or at the back of the publication, and is responsible for filling its own pages. The department is normally headed by a sports editor, who is responsible to the newspaper's editor, and who is expected to attend editorial conferences alongside the news and features editors, assistant editors and production executives.

The editorial conference determines the news agenda for the day and the space to be allocated to each department in the following day's paper. The number of pages allocated to sport tends to vary from day to day, depending on the day of the week and the sporting agenda on any given day. The sports editor must know what he intends to fill these pages with (normally a combination of news, match reports, features and opinion pieces) and who is going to provide the copy – staff reporters, freelances or agencies.

The sports team

Most sports departments will have a relatively small team of staff journalists. In addition to the sports editor there will often be a chief sports writer, whose role is normally to provide a descriptive COLOUR PIECE on the major event of the day, and who will therefore cover a wide range of sports. There may also be two or three reporters covering the dominant sport in the area, such as soccer, and perhaps a reporter covering each of two or three other major sports, such as rugby union, cricket and horse racing. Some national newspapers will have reporters covering major sports like soccer based in specific cities or areas of the country so that they can build up close relationships with clubs and individuals in the area they cover.

Other leading sports, such as rugby league, golf, tennis and athletics, may be covered by FREELANCE reporters who have contracts with individual newspapers to supply daily coverage of their particular sport. A number of other freelances, some of them perhaps former professional sports people, may have contracts to provide opinion pieces or expert analysis. Many sports desks will rely on agencies for coverage of minority sports like hockey, ice hockey and basketball. And at weekends or for significant midweek sports programmes, STRINGERS will be asked to provide additional match reports.

The copy provided by these writers is handled by sub-editors. Their role is to check copy as it comes in for factual, spelling and grammatical errors, to make sure it fits the space allocated for it in the paper and to write headlines and picture captions. Some sub-editors may also be involved in page layout and design. The staff team of 'subs' will be supplemented at busy times, such as Saturday afternoons, when a great deal of sport takes place, by 'casual', freelance sub-editors.

Writing standards

Sports writing once had the reputation of being clichéd prose churned out by lazy hacks. If such journalists ever existed, they would have difficulty getting a job today.

The quality of a newspaper's team of sports writers is a significant factor in maintaining audience share in a competitive market. The standard of writing in sports sections has risen enormously in recent years, so that it now bears comparison with the best of any other forms of journalism. This is as true at the popular end of the market as it is in the 'quality' press. Some forms of sports writing, such as the contributions of writers like Neville Cardus and Alan Ross on cricket, have a long and distinguished history. Now writers on others sports have caught up, and the best modern sports journalism is among the finest writing available anywhere.

Radio and television

The sports team in a radio or television newsroom will operate in a similar way to that in a newspaper newsroom, although the number of staff will usually be smaller. The major difference between the broadcast and print media is that radio and television cover sporting events live. This not only calls for a different range of skills; it also means much more time and effort has to be devoted to organisation. A newspaper can cover a game by sending a journalist and possibly a photographer. Radio can often get away with a commentator and summariser. But live television coverage of a sporting event is a major operation. In addition to a commentator and summariser, journalists and sports professionals may be needed to provide expert analysis, and camera operators, technicians and a director are needed to provide and mix sound and pictures. The appropriate number of outside broadcast vehicles is also needed. Much of the time of producers and researchers working in television, who often work for companies set up to provide sports outside broadcasts, is spent in organising all this.

Filling space

Journalists see themselves in many lights, from guardians of the truth and public watchdogs to entertainers and prose stylists, but the reality is much simpler than that. The basic task of any journalist is to fill space. Newspaper pages and radio and television bulletins have to be filled every day, no matter how many or how few significant events are happening in the world. Sport is a useful commodity for organisations which demand to be fed as regularly as the media because it is, in one sense at least, predictable.

We may not know when or where the next murder or terrorist outrage is going to happen, but we know well in advance exactly when and where sporting events will take place. We know they will provide the copy or pictures to fill a certain amount of space on a given day. Indeed, one of the reasons satellite television has restructured the sporting calendar is to make sure its schedules are always filled. Not all media organisations have the power to reorganise the sporting calendar to fit their needs, however.

Newspapers are the most demanding of all the media in terms of the quantity and range of sport they need to consume. But the cyclical nature of sport means that most of it tends to take place at weekends or on mid-week evenings. There is rarely much live sport taking place on a Thursday, for instance, but newspapers still need to fill their pages on Friday mornings. To make sure they achieve this, they have to vary the type of sports story they carry according to the day of the week – the emphasis being on match reports after a busy weekend of activity, but with space for more news and features on 'slack' days.

Exercises

1 Collect a week's editions of your favourite newspaper, from Monday to Sunday (including a similar Sunday newspaper if there is no Sunday edition of your chosen paper). Analyse the content of the sports sections, paying particular attention to:

- the number of pages devoted to sport on each day of the week. (Some broadsheet newspapers run tabloid sports sections on certain days. Count two tabloid pages as one broadsheet page.)
- types of story – reports of events, pre-event pieces, news stories, features and profiles
- whether the proportion of each type of article varies according to the day of the week

When you have collated the information, decide whether the day of the week influences the amount of space devoted to sport, and the types of piece used on any given day.

2 Look at the sporting calendar for the coming week. This can usually be found in the sports sections of Sunday newspapers. Try to decide how the fixtures and forthcoming events will affect the number of pages devoted to sport on each day, and how the proportions of reports of events, pre-event pieces, news stories, features and profiles are likely to vary day by day.

Handling copy

Since hot-metal typesetting, in which each letter on the printed page was manufactured in newspaper composing rooms by printers sitting at vast machines and headlines were set by hand from racks of metal type, was replaced by computer typesetting, the production of newspapers has undergone a radical change. Restrictive practices under which printers re-set every word written by journalists before newspapers could be printed were swept away in the late twentieth century. Newspapers now operate with a fraction of the staff they once did, which is one of the reasons they can afford to increase the number of pages devoted to sport. One result of this is that the involvement of journalists in the physical production of newspapers has increased.

The typed (and sometimes hand-written) COPY, from which compositors set the printed columns of our newspapers, is now a thing of the past in most newsrooms. The copy which journalists key into their computers is now what appears in the newspaper, but the process by which stories are tracked through the production system, and errors are kept to a minimum, has been largely carried over from the days of copy typed on paper.

Each story is given, by the journalist who writes it, a distinctive one-word CATCHLINE, so that there can be no confusion with other stories in the newspaper's system. Catchlines such as *match*, *race* or *winners*, should be avoided, as these names could refer to a number of events. Instead, specific catchlines such as *Bombaytest*, *Kentuckyderby* or *Olympichammer* should be used. This reduces the possibility of mistakes being made when stories are being collated on the sports desk and headlines or pictures attached to them.

The computer systems of many newspapers provide journalists with templates on which their copy should be written. These may have specific boxes for the journalist's BYLINE, the publication for which the piece is intended and the day on which it is scheduled to appear. Journalists FILING copy from outside the office, by LAPTOP computer, e-mail or by telephone to a COPYTAKER, should include their byline at the top of the copy, followed by the name of the publication the piece is intended for and the intended date of publication.

Production DEADLINES dictate that sports reports are often filed in a number of TAKES (see Chapter 5), so the status of the copy (first take, second take or whatever) should also be indicated at the top of the story. If the story is incomplete, the words *more to come* or *more follows*, should appear at the end of the copy. This is sometimes abbreviated to *mf*. At the end of a complete piece of copy, or at the end of the final take, the word *ends* should appear.

A writer's copy is always processed by a sub-editor, who checks it for accuracy and length, before it appears in the newspaper. To avoid unnecessary queries, the writer should always ensure that unusual names or unusual spellings (Phillip instead of Philip, Macmillan instead of McMillan) are followed by the word (*correct*) in brackets. This tells the sub-editor that the name has been checked and the spelling is accurate. The sub will then remove the word (*correct*) before releasing the story for publication.

Most media organisations have STYLE BOOKS, which offer guidance on such matters as the preferred spelling of certain words, punctuation (especially the style for quotations and the use of exclamation marks), grammar, and how people and organisations should be described. They may also offer guidance on how issues like disabled people in sport, or racism, should be handled.

For ease of reading copy on screen, in-house computer systems will normally use basic typefaces like *Times* or *Ariel*. Journalists filing copy by laptop or e-mail should use similar typefaces.

Copy is then processed, cut to length, given a headline and placed in the appropriate page using computer software such as QuarkXpress. It is at this stage that the typeface is changed to that used in the printed version of the newspaper. Pages will often have been designed in advance, with specific areas allocated to particular reports, although layouts can be changed if circumstances dictate it. A journalist's story does not become HARD COPY until the paper is printed.

The broadcast media have their own dedicated systems for writing scripts and putting in such information as captions and the names of the reporter, newsreader and cameraman. However, every story in a broadcast news bulletin must also have a distinctive catchline, to make sure that the correct tape is played at the right time. Spelling is less important to broadcasters (except in captions). Instead, they have to worry about pronunciation, and where mistakes can be made, scripts should offer guidance to the person who will be reading them (who will rarely be the writer):

'The winner was ridden by John Cholmondley (Chumlee) and owned by Mary Featherstonehaugh (Fanshaw).'

Presentation

Journalists normally write their copy on word processors or laptop computers with horizontal, rectangular screens. The lines of copy that appear on their screens are similar in length to those in this book. The paragraphs are only a few lines long and there is plenty of white space, which makes the screen or the page easy on the eye and attractive to the reader.

But the people who will be consuming that copy – the readers of their newspapers – will be reading it in narrow columns. A paragraph of this length would be difficult to read in a newspaper because it would appear as a solid grey mass of type, with no white space. The type would be difficult to read and readers would be discouraged from picking their way through any more than the first few lines of any story because it would be so taxing on the eye. If every story were laid out in this way, the newspaper would be unreadable and it would quickly lose readers to other newspapers which laid out their pages in a more user-friendly way.

Copy written for newspapers should be broken up into short paragraphs.

A single sentence is often enough.

A newspaper paragraph should never be more than two sentences. These should be fairly short.

Copy presented in this way in narrow newspaper columns is much more friendly to the eye.

There is plenty of white space.

This makes it easier for the eye to navigate the text and avoid missing lines or reading the same lines twice.

But the length of paragraphs will vary between broadsheet (or serious) newspapers, and tabloid (or popular) ones.

Short sentences, short paragraphs and short stories are especially important in tabloid newspapers.

They assume their readers will have a fairly low reading age.

The first paragraph of a story in a tabloid is often set in larger bold type.

The second paragraph will also often be set in larger type.

This format is another aid to easy reading. Sometimes, CROSSHEADS like the one below will be used.

Easy to read

Crossheads like these break the type up further.

They are an additional aid to guiding the reader through the story.

Media markets

Every newspaper is competing with many others in a fiercely competitive market. The way stories are laid out is one important factor in ensuring a newspaper is attractive to the readership at which it is aimed. Most media organisations exist to make money. Almost all of them are privately owned, and they have a responsibility to provide their shareholders with a decent return on their investments. To do that, they must attract readers, viewers and listeners.

Even those media organisations which operate in the public sector, like the BBC (British Broadcasting Corporation), ABC (Australian Broadcasting Corporation) or CBC (Canadian Broadcasting Corporation), must justify the licence fees or subsidies they receive from the public purse by ensuring that their product is as attractive to audiences as that produced by the private sector.

To succeed, they must be acutely aware of the market their product is aimed at. The products of the media are normally directed towards a specific sector of the market.

Newspaper markets

Mainstream newspapers are normally aimed at sections of the population that share particular characteristics. National newspapers, and those in big cities which have more than one newspaper, usually target a particular socio-economic sector of the population. They may belong to a particular 'class' (working class, middle class, professional), or share similar educational backgrounds, levels of income, age ranges or political allegiances.

Regional and local newspapers are usually aimed at the whole community. Their unique selling point is that they cover local issues (and in the case of sport, local teams and athletes) that other newspapers with a greater geographical spread cannot cover in the same detail, if at all.

These are, of course, generalisations, and the readership of particular newspapers is by no means limited to their target audiences. But it is useful (not least for the journalists who are writing the copy to fill them) to divide newspapers into the following categories.

Broadsheet
These are the serious newspapers at the top end of the market. Their target audience is better-educated people in professional managerial jobs who have, therefore, reasonable levels of disposable income.

The sports which broadsheet newspapers choose to cover reflect the perceived interests of their readership. They give extensive coverage to the most popular sports in their circulation areas, but they also give greater weight than other newspapers to those sports which tend to be enjoyed by more affluent people, such as golf, tennis, squash or rowing.

The name refers to the size of the page on which broadsheet newspapers were traditionally printed, which is twice the size of tabloid newspapers. Just as the readers of broadsheets are deemed to be capable of tackling longer stories with longer paragraphs and more complex grammar and vocabulary, they are also believed to be capable of handling larger-sized newspapers. Serious newspapers are not exclusively broadsheets, however. Some have adopted a tabloid format, and in Britain in 2003 *The Independent* began offering its readers the choice of broadsheet or tabloid sizes, an innovation which was subsequently copied by other titles.

Examples of broadsheet newspapers in Britain are *The Guardian*, *The Independent*, *The Daily Telegraph*, *The Times* and their Sunday versions (which in *The Guardian*'s case is *The Observer*). Because the United Kingdom is a small country with a highly-developed transport infrastructure, newspaper distribution is relatively quick and easy, and the newspaper market is dominated by national titles based in London. Sales of broadsheets, however, tend to be relatively low – typically less than half the sales of mid-market tabloids and well under a quarter of the circulations of the leading down-market tabloids.

In other countries, particularly those which span continents or subcontinents, newspapers tend to be city or state-based. Examples of broadsheet newspapers in the United States include the *New York Times*, *Washington Post*, *Los Angeles Times* and *Chicago Tribune*. Australian broadsheets include the *Melbourne Age* and *The Australian*, and in India, the *Times of India*.

Mid-market tabloids

These are aimed, as the name suggests, at readers in the middle to lower end of the socio-economic structure, with average levels of income and who have probably not been educated to degree level. They are usually old enough to have an interest in politics and economics, and to have outgrown the laddish frivolity of the down-market tabloids. Their content occupies the middle ground and is often aimed at the older end of the market. They sometimes also target women, on the assumption that many more affluent households will buy two daily newspapers – a broadsheet for the husband and a mid-market tabloid for his wife.

Sports coverage is also aimed at the middle ground, with the most popular sports again receiving the bulk of the coverage, but often with a slant towards sports enjoyed or played by older people with time on their hands, such as bowls or Test match cricket. Sports (or sporting events) that interest women, such as Wimbledon or Ladies Day at Ascot, may also attract extended coverage, often focused on peripheral activities such as fashion, rather than the sport itself.

Two examples of mid-market tabloids are the London-based *Express* and *Mail*, and their Sunday stablemates.

Down-market tabloids

These are aimed at a working-class, and often youthful, audience. Because the majority of the population fall into one or other of these categories, the tabloids have the biggest sales. They tend to be brash and irreverent, with news values that place sex and celebrity ahead of more serious and important events. Their stories are usually short and sharp, often personality-based, written with the simple vocabulary and uncomplicated grammar that the least literate of their readers will understand.

Sport, therefore, with its high celebrity count, dramatic content and mass appeal, is a very important ingredient in the tabloids' recipe. Major sports stories will often be flagged up on the front page. The range of sports covered is heavily biased towards the most popular, such as soccer in Britain and Ireland, baseball and American football in the USA, cricket in India and Pakistan, cricket and the locally-popular versions of football in Australia, New Zealand and South Africa. This bias tends to be followed even when the most popular sports are out of season, with reporters seeking out fairly trivial news stories to satisfy the appetites of fans, often at the expense of those sports which are in season.

Typically working-class sports like boxing, darts, snooker and racing (often slanted towards betting) can also attract more coverage than they are given elsewhere. Sports with smaller followings may only be covered if an event is too big to be ignored, but because the tabloids tend to place a high value on patriotism, athletes and teams which do well on the international stage may suddenly find themselves at the centre of tabloid interest.

Examples of down-market tabloids are the *Mirror*, *Sun* and *Daily Star* in the United Kingdom (often referred to as 'red-tops' because of the striking colour of their mastheads), the *Daily Record* in Scotland, and the *New York Post* in the USA.

Regional and local

These newspapers cover specific geographical areas. In countries like Britain they are in competition with a strong and well-resourced national press, and rely for their appeal on their strong local coverage, not least of sport. In bigger countries, as we have seen above, almost all newspapers are regionally-based. The broadsheet and tabloid newspapers produced in particular cities may have virtual monopolies, though even the continental countries have at least one national newspaper, like *USA Today* and *The Australian*.

The regional daily press in the United Kingdom has been contracting for many years, and although some cities, like Leeds, Liverpool and Birmingham, still produce both morning (more up-market and with strong national news content) and evening (middle of the road and heavily-biased towards local news) newspapers, most have just one title, normally published in the afternoon, but referred to as an evening newspaper. These try to appeal across the socio-economic spectrum and are pitched somewhere between the mid-market and down-market tabloids.

Their sports coverage is overwhelmingly local, and their reporting unashamedly biased in favour of local athletes and teams. The most popular sports again dominate, but those with a strong local following – rugby league in the north of England, rugby union in the West Country, Aussie Rules football in parts of Australia, hurling in Ireland, curling in Scotland – will also get plenty of coverage. Sports which have little following nationally will receive prominence if local athletes or teams are doing particularly well. The Sheffield *Star*, for instance, devotes a lot of space to ice hockey and basketball (neither of which are mainstream sports in England) because the Sheffield Steelers and Sheffield Sharks are the leading British ice hockey and basketball teams.

Radio and television

Radio and television channels tend also to be pitched at different socio-economic segments of the population. They often use sport as a means of maximising their target audiences. The mainstream channels try to concentrate on the most popular sports – soccer in Britain and many other countries, football, baseball and basketball in the USA, ice hockey in Canada, for instance. Those channels which are aimed at audiences higher up the socio-economic spectrum may choose to cover sports whose appeal is principally to that audience, such as rugby, golf or cricket.

The growth of satellite and cable broadcasting has led to a proliferation in the number of channels available, and to a narrowing of their focus. Many of them are devoted to specific types of programming, and sports channels are among the most popular.

This trend is closely linked, of course, to advertising, which is the media's main source of income. Advertisers tend to target niche markets, too – young men who drink beer, for example, or middle-aged women who buy washing powder. They know that certain sporting events can reach these markets in large numbers – almost any mainstream team sport attracts young men, Wimbledon, gymnastics or show jumping attract women. One way advertisers have of predicting whether the media in which they advertise will attract their target audience is to look at the sports they cover and the space or time they devote to each. Sports like rugby league, boxing or baseball tend to appeal more to the blue-collar end of the market, while followers of golf, rugby union and tennis tend to be higher up the social ladder. A few sports, like soccer, appeal to all social classes.

Exercise: Media analysis

One of the ways of differentiating the media is the way they handle specialist interests like sport. Take a selection of daily newspapers, including broadsheets, mid-market tabloids, down-market tabloids and regional titles. Analyse the content of the sports pages, making particular note of:

- the number of pages devoted to sport
- the choices of sports covered
- how the sports are covered – in-depth or personality-led
- style – how the pieces are written, use of language and metaphor
- type and length of story – match reports, news, features

Having assembled your data, analyse how coverage varies between different sectors of the market. Ask yourself:

- Do the newspapers cover the same sports, and if not, why not?
- Do they do so in the same detail and at the same length?
- Is the emphasis personality- or fact-based?
- How do these things differ between broadsheets and tabloids?
- How do regional newspapers fit into the equation?
- How does the language and structure vary? What does this say about the respective audiences?

Audience awareness

Because the national media target specific sections of the population, journalists working in it have to be aware of the level of education and income, and the range of interests, of their potential audiences. Regional newspaper, radio and television stations, on the other hand, tend to serve their entire communities, and the key distinguishing factor here is local interests.

Interest in sport is particularly susceptible to national, regional and socio-economic factors. Many modern sports were developed in Britain in the nineteenth century and have subsequently spread across the globe. With the exception of soccer, which has gained immense popularity among all classes and in most countries, the level of interest in the major sports tends to vary between countries and even regions, and between socio-economic classes.

In Australia, for instance, rugby league is the principal winter sport in some areas, rugby union in others and Australian-rules football in others. In South Africa, rugby union is the dominant winter sport among the white population, but soccer is far more popular with blacks. In Britain, rugby union is popular in rural areas among the higher socio-economic groups, while rugby league is confined almost exclusively to the industrial areas of northern England, where it has a largely working-class following. In Australia and New Zealand, cricket is popular among all classes and age groups, whereas in England, county cricket tends to have followers of retirement age, while Test and one-day cricket have a much broader appeal. On the Indian sub-continent, cricket has a massive and passionate following among all sections of the community. The North American media, however, provide little space for any of these sports. The agenda there is dominated by indigenous games like American football, ice hockey, baseball and basketball, none of which (except for baseball in Japan) has achieved the status of national sport elsewhere.

What most developed countries have in common is a growing interest in sport, particularly among men but also, increasingly, among women. Research carried out in Britain by the Newspaper Marketing Agency (NMA) showed that 54 per cent of tabloid newspaper readers turned to the sports pages first, while over a third of all broadsheet readers did the same. This figure rose to almost 70 per cent for tabloids and 61 per cent for broadsheet readers when those who scan the front page and then turn to the sports pages are included.

What they read there is important to their daily lives. Sport is one of the most hotly debated subjects and raises more passions than most others. It also has a cast of celebrities whose activities are often of interest to people who have no real interest in sport. Consequently, many people read the sports pages for pleasure – relaxation and entertainment – as much as for information.

Horses for courses

All of this, and the perceived correlation between an interest in certain sports and social rank, has significant implications for journalists. It determines not only the range of sports particular newspapers or broadcast organisations choose to cover, but the manner in which they cover them.

The choice of sports covered and the weight given to each of them will reflect the perceived preferences of their audiences. So will the style in which they are covered, from the length of individual articles to the choice of language and metaphor employed by the writers. Journalists writing for specialist journals will assume a high level of background knowledge from their readers, while those writing for general publications face the sometimes difficult task of providing audiences with all the information they need to understand the piece without 'talking down' to some readers. It is safe to assume that most people with an interest in sport in Britain will understand the basic rules of soccer and cricket, and people in other countries will have a similar understanding of their national sports. Minority sports will call for more explanation, and writers who specialise in them must avoid falling into trap of expecting their readers to know as much as they do about the sport.

Exercise

Take a copy of a tabloid and broadsheet newspaper published on the same day. Compare their coverage of a sporting event, paying particular attention to the style in which the reports are written, their vocabulary and sentence and paragraph length. Then select another sports story from the tabloid and rewrite it in the style of the broadsheet. Compare your version with that in the broadsheet. Then take a broadsheet story, rewrite it for a tabloid, and compare your version with that in the tabloid newspaper.

Sport's cultural significance

The cultural significance of sport goes wider than its importance to the leisure and media industries. In a shrinking world in which people have a high degree of social and geographical mobility, sport helps them maintain a sense of their local and national identities. When most of the population of Europe, for instance, are citizens of the European Union and share a common currency, they can cling to their roots through their local or national sports teams. Sports journalists help to establish and maintain this cultural significance. It tends to be expressed in their attitude towards the success or failure of the national teams, for instance, and sometimes in ways that are not healthy.

Peace may have broken out across the developed world, but international sport is often presented by the media as a perpetuation of old political rivalries, and even wars. This can often be detected in the language used by journalists when England are playing Germany at soccer, or India are playing Pakistan at cricket or New Zealand are playing Australia at rugby.

Conclusion

The media is one of the easiest subjects to study because we all read newspapers and magazines and see and hear television and radio every day. You would not be reading this book if that were not the case. Without the need to take time out from our normal activities, we can learn a great deal about how the media operate if we approach our daily consumption of the media actively rather than passively.

When you are listening to the radio, watching sport on television or reading the newspapers and specialist magazines, try to be aware of how specific media cater for different audiences. They all make different demands on their journalists, particularly of style. Study them carefully, and try to decide which market best suits your own style. Study the work of writers you admire and try to imitate them. There is nothing wrong with imitation as long as it does not extend to plagiarism, and a good writer's style will provide you with a useful template from which your own voice can develop.

A more analytical approach to your daily diet of sports journalism will help you to master the skills we shall be studying in the coming chapters more easily.

Summary

Sports journalism has expanded rapidly in recent years and is an important marketing tool for media organisations, especially satellite television. Sport and the media have a symbiotic relationship. The sale of media rights has increased the income of many sports organisations and led to the increasing professionalisation and commercialisation of sport. In turn, the media has changed the way in which professional sport operates. Media organisations have specific processes for producing sports journalism and aiming it at specific audiences. The media helps invest sport with certain types of cultural significance.

The sports desk

Summary Chapter Contents

The sports editor's role
The diary
Forward planning
Prospects
Processing copy

Learning Objectives

- To understand how a newspaper sports department is run
- To recognise the responsibilities of the sports editor
- To identify the roles of other key journalists
- To recognise the importance of forward planning
- To understand the newspaper production process

Because covering sport is a specialist job, most media organisations (as we have seen in Chapter 2) have dedicated sports departments which operate quasi-independently of the other editorial departments. The size of sports departments will vary according to the size of the organisation and the relative importance it attaches to sport.

The sports department is usually headed by a sports editor, who is a senior member of the organisation's editorial team, along with the news editor, features editor and possibly business, foreign, arts, fashion and other editors. Because of its self-contained nature, the sports department is responsible not only for reporting sporting events, but also for sports news and features and, in the case of newspapers, for page planning and the sub-editing of copy as it arrives in the office.

The sports editor's role

The sports editor co-ordinates the work of the sports desk. With administrative help from a sports desk secretary, the sports editor is responsible for selecting the events to be covered by sports staff and freelances, allocating assignments to reporters, commissioning features, organising freelance contributors, selecting material from agency WIRES, page or bulletin planning, copy TASTING and making sure the sports department operates within budget.

The key to the smooth running of the sports desk is the diary. Contrary to popular belief, news (and sports news in particular) is rarely something which suddenly happens. Most of it can be carefully planned for. This is where the diary comes in. As well as the obvious lists of fixtures for a wide range of sports, the diary will contain details of numerous other events which will also generate sports stories: the meetings of governing bodies, disciplinary hearings, awards ceremonies, anniversaries of major sporting occasions, and so on. Any story which is known about in advance is referred to as 'on-diary'. Stories which are not known about in advance – an athlete dying in a car crash or testing positive for a banned substance – are referred to as 'off-diary' stories.

The diary is also vital for the forward planning that is essential if the work of the sports desk is to run smoothly. Covering a major sporting event can be a complex logistical operation, requiring detailed organisation, such as making arrangements like media accreditation, travel and hotel bookings, and organising telephone lines, etc.

Forward planning

Although the sports editor is ultimately responsible for the content of the sports pages and the allocation of work to individual journalists, in practice this tends to be a much more democratic process. Other senior members of the sports team will have an input, and sports editors will be guided by the knowledge and wishes of their experts on particular sports. This is often done on an informal basis, but the formal planning forum is the sports desk conference.

The conference is the opportunity for specialist writers to make their bids for the events they would like to cover in the coming days and weeks, and to bargain for the space they believe their particular sports will need. The major sports will usually be allocated *some* space on the sports pages every day, and even out of season the most popular sports will often be given space. But the amount of space each sport gets, and the overall number of pages allocated to sport in the newspaper, will vary according to what is happening on each day. During events like a golf or tennis 'major', the Olympic Games or a world athletics championships, extra space will be made available for what are usually minority sports, at the expense of the 'mainstream' sports. But there will always be an element of bidding for space between the representatives of the major disciplines.

The views of the chief sports writer will often play an important role in the way space is allocated. The chief sports writer is usually an experienced sports journalist with strong views and a distinctive writing style, who has a roving brief to cover whatever he or she chooses. This will often be the main event of the day. The result may be a COLOUR PIECE taking a detached view of the event, which means that a second journalist – usually the chief specialist in that particular sport – will also be sent to the event to write a conventional report. Indeed, at major events such as international games, a single newspaper may also send reporters to observe the event from the perspectives of both teams, and may even commission coaches or players from the competing sides to provide their after-match impressions. These will normally be 'ghost-written' by yet more reporters.

Staff writers specialising in each of the major sports will also make their bids for space, stating which events they intend to cover themselves and for which they will need to hire freelance help. Contract reporters will also keep in regular touch with the sports editor, updating their schedules for the coming days and weeks.

Most sports desks will also call on the services of a number of journalists who are specialists in their own minor sports, such as snooker, hockey, ice hockey, basketball or bowls. They are usually freelances who may work for more than one organisation – a daily paper, a Sunday paper, a radio station and perhaps some television commentary work. They usually have excellent contacts with the governing bodies and players of minority sports, something no general staff sports reporter would have the time to cultivate. They may also cover other sports out of season.

The sports desk will also have access to copy and pictures produced by independent news agencies, some of which specialise in sport. The major agencies, such as the Press Association in Britain, provide copy to news organisations which subscribe to their services. It is available online and is constantly updated. The agencies provide sports news, reports of sports events, fixtures, previews, features and a results service. Smaller agencies operate in individual towns and cities and, as well as providing a general news service, specialise in the affairs of their local sports clubs. They accept orders to supply match reports to newspapers, broadcasters and online services.

Decisions have to be taken not only on which events are to be attended by the organisation's staff, but which are to be previewed in the form of features or profiles of the leading participants. Sports journalists not only look back on the sport which happened yesterday, but also look forward to that which is taking place today or later in the week. Previews are important not only to give audiences information on forthcoming sporting events, but also to fill space on days when there is not much sporting action. The sports supplements of Sunday newspapers, for example, will often contain almost as many features previewing forthcoming events as reports on the previous day's action.

The action that takes place on the sports field lends itself particularly well to photographs, and pictures play an important part in telling the story of an event. They are also vital to good page design. No sports editor, however, will have enough photographers to send to every event he or she wishes to cover. Although some newspapers employ a specialist staff sports photographer, many sports desks have to use general news photographers who will be assigned to cover sport at weekends or in the evenings. They rely heavily on agencies – some of them specialist sports photography agencies – for their pictures. They will also have access to a photographic library on which they can draw when a player or athlete does something particularly newsworthy.

One important aspect of forward planning is to make sure there will be enough material to fill the sports pages on quiet days when there are few events on which to report. This may involve previews of forthcoming events and profiles on the people who will be taking part in them, features on minority sports such as lacrosse, badminton or squash, which do not normally merit space, or 'timeless' features on sports issues which can be used to fill space on slack days.

Exercise

Analyse the content of a Sunday newspaper sports section. Make a list of:

- How many pages are devoted to reports of events that took place the previous day?
- How many of those events involved more than one journalist and what were their roles?

(Continued)

Exercise continued

- What proportion of space is devoted to each sport? Is this determined by the importance of the events or the perceived interests of the paper's target audience, or both?
- What proportion of the section's content has been prepared in advance? What does it consist of – previews, regular columnists, profiles, fixture lists, fitness guides, sports equipment information?
- What is the contribution of the chief sports writer?
- Has the paper used the services of current or former sports stars and, if so, in what roles?

Prospects

At the end of the sports desk conference, a set of PROSPECTS will be produced for each day of publication in the coming week. These are normally stored on the computer system so that all staff can have easy access to them.

The prospects (which some news organisations refer to as an ESTIMATE) for any given day will include a list of events to be covered, with starting times, the name of the journalist allocated to write the copy and details of any action needed to organise accreditation, transport or telephones. There may also be an indication of the time the reporter's copy can be expected in the office. When allocating stories to journalists, the sports editor also needs to allow time for the writer to travel from one place on one day to another part of the country, or even a different country, on the next.

There will also be an estimate of which major sports news stories are likely to break that day, with details of expected timings of announcements, venues of press conferences, and some suggestions for follow-up stories if that seems appropriate.

There will be a list of previews and other features, with the names of the journalists from whom they have been commissioned, their length and when they are likely to be available, together with an indication of which regular columnists will appear on the day.

When the number of pages available to sport in an edition has been finalised, space will be allocated to each event to be covered in the form of a specific number of words. The journalist involved will be told how many words to write before the event begins. A typical day's prospects for an English national newspaper will look like this:

Sports prospects – Monday, January 26

Soccer: (FA Cup 4th round) Northampton v Manchester United (Jim Smith – 800 words), Manchester City v Tottenham Hotspur (Kate Smith – 650 words), Nottingham Forest v Sheffield United (Will Bennett – 550 words – 5.30 kick-off, late copy), Everton v Fulham (Louise Brown – 650 words), Wolverhampton Wanderers v West Ham (Martin Thompson – 600 words).

Saturday match follow-ups (early copy): (FA Cup) Arsenal v Middlesborough (Jim Smith – 600 words), Birmingham City v Wimbledon (Kate Smith – 500 words), Burnley v Gillingham (freelance – 450 words), Coventry City v Colchester (freelance – 450 words), Ipswich Town v Sunderland (Martin Thompson – 450 words), Liverpool v Newcastle United (Will Bennett – 550 words), Luton Town v Tranmere Rovers (freelance – 450 words), Portsmouth v Scunthorpe (freelance – 450 words), Scarborough v Chelsea (Louise Brown – 600 words), Swansea City v Preston North End (freelance – 450 words).

Nationwide League Division 1: Bradford City v Crystal Palace (freelance – 450 words).

African Nations Cup: Congo v Guinea (James White in Tunis – 400 words – late copy).

Nationwide Divisions 2 and 3, Scottish and Women's football round-ups: (Jill Green – 300 words each).

Rugby Union: (Heineken Cup) Leeds v Toulouse (freelance – 600 words), Sale v Biarritz (freelance – 600 words), Wasps v Calvino (Simon Charlesworth – 750 words), (Parker Pen Challenge Cup) Montferrand v Saracens (Mike Watts – 700 words), (National League) Bristol v Coventry (Dafydd Jones – 500 words).

Saturday follow-ups: Gwent v Leicester (Dafydd Jones – 500 words), Stade Français v Ulster (Mike Watts – 500 words), Harlequins v Brive (freelance – 400 words).

Tennis: (Australian Open) Tim Henman, Leyton Hewitt and Justine Henin-Hardenne all playing (Marion Johnson in Melbourne – 750 words – early copy).

Snooker: (Welsh Open final) Steve Davis v Ronnie O'Sullivan – (Angus McKay in Cardiff – 400 words – ***very late copy***, result may only make final edition, or even hold over to Tuesday).

Rugby League: (Friendly) Bradford Bulls v Castleford (Eric Knowles – 350 words).

Golf: (Dunhill Championship, South Africa – David Reilly – 750 words).

Rallying: (Monte Carlo Rally – freelance – 450 words).

Boxing: (Commonwealth Heavyweight Title fight) Danny Williams (holder) v Michael Sprott (John Peel at Wembley Conference Centre – 750 words – late copy).

Racing: (Leopardstown meeting – Sandie Scott – 600 words).

Cricket: (Triangular Series, Adelaide) Australia v India (freelance – 250 words).

Photographers: Caroline Harvey at Northampton Town; Tony Milligan at London Wasps; agency pictures from Australian Open, Leopardstown racing, Commonwealth boxing and Dunhill golf.

Colour pieces: Chief sports writer at Northampton/Man U (possible giant-killing, also watching for developments on Sir Alex Ferguson's dispute with shareholders);

Features: American Football: preview of Superbowl – 1500 words – Bill Fisher in Houston – copy received; Tennis: Profile of Aussie Open semi-finalist Andre Agassi – Marion Johnson in Melbourne – 750 words.

Columnists: Sue Jones – woman's eye view; Chris Coleman – sport on television.

News estimate: Soccer: Possible developments on Ferguson row with Irish shareholders.

Cricket: Latest on debate on whether England should tour Zimbabwe.

Tennis: Greg Rusedski drug test hearing date decision.

Boxing: Lennox Lewis's next opponent announced.

To fix: Press passes for Scarborough and Northampton matches; photographer's pass for Caroline Harvey at Northampton; rail ticket and connection times to Scarborough for Louise Brown; telephone line for James White in Tunis; order Aussie cricket from agency.

What the prospects reveal

The events and sports the paper has chosen to cover reflect the interests of English readers generally and the readers of this newspaper in particular. Soccer is Britain's national sport and is followed by all sections of the community. The FA Cup, the oldest competition in the world, holds a special place in the hearts of English soccer followers and offers the possibility of high drama. Two of England's richest clubs, Manchester United and Chelsea, have been drawn to play minor teams, Northampton Town, who are a lower-league club, and Scarborough, who are not even members of the Football League. On such occasions sports journalists are always alive to the possibility of a 'giant-killing' story, and these two matches are given high priority.

But the fact that rugby union, golf and tennis – generally regarded as middle-class sports – are given substantial coverage suggests that these are the prospects of an up-market, broadsheet newspaper.

Some of the choices and priorities are personality-led. The chief sports writer has chosen to go to watch Northampton v Manchester United not only because there is the chance of a shock result, but also because the United manager, Sir Alex Ferguson, is the subject of an 'off-diary' story involving a dispute with two of the club's major shareholders. Writing about both stories offers the prospect of an interesting colour piece, especially if United lose the match.

Similarly, a relatively minor snooker event like the final of the Welsh Open would probably not command much space in a broadsheet newspaper if it did not involve former world champion Steve Davis, who has the chance of winning his first world-ranking title for nine years at the age of 46. Notice, too, that because snooker matches tend to continue late into the evening, contingency plans have been made in case the result is not known before the paper goes to press.

You will have noticed that the important events involving the most successful and best-supported teams are covered by staff writers and allocated more space. Freelances are brought in for less important events and given less space.

The fact that most of the items in the sports prospects are fixed events means that pages can be planned in advance and specific space allocated for stories and pictures.

Prospects are a valuable working tool, the 'template' on which each day's sports coverage is based, although they are constantly being added to and amended. In the event of a spectacular story breaking, such as a stadium disaster or the resignation of a major international squad coach, they can be torn up.

Crossing the divide

Sports prospects are also shared with other departments at the main editorial conference, not only to keep the editor and others abreast of what the sports section will contain, but because sport now has such an important place in western culture that the biggest stories often break out of the sports pages and find a place in the general news section. Athletes who win Olympic gold medals, national teams which win world titles, local clubs which win national titles, the appointment or resignation of national team coaches and scandals involving prominent sports figures are deemed to be of interest to readers who do not normally follow sport. They are often flagged up on the general news pages, with a cross-reference to more in-depth coverage on the sports pages.

Such stories will often involve a collaboration between sports writers and general news reporters. A sports writer will cover the event itself and the reaction of the sporting world; a general news reporter may be assigned to look at the national or local significance and report on the wider public reaction.

General news reporters and feature writers also keep an eye on the sports prospects because they often provide 'pegs' on which to hang related pieces in other sections of the paper. These pieces will often expand on the background to a particular element of a sports story, and because an essentially sporting story has crossed over into another area it is known as a CROSSOVER piece (see Chapter 7).

Exercise

This is a role-playing exercise in which a group of students can simulate the weekly sports desk conference. Someone should be appointed as sports editor, and some or all of the following roles should also be allocated (although these can be changed if other sports are more important in your own area).

Chief sports writer
Chief soccer writer
Two soccer reporters
Cricket writer
Rugby Union writer
Rugby League writer

Decide which publication you are working for – broadsheet, mid-market tabloid, red top tabloid or regional daily – as this will influence your decision-making. Find a list of sports fixtures for the following weekend. These can usually be found in the sports sections of Sunday newspapers. It should cover all the main domestic sports, and any major international fixtures which may be of interest to that newspaper's audience. Your task is to draw up the prospects for the following Sunday's paper, that is reporting on the sport which takes place on the Saturday and previewing that scheduled to take place on the day of publication (Sunday), and perhaps important events later in the week.

In addition to the writers named above, you may call on a pool of contract writers who specialise in athletics, tennis, golf and boxing, although any of them can be asked to turn their hands to other minority sports. You also have the budget to employ ten freelance match reporters.

Each writer should scrutinise the fixtures and decide which event he or she wishes to cover. They should also consider which athletes, players or coaches they would like to interview for features previewing forthcoming events. They should then prepare to make a pitch for space in Sunday's paper and argue their corner against the other journalists round the table.

The sports editor should then give each team member the opportunity to argue for his or her selections, and for the space these will occupy. The final decision will rest with the sports editor, who must balance the conflicting demands of staff with his or her own list of priorities, which will be influenced by the perceived interests of the paper's readers.

When agreement has been reached, draw up a list of prospects for next Sunday's newspaper.

Processing copy

The purpose of drawing up a list of prospects is to make sure writers know where they are going, what to do when they get there and when to file copy. The best story in the world is worthless if it misses its deadline, and unless writers and reporters can do their jobs efficiently, the complex and pressurised operation that goes into producing a newspaper will not function. Most newspapers produce a number of editions each day, for distribution to various parts of their circulation areas. Unless copy flows into the sports desk at the times it is expected, the editions will either miss their deadlines (which may mean they cannot be distributed and the newspaper will lose money) or readers will receive an incomplete sports service.

But the writing and filing of copy is only the first stage in a tight and complex process. Once the copy arrives on the sports desk, time is of the essence, so as much work as possible must be done in advance.

Some of the copy destined for the sports pages, such as previews and features, some early-breaking news stories, fixture lists, columns and so on, can be processed well in advance of the newspaper's first edition deadline. Space will be allocated and sub-editors will correct the copy, cut it to length and write the headlines. Getting these pages away early clears the decks to concentrate on the hectic task of processing the reports from events as they start arriving in mid-afternoon (weekends) or mid-evening (midweek).

By this time, most of the writers will be out of the office at the events they are covering, but extra sub-editors, many of them casual workers, some of them brought across from the newspaper's general news operation, will have been drafted in to handle the flood of copy. Each sub-editor will be allocated a number of events or stories to handle.

To make sure that copy can be processed in time for the first edition, reporters will normally be asked to file their stories in a series of separate TAKES (see Chapter 5). The task of the sub-editors is to process the various takes of each story as they arrive, checking for factual errors and mistakes in spelling or grammar. They then assemble them into a complete story, trim it to the required length if necessary, and write the headline, making sure every story for which they are responsible is ready for the press by the first edition deadline.

They must then do the same with the rewritten reports journalists file for subsequent editions. Complete pages are assembled on screen, with stories dropped into the space allocated to them as soon as the sub-editor has processed them. When a page is complete it is sent electronically to be made into a metal plate for the printing press. The late arrival of a single story can hold back an entire page and 'spare' stories are normally kept in reserve so that editions are not delayed if a piece of copy fails to appear.

Summary

The organisation of the sports content of a newspaper or bulletin is a complex process. The key role is played by the sports editor, who has the overall responsibility for the selection of events to be covered and for the allocation of personnel (both staff and freelance) to specific assignments. Sports journalists must be experts in their fields if they are to carry out their jobs effectively, and most specialise in a small number of sports. Copy is often written and processed to tight deadlines and a precise length.

Sources

Learning Objectives

- To understand how sports journalists source their information
- To recognise the importance of building up contacts
- To understand the difference between on-the-record and off-the-record information
- To identify official sources of information
- To understand the role of wire services and websites
- To recognise the importance of using other media as sources

Journalists cannot operate without a constant supply of information. So where do they get it from?

One of the key skills of general news reporters is to be able to write authoritatively on any issue, whether they have any previous knowledge of that subject or not. But journalists who specialise must quickly build up an in-depth knowledge of their subjects, not least because their audiences – in this case sports fans – will often be extremely well-informed themselves.

Sports writers often come into the job with an extensive background knowledge because they have always been interested in sport. It may be a wide-ranging knowledge of sport in general, but most sports journalists specialise in particular areas. Some of them concentrate on one sport in winter and another in summer. Only the most highly-regarded writers are given roving commissions to cover the entire sporting spectrum.

Journalists' own detailed, background knowledge of the sport they cover and the players and officials involved in it is often their most useful source. It enables them to anticipate stories and the likely reaction to them, and fill in background detail instantly from their own knowledge. It also means they know who to approach to substantiate a story and how to get hold of them quickly at any time of the day or night.

Contacts

This means cultivating a range of CONTACTS – people within the sport who are willing to speak either on or off the record about themselves and other participants, coaches or officials, or about clubs or governing bodies. Many people are naturally suspicious of the media and the exposure it can give to a thoughtless or unwitting remark. Cultivating contacts therefore involves building up trust between the journalist and the informant, who will want to know that anything he or she says will be treated responsibly. In particular, contacts will want to feel comfortable that anything they say which is background information and not for publication will not appear in print or on air. It is therefore essential that both journalist and contact thoroughly understand what each means when they use the term OFF THE RECORD.

It is generally understood that when a journalist is given information ON THE RECORD it can be used in the media and attributed to the person who has supplied the information. All journalists will assume that people are talking to them on-the-record unless they are specifically told otherwise.

Off-the-record conversations can cause greater difficulty. When a journalist is told something off-the-record it means, strictly speaking, that it is for the journalist's information only, and should not be published. However, the term is sometimes used when the information can be used but must not be attributed to the person who has provided it. This is known as UNATTRIBUTABLE information. The practice is commonly used in political circles, where a system of 'lobby' briefings is used to inform journalists of government and opposition thinking. The officials who carry out the briefings have come to be known as 'spin doctors'.

The practice is less commonly used in sport, although some athletes' agents, who want to place information in the media which might benefit their clients (such as a player's willingness to switch clubs), have been known to do so. Lobby-style briefings are also common in sports politics, especially where governing bodies from several countries may be bidding to stage a big event, such as the Olympic Games. Regular contacts will be well aware of the rules under which a conversation with a journalist is taking place, but in the early stages of a relationship it is essential to make sure that each side understands on what basis information is being provided.

Despite the suspicion with which journalists are viewed in some circles, building up an extensive list of contacts is not difficult. Many people are flattered to be courted by journalists and like to hear their voices on radio or see their names in print. Getting sport's biggest names to divulge their home telephone numbers to journalists is more difficult, however. The demands on their time from the media can be enormous, and unless you have built up a relationship with them while they were making their names, as many journalists do, the only way to make contact may be through their agents or their clubs.

Contacts books

Most journalists keep a CONTACTS BOOK in which they note the names, addresses, telephone numbers and e-mail addresses of people who have provided them with information. The same people are likely to be useful sources in the future. They will keep in regular touch with the more important of them, ringing them for a chat or meeting for a drink. A good list of contacts gives a journalist the ability to speak quickly and frankly with the most senior figures in their sport, and increases the professional status of a sports journalist. It can lead to them being head-hunted by other media organisations, with a consequent beneficial effect on their salaries. Some sports journalists build up such a good rapport with their contacts that senior figures in sport seek them out when they have something to say which needs careful handling.

Credibility and authority

The sources a journalist chooses or is able to quote will affect the credibility and authority of the pieces they produce. Quoting an unnamed source within a sports club does not have the same authority as quoting the coach or chief executive.

Similarly, the views of fans or supporters have more credibility if they seem to be representative of a wider group, such as a supporters' organisation or anti-racist group. The spokespeople for such groups can be useful contacts for sports journalists because they provide 'representation', whereas the views of individual fans are seen as being merely personal (though they can be useful if VOX POPS (see Chapter 9) are needed for a story.

Official information

Sports journalism is a two-way process. The media clearly need information to fill their pages and bulletins, but sporting organisations also need publicity to attract crowds to their events and to buy their merchandise. The best sort of publicity is free and the media have a vested interest in providing it for them.

Most professional sports clubs and bodies employ press or public relations officers whose job it is to deal with media enquiries and ensure that a regular flow of information about their clubs and the individuals who work for them reaches the media. Although this may seem like media manipulation, the demand for media access is often so great that an organised response is the only sensible way of dealing with it. It also ensures equal access for all journalists.

The top clubs provide journalists with glossy media guides at the start of each season. Press officers supplement these with regular PRESS RELEASES about forthcoming events. These are now mostly sent by e-mail and are made available on WEBSITES. They will include information on players being transferred into or out of a club, injuries and suspensions to players, the coach's views on forthcoming matches, team selection, interviews with players, and post-match quotes and verdicts from coaches and key players. They may also deal with non-playing matters like ground improvements or redevelopments and ticket availability and prices. Most major clubs produce at least one press release a day, even in the closed season, to try to keep their activities regularly in the public eye.

This information is also made available – sometimes before it is officially released to the media – on club websites. These also include useful background information such as squad lists and career details of individual players, statistics, fixtures, directions for getting to the stadium and to away grounds, and a club history. Journalists should always check the websites of both clubs before covering a match: many of the fans will have done so and journalists should always know at least as much as their audiences.

Direct access to coaches and players is usually made available regularly to journalists, who have privileged access to club training grounds and are usually allowed to approach players after training sessions have ended. Coaches will normally hold PRESS CONFERENCES a couple of days before a match to answer questions and give details of injuries and team selection.

Exercises

1 Sourcing information for a major sports event. Select an event which is due to take place in the next couple of days. Visit the websites of the teams involved and gather information about team selection, injuries and suspensions, league positions and any relevant quotes from players or officials about the forthcoming game. Write a 200-word 'preview' (see Chapter 5) of the event, based on the information you have gathered.
2 Press conference role-play. If you are part of a group, select someone to play the role of coach to a professional sports club. That person should visit the club website and gather the same sort of information as for the previous exercise. He or she should also be prepared to elaborate on that information in response to questions. (For the purpose of the exercise, it doesn't matter if this additional information is not strictly accurate.)

The other members of the group should prepare questions to ask the coach at the press conference. The coach should then make a brief opening statement about his or her team selection plans before asking for questions. You should try to ask questions that fill in the gaps left by previous questioners and that encourage the coach to give lively and useful quotes. Ask your questions in a friendly and encouraging manner. Avoid the temptation to be confrontational (which many people falsely believe to be the usual approach of journalists) unless the interviewee consistently refuses to answer an important question.

At the end of the press conference session, write up a preview piece of about 200 words as above, blending the coach's quotes into the story. The person who takes the role of coach should make feedback notes on the students' questions and the way in which they were asked.

Sponsors

Another group of people keen to keep their names in the public eye are sponsors. Sponsorship plays a major role in the finances of most sports and is the main source of income in some. In return for putting money into clubs, individual athletes or organisations, sponsors expect to see their names on shirts and on the backdrops to photographic and television sessions. Many of them also spend a great deal of money and effort in making sure the sport with which they are associated receives the highest-possible profile, and this means making journalists' lives as easy as possible.

Companies which sponsor leagues, for instance, will provide journalists with detailed, pre-season press packs, often packaged in useful shoulder-bags which can be taken to matches. This is backed up with a weekly news and statistics service, made available to reporters in the press boxes of every venue at which games are staged and sent to the sports desks of media organisations.

The sponsors of English soccer's Premier league, for instance, produce an information pack each Saturday which gives an overview of the week-end's matches. It also includes a full-page statistical preview of each game, full squad lists with the number of appearances made by each player and goals scored by them. It contains the results of both clubs' recent matches, the results of games between the two clubs in the last few seasons, the cumulative history of matches between the two sides, and the leading scorers of each club. The statistics go into fine detail, such as the average number of goals scored and conceded per game by each club, the number of corners won per game, the average time at which they score or concede goals and the average number of shots on and off target per game. Goal scoring is scrutinised in minute detail, with analyses of how many are scored with the left foot, right foot or head, how many from open play, from crosses, corners, penalties, direct from free kicks or indirectly, and own goals. There are also lists of players who have had the most shots, the most on target, the most off target, assists, crosses, offsides, fouls and free kicks won.

The pack also includes team statistics and current form for each team in the Premiership, the records of referees in issuing red and yellow cards, a fixture and results grid for the league, the latest league table, a list of leading scorers, and details of how many games each club has gone since winning, losing, drawing, scoring or failing to score.

Even the most demanding journalist could not ask for more, yet all this is supplemented at the stadium by the home club's match-day programme, which contains the manager's comments, reports on recent matches, player profiles, injury updates, comment columns, club news, profiles of opposition players and more detailed statistics on both sides. Journalists are also given a team-sheet listing the players, substitutes and officials for the game. Some clubs also provide their own statistics and copies of press reports of their recent activities.

Sponsors of big one-off events like the Olympic Games have press officers based at the venues to supply a steady stream of information to the media. Those involved with mobile events such as the *Tour de France* cycle race or Formula 1 motor racing make complex arrangements for servicing the needs of huge numbers of journalists who are moving from town to town in pursuit of the race, or from country to country.

When there's a lull in the sporting action, sponsors will stage off-field publicity events, such as manager of the month awards, to which the media are invited.

Wire services and news agencies

Media organisations do not rely for all their information on their own staff or freelance journalists commissioned by them. Some of it is supplied by wire services or news agencies.

Wire services are so-called because their reports were originally sent over telegraph wires. They are now available to subscribers online. They are the means by which news agencies circulate their material.

Most big towns have news agencies which gather local news and sell it to national media outlets. They get much of their income from sport, covering the affairs of the teams and athletes in their areas in the same way a local newspaper would. They can provide a useful link between local primary sources such as clubs, and the regional and national media, who do not have the resources to cover all clubs adequately. News agencies filter out the parochial stories and highlight those of national interest.

Some sell their stories direct to the media, but others are channelled through national news agencies, such as the Press Association in Britain, which provide a comprehensive news, preview, fixtures and results service to their subscribers.

Other sources

Most major sports have an established Year Book, usually published at the start of the season, which is a valuable source of records and statistics. The best known is probably *Wisden*, the cricketers' almanac, which has been recording the game's statistics for more than a century and which often becomes a source of news in its own right when it expresses its views on some aspect of the game in each new edition.

FANZINES and unofficial websites can be useful for assessing the mood of fans, particularly if a team is doing badly and a manager is under pressure.

Some sports journalists still prefer to keep their own records, although this is no longer essential because of the explosion in statistical information available from official and media sources.

Other media

Finally, the one source a journalist must never neglect is the media itself. The first indication of a big story will often come in a radio or television interview, or as an 'exclusive' by a journalist on a particular newspaper. The media need to watch each other carefully if they are not to be left behind on a breaking story. Monitoring your rivals is a simple and easy way of keeping abreast of what is happening in the world of sport.

Sports journalists should read as many newspapers and specialist magazines as possible. They should also listen to specialist sports radio channels, especially when travelling to cover events. News of team changes and injuries is often picked up first by radio journalists, who arrive at events well in advance of the start so that the can gather this information and use it as part of the build-up to their coverage.

Journalists should also resist the temptation to be choosy or snobbish about which newspapers they read. You may think the tabloids are sensationalist, but they often break stories first. This means that they play a major role in setting the sports agenda. The more serious newspapers and the broadcast media often follow up tabloid stories.

Conversely, you may think broadsheet newspapers are stuffy, but their coverage is often more in-depth and reliable. Radio and television stations can often be the first with stories, too. People involved in controversial events may be more willing to give interviews to the broadcast media because they know that what they say cannot be distorted.

The newsrooms of most media organisations have a full set of national and regional newspapers delivered to them every day so that they can check on the stories the opposition have produced. Freelance sports journalists should always buy a couple of newspapers, and keep up to date with what is happening through specialist radio or television sports channels, sports websites and television text news services such as Ceefax. Foreign sports news is usually accessible quickly through the websites of major newspapers in the countries concerned.

Letters to the editor in newspapers or radio phone-in programmes can also be a useful source of sports news stories, both nationally and locally. They can help journalists gauge the mood of fans, and give early warning of campaigns to oust managers or coaches, for instance.

Useful websites

www.bbc.co.uk/sport provides latest news on all major sports in Britain and worldwide, live reports, statistics and biographies of leading sports personalities.

Major broadcasting organisations in other countries, and leading newspapers like *The Guardian* in Britain, *The Australian* and the *New York Times*, also have good websites with a strong sports content. They are often free, although some may ask you to register and some charge for access.

Sports governing bodies and international federations usually have their own websites, many of them with links to leading clubs. Most major professional sports clubs and franchises also have their own sites, which are regularly updated with the latest news and have excellent statistical databases.

There are also comprehensive generic sites for many sports. The following is a selection but searching for the appropriate sport in a search engine like Google will produce many more.

American sports – www.cbs.sportsline.com – American football, baseball, basketball, golf, ice hockey and tennis.
Athletics – www.iaaf.org – site of the international governing body.
Cricket – www.cricinfo.com – news, reports and statistics from all major cricket playing nations.
Golf – www.golfonline.com – reports and statistics on all major tours.
Motor racing – www.formula1.com – fixtures, course maps, teams, drivers.
Racing – www.racingpost.com – horses and greyhounds, Britain and worldwide.
Rugby league – www.playtheball.com -- worldwide news and statistics.
Rugby union – www.scrum.com – worldwide news, plus rules and guide to the game.
Soccer – www.football365.com – news, teams, fixtures, results, previews, reports, statistics and opinion from all major European soccer leagues.

Summary

Sports journalists rely on a variety of sources for their material. Many of them are specialists, and the most important source of information is their own experience and knowledge. They also need a wide range of contacts. Keeping names and telephone numbers in a contacts book helps them get hold of the people they need to talk to easily. Sports organisations and sponsors have a vested interest in keeping journalists well-informed and provide a constant stream of material. News agencies and websites are also useful resources, and all sports journalists depend on other media to keep themselves informed of the latest developments.

Print journalism: reporting the action

Learning Objectives

- To recognise the function of sports reports
- To understand the media 'lifespan' of sporting events
- To identify the various forms of event reporting
- To understand why and how running copy is produced
- To identify the various forms of pre-event and post-event journalism
- To recognise the partiality of some sports reporting

Describing sporting events is one of the key skills of the sports writer, and provides the basic content of sports pages. Reports of events occupy more space in newspapers, radio and television than any other form of sports journalism. The ability to cover the action in a lively, informative and accurate way is an essential tool for any sports journalist.

The competitions which take place between individual athletes or teams is what sport is all about, and they are the springs from which all forms of sports journalism ultimately flow.

Often, the media will simply report the action on the day, but the more important events can command space on the sports pages for a much longer period. Indeed, major events such as the Olympic Games, the soccer, rugby and cricket World Cups, the baseball World Series or the Superbowl in American football, will occupy sports journalists for weeks or even months in advance of them taking place.

In such cases, the event itself forms only part of a continuum which, for the media, begins well before the action starts and continues after it has finished. It can consist of a number of different types of sports writing:

- Build-up or scene-setting pieces
- Previews
- 'Running' reports
- Considered reports
- Delayed reports
- Inquest pieces

The build-up piece or scene-setter

The media build-up to an event can consist of one or more pieces, often of FEATURE length, designed to generate interest in the event and provide readers with the background information they need to understand and enjoy it more fully. In setting the scene for these events, journalists will look for PEGS on which to hang their pieces, often focusing on an individual competitor as a means of injecting human interest. They may choose to write PROFILES of competitors who have a good chance of winning medals for the country in which the publication is based, or who have been enjoying a run of good form, or who did well the last time the event was staged, or who have recovered from a career-threatening injury or been in the news for reasons not directly related to sport, such as bad behaviour off the field. In the build-up to the Olympic Games or World Athletics Championships, the subject areas will range widely from the blue riband track and field events to minor sports like pistol shooting or archery, which rarely warrant space on the sports pages.

Where team games are involved the peg will often be a player or coach who has recently joined one of the teams, or who previously played for the opposition and who will therefore be able to offer insights into both camps. And because sport is often treated as soap opera by the media, scene setters will sometimes concentrate on the 'back story' to the forthcoming episode – the highlights of previous encounters, or the grudges between teams or individuals.

Build-up pieces of this kind also satisfy the fans' thirst for knowledge about sports stars and fill space on the sports pages on slack days when there is little sporting action to report. The writing of profile or background pieces of this kind is covered in depth in Chapter 7.

Exercise

Choose a forthcoming major sporting event and compile a list of people-based articles which could be used to set the scene. Select your subjects from present and former competitors, managers and coaches. Then compare your list with the pieces run by newspapers, radio and television as the event approaches.

The preview

Preview pieces focus more closely on the event itself and usually appear immediately before the event takes place. They cover topical issues such as the form and league positions of the teams involved, recent results, sequences of victories or defeats, team selection problems faced by coaches, such as injuries or suspensions to key players and transfers in or out of the club, and possible tactics and team formations. They also refer to players making their debuts, players who have played for both clubs, leading scorers, disciplinary records, the backgrounds of the officials who will be in charge, and whether the job of either coach is under threat. Sports writers rely for their information on their own expert knowledge and on the various sources outlined in Chapter 4.

Preview pieces serve the same function, in an abbreviated form, as the official programmes offered for sale at sports events.

Example

Bolton Wanderers v Charlton Athletic

Kick off: 3pm today

Referee: A. Wiley
Television: Highlights, ITV, 10.30pm

Bolton manager Sam Allardyce will bring Brazilian Emerson Thome, signed on a free transfer from Sunderland yesterday, straight into the heart of their defence. They need him, having already conceded ten goals in just three matches this season.

Injuries and suspensions: A. Barness (hamstring), B. N'Gotty (hamstring)

Probable team: (4–4–2) Jaaskelainen; Hunt, Laville, Thome, Gardner; Djorkaeff, Campo, Nolan, Okocha; Pedersen, Davies.

Charlton manager Alan Curbishley will be looking to build on an impressive start to the season which has earned his team four points from three matches. They go to the Reebok Stadium full of confidence after beating Wolves 4–0 in their last away fixture, despite the absence of the injured Italian Paolo di Canio.

Injuries and suspensions: P di Canio (knee)

Probable team: (4–4–2) Kiely; Young, Fortune, Fish, Hreidarsson; Kishishev, Holland, Parker, Jensen; Euell, Bartlett.

Forecast: Charlton too strong for Bolton's weak rearguard.

As we shall see, previews are useful not only for the readers who may be attending the event or watching on television: they are also invaluable for the journalists who will be reporting on it.

Why report sport?

The hub round which this sequence of pieces revolves is the event itself. Before we consider *how* sporting events are reported, it is worth asking *why* they are reported, because that should determine how the job is done.

What is a report of a match or a race supposed to do? If we already know the result, why should we be interested in how it was achieved? There are several reasons.

First, a report offers a *vicarious experience* for readers who were not able to attend or watch the event themselves. Reports should therefore offer vivid descriptions of the key moments of the event.

It also gives those who were able to attend or who watched the event on television an opportunity to *relive* the experience, and to compare their impressions with those of an expert observer. Reports are often read most keenly by those who were there. If we have been to a football game, the report of that game is the first we turn to in the following day's newspapers. People who live in towns which still have Saturday evening sports papers, often printed on coloured paper and with names like the *Sporting Pink* or *Green' Un*, which provide running reports (see below) of matches, will often buy a copy on the way home from the stadium. They do so to read a move-by-move account of the game they have just watched and relive it over again, perhaps picking up additional information they missed earlier. Reports must be accurate and well-informed if they are to impress the reader who has witnessed the event.

Some readers also want to test the *opinions* they formed while watching the event against those of an expert. Reports can generate debate and provide a printed equivalent of the post-match discussion in the pub.

People also read reports for *information* – that an athlete recorded a personal best, that a batsman has scored his thousandth run of the season, that a team has won promotion to a higher league.

Many people read reports for *entertainment*, even though they may not be especially interested in the outcome of the event. They read them for the quality of the writing, for the wit or humour or wisdom of a talented writer who happens to be a sports journalist.

Reports should also offer *analysis* and *criticism* of tactics and performances, and put the outcome of the event into *context* – what does it mean for a team's prospects for promotion or relegation, or an athlete's chances of qualifying to take part in the Olympic Games?

Reporting the event

Covering a sporting event for a daily newspaper is one of the most demanding and pressurised jobs sports writers have to do. It involves writing a predetermined number of words quickly and accurately while the action on which they are reporting is still unfolding before their eyes. It demands not only a comprehensive knowledge of the sport being covered, its rules and history, and a similar knowledge of the individuals taking part, but also the ability to write accurately and entertainingly against tight deadlines and to a specific length. The production demands of newspapers may also require reporters to write two or more different versions of their reports within a very short space of time.

Production demands

Because professional sport is a branch of the entertainment and leisure industry, most sporting events take place at the most convenient times for the public to watch – weekends and midweek evenings. This places difficult demands on daily and Sunday newspapers wishing to cover the events. Their first editions may go to press less than an hour after games and meetings end.

To enable them to carry reports of these events in their early editions, sports desks must take in and process the copy produced by their reporters quickly and efficiently. This depends to a large degree on forward planning by the production staff on sports desks in newspaper offices and fast work by reporters in the field.

Once the events to be covered have been chosen, sports pages are planned in advance, with a specific amount of space allocated to each match. This means that reporters at the stadiums can be told the precise number of words they must file on their event. And to maximise the time SUB-EDITORS on sports desks have to process the large volumes of copy flowing in on a busy afternoon or evening of sport, reporters are expected to file their first reports as RUNNING COPY.

Running copy

Running copy (often referred to by journalists as 'a runner') involves filing copy in a series of TAKES by telephone to a COPYTAKER, or from a laptop straight into the newspaper's computer system. A journalist will phone the office from the press box before the event begins to be told how many words to write.

It is important that the correct number of words is filed. If not, a sub-editor will have to cut or add to the copy to make it fit the space available, wasting valuable production time. Reporters filing copy electronically can get an accurate word count from their laptop computers. Those dictating copy straight from their notes will ask the copytaker to give them a word count from the computer into which the copy is being keyed. Those writing copy by hand before dictating it can calculate the length quickly by writing it at five words per line in their notebooks.

If a reporter is asked to write a 550-word 'runner' on a soccer match, for instance, he or she will be expected to file the first take of 250 words at half time, the second take of 250 words ten minutes from the end, and a final take of 50 words, together with the scoreline, the moment the referee blows the whistle at the end of the game.

An even more extreme example of this is the report written for the Saturday afternoon sports papers produced in some large cities, which are printed within minutes of games ending so that they can be sold to fans as they go home from matches. The reporters involved are in constant telephone contact with their offices, and report the game incident by incident as it happens.

In both cases, journalists are essentially reporting the key moments of the match in chronological order, as they unfold before them on the pitch, without knowing what the final result will be. The final 50 words will sum up the game and serve as the INTRO (introduction) to the piece. It will be placed at the top of the copy by the sub-editor who handles it.

Example

Running copy – 550 words

First take – 300 words at half time

Given the state of both his goals against column and his treatment table, it was no surprise that the Bolton manager Sam Allardyce brought experienced defender Emerson Thome, signed on a free transfer only 24 hours earlier from Sunderland, straight into his starting line-up.

With Anthony Barness and Bruno N'Gotty both suffering hamstring injuries in the Portsmouth debacle, Nicky Hunt came in alongside the Brazilian at the back. But despite Charlton fielding an unchanged side in the continuing absence of Paolo di Canio, they were the first to wobble. Left back Hermann Hreidarsson brought down striker Kevin Davies a couple of yards outside the penalty box, and when Bolton were given a second chance at the free kick after the Charlton wall failed to retreat the full ten yards, captain Jay-Jay Okocha curled the ball beyond the unsighted goalkeeper Dean Kiely, only to see it cannon back off the crossbar before being scrambled away for a corner.

Hreidarsson was then booked for chopping down Ivan Campo in midfield before Thome made his not inconsiderable presence felt in attack, bundling the ball just wide of a post.

More than 20 minutes had elapsed before the seams of Bolton's patched up rearguard were seriously tested. Scott Parker ran on to Jason Euell's flick to slip clear of the back four, only to try to stroke the ball past Jussi Jaaskelainen, who spread himself wide enough to deflect the effort.

The Bolton goalkeeper looked less assured when he flapped at Claus Jensen's floated free kick. It was striker Shaun Bartlett who made the solid contact, but his header flew narrowly over.

Second take – 200 words, ten minutes from the end

For a while Bolton's defensive frailties showed again, and the back four was caught square by the Charlton captain Matt Holland, who was anxious not to repeat his midfield partner Parker's mistake when left one-on-one with the goalkeeper. He struck the ball hard to Jaaskelainen's right, only to be foiled by his flying, one-handed save. But having kept the sheet clean the goalkeeper blotted his own copybook by getting himself booked for protesting too vigorously that he had been fouled in the melee that followed his save.

Bolton had clearly taken Allardyce's demands for greater application in the wake of their four-goal drubbing at Portsmouth to heart, but despite ample possession and Okocha's persistent prompting, they found it difficult to fashion clear-cut chances of their own from open play.

But when Stelios Giannakopoulos replaced Henrik Pedersen after the break the attack began to look sharper. The little Greek international's pace and guile complemented the bulky Davies' more old-fashioned approach and between them they began to pose a serious threat. Davies forced Kiely into a reflex stop at his near post, and the goalkeeper was soon flinging himself towards his other upright to deflect an angled shot from the Greek.

Now it was Charlton who were reliant on set-pieces, but Jensen's free kick was over elaborate and over the bar.

Intro – 50 words at the final whistle

Bolton Wanderers 0 Charlton Athletic 0

Keeping a clean sheet is one thing, and Bolton did that admirably here, but if they are to avoid the perennial struggle against the drop they must take their chances against the likes of Charlton.

They could and should have recorded their first victory of the season, but just could not score. Defence sorted: now to find a striker.

Discussion

The time constraints imposed on journalists writing running copy mean that they may have to write much of it before anything of real significance has happened. In this example, the reporter has filled the first two paragraphs with background material about team selection and a new signing – material which would have been gathered for the preview piece discussed earlier. This is followed by a description of key moments in the first half of the match, to make up the number of words required at half time. Notice how the reporter has linked the background material smoothly to the action with the sentence: *'But despite Charlton fielding an unchanged side in the continuing absence of Paolo di Canio, they were the first to wobble.'*

Providing bridging passages like this avoids the jerkiness that would otherwise result from an abrupt change of direction in the piece. Although the overall word count is fixed, reporters are permitted a certain amount of flexibility in the length of their separate takes. In this example, the reporter has padded out the action with background material because there were no goals in the first half and little else of note on which to report. If several goals had been scored, however, and there had been a number of other notable incidents, the reporter may have chosen to file 300 or even 350 words at half time. But the second take would have been reduced in length accordingly, to avoid exceeding the overall word count for the piece.

The challenges facing sports reporters vary according to the way the events they are watching unfold, and sport by nature is unpredictable. In this example, the dearth of goals or any other exciting incidents means the challenge is one of producing an interesting and readable piece out of scant raw material. In the second take, the writer has again strayed outside the confines of the action to introduce an element of 'back-story' – Bolton's heavy defeat in their previous match – to put their defensive performance on this occasion into context. At many sporting events, however, the challenge is to condense a great deal of action and incident into a relatively small number of words.

The final take of a running match report will often demand the ability to condense the entire event into a couple of sentences, as well as putting the result into perspective. This final take will appear in the newspaper as the introduction to the report, and it is the function of an intro to distil the essence of the story while grabbing the attention of readers and making them want to read on. In this example the writer has turned the lack of goals in the game to advantage by using it as the basis for his analysis of the teams' performances.

Finally, it is worth remembering that journalists are expected to stick to the number of words for which they have been asked, no matter how many or how few goals have been scored, and no matter how exciting or dull the match.

Exercise

Watch a game on television, either live or recorded on videotape. Before you do so, study preview pieces in newspapers, on teletext or on the internet, making notes of any background information which may be useful in a running report. This should include the names of the players on both teams and their shirt numbers, so that you can identify them easily. Set yourself an overall length for your piece of 500 words and write a report on the game as you watch, in takes of 250 words (to be completed by the end of half time), 200 words completed 10 minutes before the final whistle and a 50 word intro, completed as soon as the game ends.

You will find it more realistic, and less distracting, if you turn off the commentary. You will still have the advantage, not always available to reporters in a press box, of action replays of the key moments. But you will not, of course, have access to the shared expert knowledge available among the pool of experts covering the match at the stadium.

Take care to hit the deadlines and 'take' lengths you have been set. Compare your finished piece with reports of the match in the following day's newspapers.

The reporter's notebook

While games are in progress, reporters should make notes of the key incidents, together with the times at which they happened, in their notebooks. Some reporters dictate running copy straight from their notes, though most write out their takes before dictating them.

It is vital to take an accurate note of the action, as journalists will almost certainly have to refer back to them at later stages of the reporting process. The first thing most reporters do is make a note of the team formations, using the players' shirt numbers as shorthand. Players names are also written in shorthand form, so that the reporter misses as little of the action as possible while jotting down the key incidents. Journalists organise their notebooks in different ways, but a typical page of notes from the match covered above would look like this:

Example

Bolton	Charlton
22	1
18–17–35–11	19–24–6–12
6–16–4–10	2–8–7–10
8–14	9–17
(4–4–2)	(4–4–2)

Hreid brings down Davies, 20yds (10 mins)

Hreid booked – foul on Campo (12)

Okocha free kick – into wall – not 10 yds – taken again – hits bar, gk unsighted, scrambled for corner

Euell – Parker – clear – weak shot – gk deflects for corner (22)

Thome just wide (15)

Jensen free kick – gk misses – Bartlett firm header – just over bar (30)

Okocha cross, Kiely punches away (32)

Half time 0–0

Holland put clear by Euell – shoots right, keeper saves (41)

Gian (sub) on for Pedersen

Gian sets up Davies – Kiely saves near post (50)

Goalmouth scramble – gk injured – protests – booked

Gian shot, Kiely diving save (54)

Jensen free kick – too clever – over bar (62)

Djork shot, kicked off line by Hreid (88)

Full time 0–0

When reporting matches, many reporters divide their notebooks into two columns, one for each team. This makes it easier to locate notes of specific incidents when writing their reports.

The figures at the top of each column are the shirt numbers of the players and the positions they occupy on the field. Most newspapers carry this information at the end of match reports, and a visual record of the team formations helps reporters identify players during a match.

Reporters make brief notes of key moments in a match, together with the time at which they happened. They will often shorten the names of players or their positions (gk = goalkeeper). This cuts note-taking to a minimum and allows them to concentrate on the action and writing their reports.

Considered reports

The constraints under which running copy has to be written can sometimes produce unbalanced accounts of the event, with formulaic intros and abrupt conclusions. Given time to reflect on the match as a whole, journalists can produce better-balanced, more reflective and more thoughtfully written accounts. They can also include the post-match views of the coaches and players on the performances of their teams. The time available between the first and final editions of their papers, (although this may be as little as an hour) gives them the chance to do this. During that time they have to rewrite their pieces and carry out their interviews.

Fortunately, the administrators of professional sports are aware of these time constraints and do what they can to accommodate the post-match needs of journalists. Most sports organisations require managers and coaches, and in some cases players, to make themselves available for media interview within a reasonable period after games end. Major stadiums have press rooms or media centres in which journalists can work, and many have specially equipped interview theatres to which coaches and players will be brought after a game. In smaller stadiums, however, post-match interviews can take place in the manager's office, the players' tunnel or even on the pitch. In America, journalists often have free access to the dressing rooms, where they can talk to anyone they wish.

The purpose of post-match interviews is to give journalists the opportunity of questioning the key figures about major incidents and report their views on the significance of the result and the performances of individuals. It also allows them to gather information and responses on any injuries sustained or disciplinary action taken by match officials, and to seek comment about controversial aspects of the game. The appropriate quotes can then be included in a considered rewrite of their earlier running reports.

If time is available, many journalists will produce a completely fresh report for the later edition, interweaving quotes with a more balanced account of the most significant moments in the game and some comment and analysis of their own. Others may choose to retain some of their earlier material, cutting and condensing it to focus on the most significant aspects of the match and making space for quotes, analysis and action from the latter part of the game that they did not previously have time or space to report. They will often spend much of their time polishing the opening of their reports, to make them more balanced, to take in significant post-match quotes and to sharpen the impact on their readers and make them want to read on. Reporters who work for newspapers which produce regional editions may have to provide two versions of their considered reports, written from the point of view of each of the teams involved.

These considered pieces are usually expected to be of the same length as the earlier running copy, although sports editors will sometimes give reporters at particularly eventful games more space for their rewrites, while those at less eventful ones may have the space available to them reduced.

Here is the considered rewrite of the game for which we have already seen the running copy.

Example

Bolton Wanderers 0 Charlton Athletic 0

After shipping four at Portsmouth in midweek, the goal rush has abated for Bolton, but the tide has yet to turn. Plugging a leaky defence is one thing, and Bolton proved admirably watertight here, but if they are to avoid their usual struggle against the drop they must do more than that against small fry like Charlton.

They could and should have recorded their first victory of the season, but despite a second half of almost constant pressure, they could not score. Defence sorted: now Sam Allardyce must find some penetration.

'We sorted out one end today and the midfield was different class,' Bolton's manager said afterwards, 'but the front end wasn't there, unfortunately.'

Given the state of his goals-against column and his treatment table, it was no surprise that Allardyce brought the experienced defender Emerson Thome, signed on a free transfer only 24 hours earlier from Sunderland, straight into his starting line-up. With defenders Anthony Barness and Bruno N'Gotty both suffering hamstring injuries in the Portsmouth debacle, it was all hands to the pumps as teenager Nicky Hunt was drafted in alongside the Brazilian.

With Charlton sweeping into the Reebok Stadium on the back of a four-goal victory of their own, Allardyce's first priority was to batten down the hatches. But despite fielding an unchanged side in the continuing absence of the injured Paolo di Canio, Charlton never looked like repeating their drubbing of fellow strugglers Wolves.

More than 20 minutes elapsed before the seams of Bolton's patched up rearguard were seriously tested. Scott Parker ran on to Jason Euell's flick to slip clear of the back four, but tried to stroke the ball past Jussi Jaaskelainen, who spread himself wide enough to deflect his effort.

The Bolton goalkeeper looked less assured when he flapped at Claus Jensen's floated free kick and was relieved to see striker Shaun Bartlett's header sail over the bar. When Matt Holland caught the back four square again it looked as though Bolton's defensive frailties might return, but Jaaskelainen flung himself to his right to palm away the shot and Charlton's most dangerous spell was over.

'It was a very hard-fought and scrappy game and chances were few and far between. We were happy with a point,' said their manager, Alan Curbishley.

That's not the way they saw it from the other dugout.

Bolton almost scored early on, when Hermann Hreidarsson brought down striker Kevin Davies a couple of yards outside the box. Captain Jay-Jay Okocha curled the ball beyond the unsighted goalkeeper Dean Kiely, but it cannoned back off the crossbar.

And when Stelios Giannakopoulos came on after the break Bolton seemed to have found the cutting edge they needed. The little Greek's pace and guile complemented the bulky Davies' more direct approach, and Charlton were on the back foot. Davies forced Kiely into a reflex stop at his near post, and the goalkeeper was soon flingng himself towards his other upright to deflect an angled shot from the Greek.

When the goalkeeper was beaten by Youri Djorkaeff in the dying minutes it seemed as though Bolton's ship had finally come in, but Hreidarsson kicked his goal-bound effort off the line and their hopes were sunk once more.

Exercise

Try to identify the main differences between the running copy and the rewrite.

(Continued)

Exercise continued

Suggested answer

1 The writer has reworded the opening paragraph, introducing an extended metaphor about shipping and water, suggested by the reference to the naval town of Portsmouth. It is picked up again at various points throughout the piece. The intro is now more powerful and effective, summarises the outcome of the match neatly and leads strikingly into the main body of the report.
2 The second paragraph has also been sharpened up, and the quote from the Bolton manager in paragraph three has been chosen to support the reporter's own verdict on the match.
3 The following two paragraphs have been recycled, with minor alterations, from the running copy because they provide the context against which the subsequent action must be seen.
4 That action, however, has been repackaged. Instead of the chronological account of the ebb and flow of play, we now have separate accounts of the attacking performances of each team. The less important incidents, which were included in the running copy to fill space, have been removed to make way for managerial quotes and important action, such as the last-minute goal-line clearance, which the reporter had no space for in the original piece. As before, the Charlton manager's quote immediately follows the account of his team's performance and comments on it. The reporter then makes a smooth transition from his account of one team to that of the other by switching the point of view from the Charlton manager to the Bolton dugout.
5 Whereas the running copy ended rather abruptly on a wasted free kick (although the reporter tried to soften the blow with a little cadence – *over elaborate and over the bar*), the considered piece is rounded off neatly. The use of the words *ship* and *sunk* in the final paragraph end the piece as it began, with a maritime metaphor, and give it a feeling of unity.

Delayed reports

Considered pieces like this usually appear in the following day's newspapers. They are the first written accounts most readers will have seen of the event, and they will expect the action to be thoroughly covered. However, newspapers sometimes decide or are compelled to carry reports some time after the event has taken place. Daily newspapers which do not publish on Sundays often choose to carry reports of Saturday's matches on Mondays, and weekly newspapers are often compelled to carry reports several days after the event. The time difference between the place where an event is happening and the place where a newspaper is published will sometimes result in reports appearing up to 36 hours after the event. Accounts of the first day's play in a Test cricket match in Australia, for instance, will not appear in British newspapers until after the second day's play has been completed.

By the time these reports appear, the reader may well have seen highlights of the event on television or read reports in other newspapers, on teletext or the internet. Delayed reports, therefore, have to take a different approach and find ways of offering a fresh perspective on the event. There is still the need to provide basic information about the event, such as the result, the scorers and other key incidents, but the main aim should be to provide readers with fresh information the contemporaneous reports did not supply. This may involve deeper analysis, a more in-depth look at controversial or key incidents or the performances of individual players, the effects of injuries on the respective squads, a consideration of forthcoming matches in the light of what happened in the one being reported, or a piece devoted largely to the thoughts of the coaches or players after the game.

Because they are aware of the needs of the media, many coaches and managers will give separate interviews, after the normal post-match press conference has finished, for journalists writing delayed reports and who need to find fresh angles around which to base those reports.

The following is a delayed report of the soccer match described above. The game took place on a Saturday afternoon, but the report was written for the Monday morning edition of a British national broadsheet newspaper, and would be read almost two days after the event took place. Compare it with the considered report of the same match printed above, looking particularly at what proportion of the delayed report is devoted to incidents in the game itself, and how much is given over to quotes, analysis and discussion of points which arose as a result of the game.

Example

Bolton Wanderers 0 Charlton Athletic 0

The managers of high-profile clubs like Manchester United and Arsenal look on next weekend's break from Premier League action as a mixed blessing. On the one hand, they are delighted to have so many players in their squads who merit selection for their countries. On the other, they believe it merely gives their star players – whose considerable wages the clubs are paying – the chance of getting crocked on international duty.

But the less fortunate members of the Managers' Union take a different view. Neither of these clubs is likely to be inconvenienced unduly by the call-up for national service, and both managers welcomed the two-week lay-off as a period of convalescence for players they hope might make up for the short-comings so evident here.

The season may be barely a fortnight old, but the talk at the post-match inquests is already turning to how much easier life would be if only key players were fit.

'It was a point on the board,' was about all Charlton manager Alan Curbishley had to say about this scrappy stalemate before turning his thoughts to the treatment room. 'We now have a two-week break when hopefully we can get one or two players fit.'

He had in mind Paolo di Canio and the on-loan Carlton Cole, whose creativity and nose for goal were sorely missed. Charlton made few chances, and when they did Scott Parker did his own hopes of a return to the England squad no service when he tamely muffed a one-on-one with Bolton goalkeeper Jussi Jaaskelainen.

Skipper Matt Holland let a similar opportunity go begging and Charlton were lucky to get away with a point after an aimless performance that cried out for someone to take charge on the pitch and stamp his authority on the game. 'If Richard Rufus and Gary Rowett come back in, hopefully it will make the squad that much stronger,' said Curbishley. 'We hoped that if we got on top our midfield would come into its own, but as soon as we won the ball, we gave it away again.'

Though disappointed with the result of a match they should have won, Bolton manager Sam Allardyce at least had some grounds for satisfaction. His team has now stopped leaking goals, thanks partly to the arrival of Brazilian central defender Emerson Thome.

'He had an excellent debut. He is in magnificent condition and he didn't look like he had been out of Premiership football for as long as he has,' said Allardyce.

His main concern is now at the other end of the park. The influential Jay-Jay Okocha hit the bar with a first-half free kick and Youri Djorkaeff had a goal-bound effort cleared off the line, but Bolton should have had more to show for their hard work.

Striker Henrik Pedersen was taken off at the interval and though his replacement, the nippy Greek international Stelios Giannakopoulos, looked a more dangerous partner for the burly Kevin Davies, Charlton goalkeeper Dean Kiely was equal to whatever they threw at him.

Allardyce is now pinning his hopes on getting Thome's compatriot Mario Jardel, twice Europe's top scorer while with Sporting Lisbon, down to his fighting weight after a six-month lay-off.

Although he was given half an hour on the pitch in the midweek defeat at Portsmouth, Jardel wasn't even on the bench on Saturday, and Allardyce hopes the two-week break will complete his rehabilitation.

'He's put on a bit of weight sitting on the beach in Rio,' he said. 'We need to get him lean and mean again.'

With Bolton's first victory still eluding them, perhaps his entire squad needs to take advantage of the two-week break to put their dismal opening to the season behind them and start again as they mean to go on.

Discussion

In the intro, the reporter is already looking forward to the following weekend, when there will be a break in the League programme to allow many players from the leading clubs to play for their countries in international matches. This also has the effect of broadening the appeal of the piece beyond the supporters of the two clubs involved. Most clubs at this level will be affected by having players drafted into their national teams, and because the leading clubs employ the best players from many countries, a large proportion of their squads may be involved. The report picks up on a current RUNNING STORY – the tensions between club and national coaches over the exposure of highly-paid players to injury in 'friendly' international matches – before focusing on the injury problems of the two clubs involved in this match.

The contrast between the views of their coaches and those of wealthier clubs like Manchester United and Arsenal brings their positions in the pecking order, and the shortcomings of their performances as revealed in this match, into sharp focus. The bulk of the remainder of the report is taken up with the views of the respective managers on their injury problems, with reference to the key players involved. The reporting of the match action is limited and is used to illustrate the points being made by the managers.

Exercise

Using your own analytical skills, and quotes derived from the media or club websites, write a delayed report on the event for which you have already produced running copy and considered pieces, for publication 24 hours after the event.

Inquest pieces

Some sporting events, such as international matches or the finals of major competitions, acquire such significance that the media will take the process further by devoting space in the days following their initial reports to deeper analysis. This may focus on what the performance and result mean for the future of the team or athlete involved, or extend to wider issues such as the state of the sport nationally or worldwide.

Example

England's victory in the second Test match in Port of Spain not only ensures their best performance in the West Indies for decades, it may even signal a shift in the order of world cricket.

England have exorcised the ghosts of all those thrashings at the hands of the outstanding West Indian fast bowlers of the past, and they have now found two of their own who may have the future of international pace bowling in their hands.

In doing so they have confounded the experts who predicted that this series would be dominated, as has so much international cricket recently, by batsmen, with the Windies' captain Brian Lara leading the charge.

Instead, Steve Harmison and Simon Jones have taken 26 wickets in four innings while Lara, one of the world's greatest batsmen, has faced just 58 balls and scored a mere handful of runs.

On this tour, Harmison and Jones have developed into England's best fast bowling partnership since Darren Gough and Andrew Caddick. This was a department in which the West Indies led the world for decades, but no more.

Michael Holding, Andy Roberts, Joel Garner and Malcolm Marshall are long gone, and the latest crop of West Indies pacemen have yet to live up to the weight of expectation which has been placed on their shoulders.

And what of the rest of the world? Australia's Glenn McGrath and South Africa's Allan Donald are both off the scene and Pakistan's Shoaib Akhtar, though blisteringly fast, is equally wayward.

Recent history has shown that pace bowlers, more than anyone else, win Test matches, and with Yorkshire's Matthew Hoggard also on the brink of fulfilling his potential, England may soon be the side that instils fear in batting orders around the world. Indeed, if the trio can stay clear of injury, they may develop into the best pace attack since the golden era of Fred Truman, Brian Statham and Frank Tyson.

The one place where pace is not necessarily the weapon of mass destruction is on the spinners' wickets of the Indian sub-continent, as Sri Lanka's Muttiah Muralitharan regularly demonstrates. But only he and that other 500-test wicket spinner, Australia's Shane Warne, stand undisputedly ahead of England's new generation of quick bowlers.

If only England could find a couple of spinners to match those others from the golden era of English bowling, Jim Laker, Tony Lock and Johnny Wardle, they could walk confidently down the steps of any cricket pavilion in the world.

Discussion

This piece uses the peg provided by England's victory to examine the state of fast bowling across the world of cricket. It ranges back over the previous half-century, and also looks forward to what the future may hold. It moves way beyond the West Indies v England Test match, out of which it arose, to include players from most of the world's other major cricketing nations.

Favouritism or neutrality

Although sports reporters are normally expected to behave like other journalists and produce even-handed and unbiased stories, there are occasions when they are permitted – and expected – to stray from absolute neutrality. The readers of local newspapers will largely support local teams or athletes, sometimes with great fervour, and they expect to have their prejudices reflected by the local media. If a team from within a newspaper's circulation area is playing one from elsewhere, the event would normally be reported from the perspective of the local team. Similarly, national newspapers will report events involving a 'home' team or participants from a national perspective. But when reporting domestic events in which they have no way of knowing which, if any, of the participants the reader supports, reporters should remain strictly neutral.

Summary

Reporting the action at sporting events is one of the key roles of sports journalists. It involves a wide range of activities, from previews and build-up pieces which set the scene for the event, to 'instant' reports of the action, more considered accounts, and reflective pieces written after the event. It demands the ability to write quickly and accurately, and within strict space limitations.

Print journalism: sports news and photography

Summary Chapter Contents

Writing news stories
Writing intros
The five Ws
What not to do
News story structure
Writing style
Running stories and follow-ups
Journalistic ethics
The role of the sports photographer

Learning Objectives

- To learn the basic principles of news story writing
- To understand the importance of the intro
- To know how to structure a news story
- To recognise the stylistic demands of a news story
- To understand the nature of running stories and follow-ups
- To appreciate the role of the sports photographer

Reports of the action on track or field form the staple diet of the sports pages, but when there is little action to report, and when big stories are breaking outside the arena, other journalistic skills are called for. In addition to the specialist skills of a sports reporter, the sports journalist must also be able to handle the most fundamental of journalistic skills – researching and writing news stories.

The action off the field is almost as important as that on it, and there is always a steady flow of news stories awaiting the attention of the sports journalist. There is the movement of players from one club to another, the hiring and firing of coaches, the signing of sponsorship deals, the off-field behaviour (or misbehaviour) of players and fans, changes to the rules of sports, the financial difficulties in which clubs and governing bodies some-times find themselves, drugs tests, and the daily activities of sports people who have become personalities and celebrities in their own right. Covering these stories demands the same nose for news and the same tenacity as that needed by any other reporter on a newspaper or broadcasting station.

Writing news stories

The news story is the basic building block of all journalism. News stories follow a simple structure, and anyone who can write a good news story can communicate clearly about anything. It is worth spending time learning how to do it well.

The secret of writing a good news story is knowing how to condense the essence of the story into the intro – into a single sentence or short para-graph. Additional information can then be added, in order of importance. The essence of a good news story is that, at whatever point the reader chooses to abandon it, what he or she has read will make complete sense.

There are two reasons why news stories are written this way. The first is that it allows readers to take as much or as little as they wish from the story before they move on to the next one. The second is more practical: if space is tight, a sub-editor can cut the story at any point, from the bottom up, without having to rewrite it, knowing that it will be understood by the reader. For this reason, news reporters must learn to swallow their pride. Those who write sports news stories should *expect* to have their copy cut by sub-editors, and they should always be written so that they can be cut easily.

At first, many students find it difficult to write a simple news story. This is because the news story's structure is, in many ways, the opposite of how they have always been taught to write. A school or university essay often begins with a statement of what it intends to achieve, goes on to provide a series of facts in support of an argument, and ends by drawing a con-clusion from them. The news story, on the other hand, *begins* with the conclusion – with a statement of the essential things the reader needs to know. It then goes on to provide additional information to justify and explain what we have already been told in the opening paragraph.

Writing intros

The intro, or opening paragraph, is the key to a good news story. It should condense the story to its basic facts and make the reader want to know more. Achieving this is not as easy as it sounds, and for most people it only comes with practice.

The simplest way to grasp how an intro should be written is to imagine you are telling the story to a friend. When we have some interesting news, it is natural to blurt out the key points first: 'Did you hear that Nasser Hussain has resigned as England cricket captain? Michael Vaughan is taking over.'

With only minor modifications, this would serve as the intro for the story in the following day's newspapers:

> *Nasser Hussain yesterday resigned as England cricket captain. Michael Vaughan will take over for the second Test which starts on Thursday.*

Those two short sentences contain all we need to know to understand the essence of the story. Additional facts will put what has happened into perspective and explain the reasons behind it, but if we never read any further, we will understand the essential points.

The five Ws

A more systematic way of achieving the same thing is to answer the following questions, sometimes referred to as the five Ws.

- Who?
- What?
- When?
- Where?
- Why?

Answering these questions – and the supplementary question How? – usually allows us to assemble all the information needed to understand a story, although it is not always necessary to answer all of them in the intro.

The example above answers the first three questions in the brief opening sentence. Nasser Hussain (*who*) yesterday (*when*) resigned as England captain (*what*). The second sentence answers the same questions about his replacement. Michael Vaughan (*who*) will take over (*what*) for the second Test on Thursday (*when*).

Having written the intro, the essence of the story can then be amplified in the second paragraph, which in this case might read:

> *Hussain told England coach Keith Fletcher of his decision immediately after his side drew with South Africa in the first Test at Edgbaston. 'I wasn't quite the captain England needed or wanted,' he said.*

This paragraph answers the other three questions not dealt with in the intro. Hussain told the coach (*how*) at Edgbaston (*where*) because he was not up to it (*why*). If a story is just breaking, the *why* aspect may have to be missed out because it involves analysis or demands information that is not immediately available to the reporter. Follow-up stories (see below) will often concentrate on *why* something happened.

Intros should always start with the main point: in this case, *Nasser Hussain resigned*. Do not attempt to lead up to the main point with explanation. Something like: *After England struggled to draw with South Africa in the first Test at Edgbaston yesterday, their captain Nasser Hussain submitted his resignation*, merely delays the impact of the story and makes the intro unfocused. All explanation and description should be saved until after the reader has absorbed the main impact of the story.

In most sports news stories this will mean that the intro will focus on people: the quarter-back who has been traded, the coach who has been sacked, the jockey who has been suspended, the athlete who has failed a drugs test.

What not to do

Avoid starting intros with questions or quotes. Readers want to be told what has happened, not cross-examined. Quotes in a news story slow down the process of absorbing the main facts.

Care should also be taken about saying *when* a story took place. To use the word 'yesterday' in a morning newspaper is acceptable because readers know that they are reading yesterday's news. But few evening newspapers would use the word – even though many of their stories happened the previous day – because it draws attention to the fact that the story is 24 hours old and robs it of the immediacy news stories strive for. Similarly, a weekly newspaper published on a Friday would try to avoid saying that the story had happened on Monday. One way round this, and of restoring immediacy to a story, is to find a way of getting the word *today* into the intro:

> *England opener Michael Vaughan is today coming to terms with his new responsibilities as captain after Nasser Hussain dramatically quit the job at the end of the first Test match against South Africa.*

News story structure

Having summarised the main points of the story in the intro, the reader should then be provided with the detail in order of its importance. In this case, Nasser Hussain is the key figure, and his resignation and the reasons for it should now be amplified.

> Example
>
> *Though the 35-year-old Essex batsman has ended his four-year reign as England's Test captain, he intends to continue playing for his country under Michael Vaughan.*
>
> *He said: 'Being captain of England is something you have to do one hundred per cent, and there are only so many times you can go to the well and dig deep for the team. The last thing they want is a tired leader.'*

The second most important figure is the man who will replace him as captain, Michael Vaughan. We now need to hear his reaction and, for the benefit of readers with a limited knowledge of cricket, learn something about him.

> Example
>
> *That mantle has been thrust on 28-year-old Michael Vaughan, who also succeeded Hussain as one-day captain.*
>
> *The Yorkshire opening batsman, who has already led England's one-day side through two victorious series, said:*
>
> *'It's going to be mentally tough and a lot more mentally tiring, but I feel I'm ready for the job.'*
>
> *'Nasser has had four years at the top and I'm really pleased he has given me this team.'*

If space is limited, the story could end here, but because the success of their national sports teams is important to readers, a British newspaper would want to run the story at length. The scope of the piece would therefore be widened to include the reactions of other key figures in English cricket, like the national team coach and the Chairman of the selection committee, and opponents such as the captain of the South African team which has precipitated the resignation. The backgrounds of the two key figures would have to be explained, and journalists might also seek the views of respected analysts on Hussain's captaincy and the prospects for the team when Vaughan takes over.

The remainder of the story might run something like this:

Example

David Graveney, Chairman of the England selectors, said Hussain's decision to remain part of the team would be helpful to Vaughan.

'Michael Atherton found it useful to have Graham Gooch to turn to for advice and in turn Alec Stewart leaned on Michael.

'But the important thing is to allow the new captain space to do his own thing. He must be allowed to make his own decisions.'

David Byas, who was Vaughan's captain at Yorkshire, said: 'He will handle the pressure of the job as well as anyone. He will relish the challenge.

'The important thing is that he should continue to get runs. If he has a dip in form, people will put it down to the pressures of the captaincy.'

Hussain made his Test debut in 1990 and became England captain in 1999. Under him, England went from being one of the weakest to one of the strongest teams in the world. They won 17 and lost 15 of his 45 Tests as captain.

But a heavy defeat in the Ashes series in Australia last winter and a poor showing in the World Cup prompted speculation about his future.

Vaughan, who is widely-regarded as England's best batsman, scored 156 in the First Test and described it as his best-ever century. He rose to the top of the world batting rankings last year, and took over as one-day captain after the World Cup.

Under him, England have won the Natwest Challenge against Pakistan and the Natwest Series against South Africa and Zimbabwe.

Weaving in the background

An important news story will draw on a wide range of sources and include a lot of background detail and analysis. All of this must be structured logically and flow smoothly. To avoid interrupting the flow of the story with chunks of background detail, this should, where possible, be woven into the breaking news.

> **Example**
>
> *The Yorkshire opening batsman, who has already led England's one-day side through two victorious series, said: 'It's going to be mentally tough and a lot more mentally tiring, but I feel I'm ready for the job.'*

This sentence provides a lot of background information (Vaughan plays for Yorkshire, he is an opening batsman and he already captains the national one-day team) which some readers will need to be told if they are to understand the story fully. But it is used unobtrusively (as an alternative means of referring to Vaughan) to introduce a fresh quote, so readers who are familiar with Vaughan's background will not feel they are being given a lot of information they already know.

Weaving background information into the body of the story in this way avoids any impression of talking down to the reader. It is often difficult, particularly with sports stories, to gauge how much knowledge readers already have. Keen cricket followers will know much of the background to this story already, but many readers may not. Slipping it into the story in this way helps to disguise the fact that some readers are being fed a lot of unnecessary background. It also means that, although the story has a rigid structure, it is not apparent to the reader, who merely sees a smooth flow of copy. The structure of a news story only becomes apparent to the reader if it is confusingly written.

Writing style

Students who are used to writing essays often find other difficulties when they are asked to write news stories for the first time. These usually involve length, style and the admissibility of the writer's own opinions. Essays can be long and opinionated: news stories should be written as concisely as possible, and their writers should keep their opinions to themselves.

A 1500-word essay has the space to allow the writer to be expansive and even florid: a 150-word news story does not. News stories should be written tightly, leaving out superfluous words, stylistic flourishes and unnecessary information. Every word has to earn its place.

Cutting out unnecessary words means that more information can be packed into the story, or more stories can be squeezed into the page. A journalist should always go back over the first draft of a story to see how the writing can be tightened up. It almost always can. Many common phrases can be reduced to a single word, such as 'in order to' (to), in the region of (about), despite the fact that (though), 'in view of the fact that' (because). Avoid tautology such as 'fastest *ever*' and '*final* result', and meaningless descriptive words such as '*pretty* impressive' and '*very* powerful'. Cutting out superfluous words can save a lot of space in a news story.

Exercise

Rewrite the following story, reducing it to half the number of words without losing any of the information it contains.

The two teams who will meet to contest the XXXVIII Super Bowl at Houston, Texas, on February the 1st have been decided. They will be the New England Patriots and the Carolina Panthers.

The Patriots got there by beating the Indianapolis Colts by a margin of 24–14 in the play-offs of the AFC, while the Panthers booked their place in the Super Bowl by defeating the Philadelphia Eagles by no fewer than 14 points to 3 in the play-offs of the NFC.

In view of the fact that the New England Patriots appeared in the Super Bowl only two years ago, their appearance for the second time in three years should come as no surprise.

Carolina Panthers, on the other hand, were not expected to get this far in view of the fact that only two years ago they lost 15 straight games in a row. Their opponents, Philadelphia Eagles, however, had been defeated in the play-offs in both the previous two seasons and were confidently expected to make it third time lucky.

Suggested answer

New England Patriots will meet Carolina Panthers in the XXXVIII Super Bowl at Houston on February 1.

The Patriots, who also reached the Super Bowl two years ago, beat Indianapolis Colts 24–14 in the AFC play-off, while the Panthers sprang a surprise by beating Philadelphia Eagles 14–3 in the NFC play-off.

Two seasons ago, the Panthers lost 15 successive games, while the Eagles were in the play-offs for the third year running.

The first story contains 173 words. The second contains only 72. Yet it retains all the facts and is easier to read. The space saved will create room for the writer to develop the story further, or allow the sports editor to get another story on the page.

Keeping it simple

The grammar of a news story should be simple and uncluttered. Complex sentences, with subordinate clauses, should be avoided. Sentences should be short and direct. They should run to 30 words or less, and paragraphs should be no more than two sentences. Longer paragraphs look grey and daunting and difficult to read when set across the narrow columns of a newspaper page (see Chapter 2). Try to avoid clichés and euphemisms, and if one appears in your story, search for an alternative. People don't 'pass away', they die; teams don't 'get a result', they win.

While avoiding euphemisms, you should ensure that the tone of your story is appropriate to the subject matter. Humour can be a useful tool in the writing of some stories, but should be avoided where it might cause distress or offence.

Judging what might offend or distress readers when reporting tragic events such as a stadium disaster or a fatal accident to one of the competitors in a sporting event can be difficult. Always bear in mind that the relatives or friends of those involved may be reading what you have written. Stick to the relevant facts, do not go into unnecessarily unpleasant detail (even when this will show how thoroughly you have done your job), avoid sensationalism and resist the temptation to apportion blame or rush to judgement.

Avoid using jargon. Find a way of saying the same thing in plain English. And do not use acronyms without explaining what they mean (MCG – Melbourne Cricket Ground; IOC – International Olympic Committee) unless you are sure your readers will understand them.

In some cases it may be necessary to amplify the official titles of sporting organisations or competitions, especially when some British sports are being covered in non-British media. The British invented or codified many of the world's leading sports, and just as the United Kingdom does not put its name on its stamps because it was the first country to introduce a modern postal system, so many British sports' governing bodies and some of its (and the world's) major sporting events do not include the words British or English in their titles. The body which runs soccer in England is simply The Football Association. Britain's golf 'major' is officially The

Open, its tennis grand slam The Championships. The latter is universally known as Wimbledon, but non-British audiences may need to be told that you are referring to the (English) Football Association or the (British) Open golf tournament.

Exercise

Rewrite the following story so that it is simpler and easier to read. Remove any clichés, euphemisms and jargon, and explain any acronyms. Remove any of the writer's own opinions or prejudgements, and make sure that nothing in the content or tone of the story will cause unnecessary offence or distress to readers.

F1 is likely to claim another victim today as legendary driver Jim Smith, who was the youngest man ever to win a GP and who, according to many judges, was destined to become world champion, lies in a hospital bed on the verge of death.

The Aussie speed merchant met his Waterloo when, in only his second race in Britain and in weather conditions rarely experienced Down Under, he spun off the Loamshire track and, as the crowd watched in stunned silence, smashed sickeningly into the trackside barriers.

The initial speculation was that the Aussie, who's just 23 and engaged to top pop songstress Sonja Green, who was watching in horror from the stand, had passed away on the spot.

He was rushed to LGH in a chopper, and fans feared he would be pronounced DOA but, much to their relief, medics later declared he was in ITU with a depressed cranium and fractured tibia and scapula.

It was obvious there were two reasons for the incipient fatality, the first being that Bob Black tried an overtaking manoeuvre that would have made a Sunday driver on a wet Bank Holiday look competent, and clipped his rear wheel, while the second was that the powers that be failed to make sure the circuit was fit to race on, with the unacceptable level of oil on the track undoubtedly contributing to the near-fatal skid.

Experts at the HSE have launched a thorough investigation.

Discussion

Several of the paragraphs are far too complex, with sub-clauses that interrupt the flow of the story and inhibit our understanding of it. They should be broken down into shorter sentences, with the less important supporting information used further down the story.

The writer's assumptions about the likely fate of the driver and the causes of the accident are opinion, not fact. They have no place in a news story (although the opinions of doctors at the hospital or race track officials could be included if they were properly attributed).

The writer's speculation that the driver will die is not supported by any medical opinion and will cause distress to those close to him. When injuries are life-threatening it is better to describe the victims as fighting for their lives.

Initials and acronyms like F1 and HSE should be spelled out, at least in the first instance, as should abbreviations like GP and DOA. Not every reader will know what they mean.

The word 'legendary' is misused – a legend is a traditional story, often untrue.

Slang like 'speed merchant' and 'Down Under' and clichés like 'met his Waterloo' and 'stunned silence' should be avoided, especially in stories with subject matter as serious as this.

Descriptions like 'watched in horror' (how else would his fiancée view the accident?) and 'sickeningly' are unnecessarily sensationalist, while 'top pop songstress' and the reference to Sunday drivers are too flippant to be used in this kind of story.

'Passed away' is a euphemism, and cranium, tibia and scapula are medical terms which should be replaced by the common descriptions. We don't need to be told that the investigation will be thorough: nobody would expect it to be slipshod.

Suggested answer

The Formula 1 racing driver Jim Smith is fighting for his life today after his car spun off the Loamshire circuit and hit crash barriers.

He was taken by helicopter to Loamshire General Hospital, where he is in intensive care suffering from a fractured skull and broken leg and shoulder blade.

The Australian was taking part in his second race in Britain when he spun off in heavy rain. His fiancée, the pop singer Sonja Green, was watching from the stand.

The accident happened when another driver, Bob Black, tried to overtake and seemed to make contact with Smith's rear wheel. The Health and Safety Executive is investigating.

Smith (23) is the youngest man to win a Grand Prix and was regarded as a future world champion.

Stick to the facts

Opinion has no place in a news story. Stick to the facts and let the readers draw their own conclusions from them. When writing a news story, a reporter should always follow the principles of accuracy, objectivity, neutrality, balance and fairness, and make sure that fact is always clearly distinguished from opinion. The only exception to this is if you are writing for a local newspaper covering a local team or individual, or a national newspaper writing about the country's sporting interests. In such cases you will know where the interests of your readers lie and can write the piece from their point of view. But no matter what publication a story is being written for, accuracy, fairness and the separation of fact and opinion remain sacrosanct.

The information on which a sports story (or any other piece of journalism) is based should always be checked carefully. Being 'fairly sure' that what you are saying is accurate is not good enough. Journalists have a duty to their audiences to make sure that what they are saying is correct. They also have a duty to themselves and the organisations they work for to make sure that what they say does not lead to court proceedings. Seemingly trivial inaccuracies can make a story libellous. Minor errors can have expensive consequences.

The facts of a story should always be verified by reliable sources. Never base a story on hearsay evidence or rumour, and no matter how good a story seems to be, do not use it until you have checked it. The most sensational stories are often those which are likely to be inaccurate. Even inconsequential errors of fact can make you look foolish. If you 'think' a sportsman is a Czech and he turns out to be Slovakian, you will not be sued. But the fans of the club for which the Slovakian plays will know you got it wrong, and they will start to doubt the accuracy of everything else you say. It is much safer to check on the Czech. The golden rule you must always follow is: IF IN DOUBT, LEAVE IT OUT.

Similarly, you should never make assumptions without checking that they are correct, no matter how obvious they seem to you. For instance, if a cricketer with a well-documented history of marital difficulties suddenly pulls out of an overseas tour 'for family reasons', it is tempting to assume that his marriage is on the rocks again. Yet it could be that one of his parents or children is seriously ill. Jumping to the wrong conclusion could be extremely insensitive and embarrassing. The dictum to remember is: Never ASSUME – it makes an ASS out of U and ME.

Running stories and follow-ups

Some news stories are self-contained. Once we have read them there is nothing more we need to know. But many breaking stories are merely starting points. As time goes by the story will develop, or will have consequences which can lead to follow-up stories being written. Such stories fall into two categories – the RUNNING STORY and the FOLLOW-UP. A running story is one which develops over time. It may begin with an announcement by a drugs testing agency that an athlete has failed a drugs test, but from that point the story may 'run' for weeks. That announcement will be followed by a statement from the athlete accepting or denying guilt. Once the athlete's club or the sport's governing body has had time to consider the news, it will make a statement about whether the athlete is to be suspended from competition. The governing body will announce when its disciplinary committee will meet to hear the case. Fellow athletes will enter the debate with statements of support or criticism. The hearing will take place, a decision will be announced and a punishment may be imposed. There will be further public debate about whether the decision was just or the punishment is appropriate, and about the effects on the sport. The athlete may appeal against the decision or the punishment. If he or she is an international athlete, there may be consequences for the national team. The appeal will be heard. The national and international governing bodies may change their rules on drugs and drugs testing as a result of the case. A story which began with a simple announcement can often run for weeks or even years.

Follow-ups tend to be more limited in scope, maybe filling in some of the background or looking at the consequences of the original story. For instance, if a player moves from one club to another, a follow-up story may focus on how his original club intends to replace him in the team and what it intends to spend any transfer fee on. Or it could be angled on the role the player will be expected to perform at his new club, and the consequences of his arrival for any of his team-mates there.

Looking for a follow-up to a story can be a useful way of generating copy when there is not much other news around. The news content of many Sunday newspapers can consist largely of follow-ups to that week's news.

Journalistic ethics

Gathering information for and writing sports news stories will inevitably involve questions of journalistic ethics from time to time. It is rarely, if ever, acceptable for a journalist to resort to lies or deception in pursuit of a news story, or to secretly tape or film interviews. (Exceptions have been made when serious wrongdoing has been investigated, but only after careful consideration and consultation with senior news executives.)

Privacy

Issues of privacy are more difficult to handle. Sports men and women are necessarily in the public eye, they are often well rewarded for their skills, and many have been accorded celebrity status by the media. Public interest in them is, therefore, greater than it is in ordinary citizens. That does not, of course, mean that they are not entitled to their privacy, but it does mean that their activities are more closely scrutinised. Indiscretions involving drink or drugs or sex, or illegal activity which might go unnoticed in other people can become big stories as media organisations compete with each other for fresh revelations. There is an argument that 'sleaze' stories of this kind are in the public interest because the subjects are role models, especially for young people. However, the line between the right to privacy and the public's right to know is a fine one, and many of the discussions about journalistic ethics are around where that line should be drawn. The debate is especially fierce around kiss-and-tell stories, and whether the media should pay for bedroom revelations about sporting celebrities. Does the fact that someone is willing to reveal intimate details of a relationship give the media the right to invade the other partner's privacy?

Contempt of court

The indiscretions of some sports personalities lead to appearances in court. In one sense, this makes the journalist's job easier. Court hearings are public events which the media are entitled to report. Indeed, the involvement of the media is enshrined in the notion that justice should not only be done but should be *seen* to be done. However, the public's thirst for knowledge about celebrities should not tempt journalists to exceed their rights and responsibilities in relation to court proceedings. They need to take special care about what they publish in advance of any trial, or they may find themselves in contempt of court.

In Britain and some other countries, once a person has been charged with an offence there are strict limits about what the media can report before it is mentioned in court. For instance, a case involving the Leeds United footballers Jonathan Woodgate and Lee Bowyer over an incident outside a night club was halted by the Judge and had to be retried after an article appeared in a national newspaper.

Quotes

Direct quotes should never be altered, except in the interests of clarity or to correct an obvious error made by the person being quoted. They should never be edited or condensed without clear acknowledgement, and only then if the sense is unaltered.

Embargoes

An EMBARGO should always be respected, unless it has been imposed with the clear intention of delaying publication of a matter of public interest which would otherwise have appeared in the media earlier. It is common (and perfectly legitimate) for organisations to issue embargoed information to journalists in advance of the time at which it would otherwise have been made public. This gives the media an opportunity to prepare their stories thoroughly and dissuades journalists from publishing incomplete or inaccurate stories in order to avoid being beaten by their competitors. Indeed, most journalists find the embargo system useful, as it avoids the need for an unnecessary competitive scramble and gives them time to seek reaction to the story in advance of publication.

Embargoes are not legally binding, but most journalists abide by them because if they don't, they may fall victim to someone else's embargo-busting in future. However, if a journalist has obtained the same information from another source before the embargoed material arrives, he or she need not feel bound by the embargo. The simple rule with embargoes is to play fair by your journalist colleagues, but not to allow the subsequent release of embargoed material to deny you an EXCLUSIVE you have worked for and obtained through your own contacts.

Sensibilities

Sports journalists should always take care not to offend the sensibilities of others. They should take particular care to avoid sexism, racism, ageism and issues around disability creeping into their writing. The sports people about whom they write are predominantly young, white and male, and it is easy to overlook the interests of people who do not fit into that category.

Recent changes in sport and sports journalism mean that some prejudices are gradually being tackled. There is now more coverage of women's sport, particularly sports like football, cricket and rugby, which have been traditionally associated with men. There are also more female sports writers and presenters, although the balance in both cases is still overwhelmingly male. Similarly, black players and competitors have now established themselves and become successful in most professional sports, though the number of black sports journalists is still quite small.

The problems of racism in sport, and in sports journalism, have not disappeared, however. Racial taunts are still common among some sections of crowds at sporting events, while the refusal of a white South African rugby player to share a hotel room with one of his black colleagues, and the difficulties experienced by some white Zimbabwean cricketers, show that it is still endemic in some sports. Remarks made by an American television commentator about black gridiron football players show that it has not been entirely eliminated from the media, either.

The media still has a tendency to ignore events for disabled people or sports played mainly by older people (such as bowls), or to consign them to their own little ghettoes on the sports pages.

Influence

The relationship between sports journalists and the sports they cover is inevitably a close one. They must never allow it to become incestuous. Journalists are almost always given free access to events. They also get privileged access to competitors, players, coaches and administrators. They are sometimes provided with free travel and accommodation by event organisers or sponsors. They can be entertained or offered gifts of various kinds. All of this is perfectly legitimate, so long as journalists do not allow it to affect their objectivity or inhibit them from critical coverage when it is necessary.

The role of the sports photographer

The technical skills of the sports photographer are outside the scope of this book, but photography plays a vital part in the sports coverage of newspapers and websites. Photographers and journalists often work closely together on stories and features, the work of one complementing that of the other.

The role of the sports photographer is a difficult one. It often involves standing out in the cold, at a less-than-perfect vantage point, trying to keep an eye on the action and not miss important incidents like goals, while also looking for the unusual or dramatic picture. The sports photographer will usually be working alone, covering an event on which television may be focusing half a dozen cameras. It is an unequal contest.

For that reason, many photographers do not try to compete with television, which can cover the key moments from a number of different angles. Instead, they try to create their impact through the composition of their pictures and the action taking place in them, the expressions on competitors' faces, the contortions of their bodies, or maybe the flashpoint of an argument between opponents. Sometimes the most telling pictures are taken off the field of play and away from the competitors, concentrating on referees or umpires or the reaction of the crowd.

Most major newspapers employ specialist sports photographers, but many have to double up as news photographers on weekdays, and turn out to sporting events in the evening or on Saturday afternoons. They often face deadlines even tighter than those of their journalist colleagues, though sending pictures back to base is now easier since the arrival of digital cameras and modems. Photographers who, until recently, had to leave an event early and go back to the darkroom to process their pictures can now send them direct from the stadium. They can also preview the images they have taken and select those which work best.

However, like writers, once a photographer's work has been filed, it is out of his or her hands. The final decision about which picture to use will be taken by a page designer or sub-editor. In the end, picture selection will depend on the space available on a page, and whether an upright or portrait shape works better than a landscape. Only in exceptional circumstances will pages be redesigned to accommodate a really good picture.

Summary

The ability to research and write news stories are two of the key skills of the sports journalist. News stories are written to a formula, with the key points summarised in the opening paragraph (intro) and elaborated in order of importance in the main body of the story. They should be written so that they can be cut from the bottom to fit whatever space is available and in such a way that they make sense no matter where they are cut. Style and language should be as simple as possible, stories should stick to fact rather than opinion, and they should be accurate and fair to those involved.

7

Print journalism: sports features

Learning Objectives

- To understand the differences between features and other forms of sports journalism
- To recognise pegs and angles around which features may be written
- To know how to construct a feature and write in the appropriate style
- To understand the principles of writing profiles, opinion pieces and participation features

What is a sports feature?

Features are longer pieces of journalism which give writers the opportunity to treat a subject or individual in-depth, and often with style and wit. A feature-length article allows more space for background information, contributions from a greater number of sources covering a wider range of issues, and an opportunity to provide more comment and analysis. It also allows the writer to abandon the tight constraints of news story construction and write in a more colourful way. Because features need to sustain the interest of the reader over a longer period – anything from 500 to several thousand words – they need to be written in a bright and entertaining style.

The golden rules for writing features are:

- Grab their attention
- Keep their attention
- Leave them satisfied

Finding a peg or angle

Any piece of journalism needs a subject, but it is not enough simply to write about your favourite athlete or team. There has to be a reason for doing so, to engage the interest of readers. The subject around which a feature is written is normally in the news, or in the public eye, for some reason. An important sporting event may be coming up; a team or athlete may be doing particularly well or especially badly; a coach may have been fired; a player may be involved in a drugs scandal; someone may have been killed or injured at a stadium; a group of fans may have been involved in hooliganism or racist behaviour.

Any of these (and many other) events provide journalists with the subject matter for features. The events on which features are based are known as PEGS – they are the things on which the features are hung.

Having found a peg, the journalist must then find an ANGLE from which to write the piece. In the run-up to a big game, for instance, the feature writer may choose to focus on previous meetings and the rivalry between the two teams, or base the piece around a current or former player who has represented both teams, or look at the action the police are taking to prevent rival fans clashing. News that a coach has been sacked may prompt features about what makes a successful coach, an analysis of which other coaches may be in the firing line or a retrospective look at those who have already been fired this season, and whether a change of coach makes any difference to a team's success. Some journalists even take part in training sessions or competitions to try to give an insider's view of a sporting event.

Constructing a feature

The intro

Features are written in a more colourful style than news stories, and the same applies to intros. The function of the intro remains the same – to grab the reader's interest – but this can be done in a wider variety of ways than merely presenting the most important facts. The more expansive form of the feature allows journalists to approach the subject matter in a more subtle manner. Feature writers have come up with a range of ways of engaging the reader's interest and teasing them into reading on. Here are some of them:

Dropped intro

This delays the punch, so that the reader is left wondering who or what is the subject, which is then revealed some way into the feature:

> *When he walked through the door of the restaurant in a baggy, slightly-crumpled suit, he looked a small, deferential figure, who waited patiently for a waiter to show him to my table. It was difficult to believe that the weight of a nation's expectations would be resting on those slight shoulders.*
>
> *But tomorrow afternoon, with a pack of 20-stone All Blacks forwards bearing down on him, scrum half Will Smith will be the calm eye at the centre of the most ferocious storm of the international rugby season.*

Quote intro

News stories rarely begin with quotes because they get in the way of the facts, but a powerful quote can be a good way into a feature, painting a picture of the person who is speaking and sketching in some of the background before we meet them:

> *'When I missed that penalty in the semi-final of the World Cup I knew I had cost my team a place in history. But in an odd way it made me a stronger player, and if the Boss is looking for volunteers to take a penalty again this time, I'll be the first in the queue.'*

Historical intro

Some features demand to be set in historical perspective. A news feature on a stadium disaster or a gambling scandal might begin with a retrospective look at other disasters or scandals. Similarly, many sporting achievements assume extra interest because of the other achievements – or lack of them – that preceded them:

> *Anybody who can remember the last time the Giants won the Cup will qualify for concessionary entry to tomorrow's final, because it is seventy years since they last lifted the trophy.*

Contrast intro

Another teasing way into a feature is to make use of any contrasts the subject throws up. This might mean contrasting a giant defender on one team with a small but nippy forward on the other. Or it might be to contrast the past life or fortunes of a participant with the personality who is about to occupy centre stage:

> *Though he's never played at the Millennium Stadium, Mark Jones will feel perfectly at home when he walks on to the pitch. A year ago, as a brickie, he was helping to build the place with trowel and cement: tomorrow, as a pro, he'll be holding another wall together, as the keystone of the United defence.*

Question intro

A question would reduce the impact of the intro of a news story, but in a feature a question can again be used to whet the reader's appetite and coax them into discovering the answer:

> *How much would you pay to see your favourite team get slaughtered? Well, the fans of non-league Gresford Rovers, who normally pay three pounds to see their team's home matches, are willing to pay three hundred pounds for a ticket for their team's visit to the European champions in the next round of the cup.*

This is just a selection of the ways in which features can be introduced. What they have in common is that they make the reader sit up and take notice. There are innumerable variations on these themes, and two or more intro types can sometimes be combined. Always read the intros to features carefully and try to work out what the writer is doing and how he or she is luring you into reading the rest of the piece – the main body of the feature.

The body of the feature

Because most features have a news peg, we can almost take the news angle as read – that this pitcher is about to play in the World Series, that this jockey is riding the favourite in the big race, that an athlete has tested positive for drugs in the Olympic Games. The purpose of the body of the feature is to fill in the background to the news angle, by painting pictures of the people involved, by analysing the consequences of a newsworthy event, by trying to predict what will happen in the future. And to maintain the reader's interest over the longer distance, it is important that the writing should be colourful and varied, moving smoothly through a range of elements, from description to quotes to background detail to analysis, with bridging passages to link the various elements. There are examples of all these things later in this chapter.

The outro or payoff

The final paragraph of a news story is the least important, the first to be cut if the piece is too long. But because a feature must strive to maintain the reader's interest to the end, the final paragraph is not expendable. After the intro, it is perhaps the most important in the piece, because it is the one that will leave the final impression on the reader. The last paragraph of a feature is called the OUTRO (the opposite of an intro) or PAYOFF, and should round the piece off in a satisfactory way, just as the final paragraph of a novel does.

There are various ways of achieving this sense of wholeness. One of the most common is to bring the piece full circle, finishing it where it started:

> Intro: *Stratford striker Steve Strong is no stranger to finding his way through congested areas. His day job is a bus driver in London's northern suburbs.*
>
> Outro: *So after ninety minutes trying to find a way through the Liverpool defence, coping with rush hour on the North Circular will seem like child's play.*

An analytical piece may end by summarising the arguments it has covered, reach a conclusion or end by asking a question. A profile may end with a telling quote.

The standfirst

To give the reader a flavour of what the piece is about and to add visual interest to the page on which it appears, a feature is often preceded by a STANDFIRST. This is a short paragraph which outlines the thrust of the piece. It usually contains the writer's byline. Although it is the first thing (other than the headline) most people will read, it tends to be the last thing to be written, and will often be provided by a sub-editor rather than the journalist who wrote the piece.

Example

The Olympic Games return to their birthplace this year, but the facilities may not be ready on time. Summer spectacular or Greek tragedy? **Barbara Brown** *reports from Athens.*

Profiles

The most common form of feature found on the sports pages is the PROFILE. A profile is a biographical piece on an athlete, coach or administrator who is currently in the news. A profile can be as short as a few paragraphs or can fill a couple of pages. By definition it is a human-interest story, often with a celebrity at its heart, and therefore doubly popular with readers.

As explained above and in Chapter 5, the peg on which a profile is hung will often be the subject's involvement in an important forthcoming sports event. The piece will be written as part of the build-up to the event and the subject chosen because, of all the players taking part, he or she is of particular interest. The person may have played for the opposing team at some stage in the past, or be in a rich streak of form, or on the verge of breaking some sort of record, such as the number of goals or points or runs scored in the competition.

The most common way of gathering information for a profile is to interview the subject, and get his or her views on the forthcoming events and on the strengths and weaknesses of his or her own and the opposing team. (Interview techniques are covered in the next chapter.) But the best profiles, particularly those which aim to present a rounded picture of the subject rather than simply to elicit the person's views on a particular event, will look wider than this. They will also include the views of team mates or opponents who know him or her, coaches who have worked with the person and can assess his or her strengths and weaknesses, and background information on the subject's past achievements. This is one reason why a sports journalist needs a wide range of contacts.

If you can't get an interview with the subject of your profile (and it can be extremely difficult to arrange a one-to-one interview with leading sports personalities), it is possible to obtain their views from other sources. Many of them are contractually bound to attend press conferences before or after the events in which they are taking part, when you may be able to put some of your questions. Quotes they have made previously can be obtained from cuttings or from online archives, and many of them have their own websites, on which they give their views about a range of issues. When using material from these sources, however, you should take care not to infringe copyright laws (see Appendix 3).

Example

The following is a profile of the American tennis player Andre Agassi. The paragraphs are numbered for ease of reference in the discussion which follows.

1   It's obvious Andre Agassi is over the hill.

2   Watch him. He doesn't cover as much of the court as his younger opponents, but plays off the same two or three yards of the baseline.

3   After 19 years on the tennis circuit, the long hair that was his trademark is gone, his head shaven to hide the baldness of advancing years.

4   The excesses of his hot-blooded youth are things of the past, too.

5   He has two children now, and a string of lucrative advertising contracts. Marriage to another tennis superstar, Steffi Graf, has made him half of the richest family on the circuit, and can't have done much for his motivation.

6   But the trouble with Agassi is that he just doesn't look in the mirror.

7   At the age of 33, when other great champions like Bjorn Borg had been retired six years, Andre just keeps on winning.

8   'My age is irrelevant to me when I'm on court. My tennis speaks for itself,' says the man from Las Vegas. And at the moment, it's speaking as eloquently as ever.

9   We're midway through the Australian Open, the first Grand Slam of the year, and Agassi is still there. Indeed, it's difficult to remember when he wasn't. He hasn't been beaten in Melbourne for four years. He's now won 25 straight matches there (he didn't enter in 2002) and who would bet against him picking up his third Australian title of the new millennium?

10   'I've experienced every part of my game in the first week and liked the levels I've hit. I feel I'm in a position to go further and take it higher,' he says, his eyes twinkling, his enthusiasm undimmed.

11   So how does a man of Agassi's relatively-advanced years, who looks smaller and frailer than his five-feet-eleven frame, and who travels with his wife, two-year-old son Jaden and three-month-old daughter Jaz, go on beating men younger, bigger, stronger, hungrier and less encumbered than he is?

12   'I try to make sure everything is sharp, to have a game plan. I know that if I'm fit and strong and moving well I'm going to get more opportunities to do the things I do well.'

13   And that takes sweat and dedication. When he is not working out in the gym with his strength trainer Gil Reyes, he is running up and down a thousand-foot hill near his home in California every day. And that includes Christmas Day and New Year's Day.

14   'He does it in the rain, in the heat, in the cold,' says Reyes. 'He's stronger now than he's ever been in his life. Andre sprints until his legs burn and his entire body aches. That's when you see what he's all about.'

15   Agassi puts so much effort into maintaining his fitness because, after so long in the game, he has nothing more to learn about technique.

16   As he says: 'It's impossible at 33 years old that I'm going to hit a tennis ball better than I already hit it.'

17   So now you know why Agassi doesn't move far from the middle of the baseline. The sheer pace he generates means he doesn't have to. It's his opponents who do all the running.

18   But that kind of technique took a lot of acquiring.

19   One of his old adversaries, the former Swedish player Mats Wilander (yes, Agassi is old enough to have played against him), once famously accused the American of not knowing how to construct points on a tennis court.

20   But now Wilander says Agassi knows his own game better than any other player, knows exactly what he needs to do to win.

21   'He has honed his tennis brain. That's why he's able to be so fresh so late in his career – because it's so new to him,' he says.

22   The precocious kid who burst onto the circuit as a brash teenager soon learned how to construct points well enough to win eight Grand Slams and 50 other singles titles.

23   When he won the French Open in 1999, Agassi joined Fred Perry, Don Budge, Rod Laver and Roy Emerson as one of only five men to win all four Grand Slam titles. And there could be more to come.

24 His coach Darren Cahill, who has also coached the youngest Number 1, Lleyton Hewitt, seems to think so. Rumour has it that Wimbledon champion Roger Federer would like to employ him, but for the moment Cahill is sticking with the older man.

25 And Reyes believes Agassi can stay at this level 'for another two or three years'.

26 But even Andre knows he can't go on for ever. 'The day I feel I can't get any better, I'll be pretty clear about that,' he says.

27 'It gets harder every year. I have a lot of belief in my training programme, so I don't struggle with the motivation. But you struggle with getting older.'

28 Try telling that to Agassi's latest victim, the young Paradorn Srichaphan from Thailand, who surprisingly beat him in straight sets in the second round at Wimbledon two years ago.

29 'He's really playing well and was moving me a lot from side to side,' said Srichaphan when they came off court yesterday.

30 Agassi won in three sets, extending his unbeaten run in the tournament to 25 matches.

31 Over the hill? Agassi just goes on tramping up the mountain.

Discussion

Paragraph 1: The intro grabs the attention because it flies in the face of the facts. The reader will know that Agassi is in excellent form, and will therefore want to read on to see how the writer will justify the opening sentence, the more so if the reader strongly disagrees with the assertion that is being made.

Paragraph 2: The brief sentence: 'Watch him' serves two purposes. First, it includes the readers in the story, invites them to become part of the argument, mentally transports them to the courtside in Melbourne. Secondly, it invites them to paint a picture of the player in the mind's eye, a picture which the subsequent three paragraphs flesh out with detail about his appearance, his playing style, his family.

Paragraph 6: 'He just doesn't look in the mirror.' Looking in the mirror is the way most of us realise, sometimes with shock, that we are getting older. The metaphor underlines the fact that Agassi is ignoring the ageing process.

Paragraph 7: Agassi keeps on winning. The false assertion of the intro is overturned and, having been tricked into reading this far, we discover what the piece is really about. Note how here and in subsequent paragraphs, background details like his age, his record and comparisons with other well-known players like Borg, are woven smoothly into the text. It would have been easier simply to have dropped these details in as a free-standing paragraph, but this would have interrupted the smooth flow of the text and perhaps discouraged some readers from reading on.

Paragraph 8: Having introduced the subject of the profile, we now hear directly from him. Clearly, it is important to quote the subject if possible. It can be difficult to get a one-to-one interview with leading sports figures because of the demands on their time, but many of them are regularly available at post-match press conferences.

'At the moment its speaking as eloquently as ever' provides a smooth bridge between Agassi's comment and the following paragraph, which provides more background on the tournament in which he is currently playing.

Paragraph 9: Note the present tense, which gives a sense of immediacy. The piece is about what's happening *now* rather than what happened yesterday. The rhetorical question with which the paragraph ends leads us smoothly back to Agassi and his views on his chances of winning the tournament.

Paragraph 10: 'His eyes twinkling, his enthusiasm undimmed.' Unlike a radio or television interview, in print we can't see or hear the person who is talking. But a person's body language and general demeanour often helps us interpret what they are saying and helps paint a picture of the person in our minds. The reader, therefore, needs to be told.

Paragraph 11: Inserting a question into a profile is a useful way of holding the reader's interest. In this case, the question also encapsulates further description of Agassi and some information about his family the reader may not know. Introducing it like this is preferable to spoon-feeding the reader with gobbets of fact. And having been asked these questions, the reader is more likely to stay with the piece to find out the answers.

Paragraph 13: Agassi's remarks about fitness are linked smoothly to a comment from the man who helps keep him in shape. If a profile is to provide a rounded picture of its subject it should also include the views of other people who know them well.

Paragraph 14: Reyes' comment has been selected not only for what it says but because of the graphic way in which it is said. It paints a vivid words-picture of the athlete in training.

Paragraphs 15/16: The writer introduces his own view about Agassi as a tennis player, which is given added weight when it is immediately confirmed by Agassi himself.

Paragraphs 17/18: More of the writer's analysis, but this time explaining the apparently critical reference in the second paragraph.

Paragraphs 19–21: A second 'outsider's' view is introduced, and it is an important one. We would expect Reyes, as an employee of Agassi, to say supportive things about him, but a former opponent might take a more objective view. Indeed, Wilander has been critical of Agassi in the past, and is therefore ideally placed to offer a view on why he is now so successful. And reminding the reader that Agassi played against a man who has been retired for many years helps underline the longevity of his career.

Paragraph 22: The description of Agassi's younger self, with appropriate adjectives – precocious, burst, brash – helps to illustrate Wilander's point, offers a stark contrast with the player he has now become and prepares us for the success the change has brought, which is outlined in the following paragraph.

Paragraph 24: Mention of Agassi's coach and his involvement (or lack of it) with younger players helps cement the article's contention that Agassi is still at or near the top of the pecking order.

Paragraph 26: The question of how long Agassi can remain at the top has been hanging over the entire piece, and the reader has been kept waiting for the answer. Now, towards the end of the piece, this tension is relieved and the answer is supplied by the man himself.

Paragraph 28: The piece concludes by telling us that, in contrast to the gradual decline Agassi himself suggests will set in sooner or later, he is still getting better, beating a younger man who beat him two years previously. Reference to his most recent match also restores the piece, which has necessarily dealt with the past a good deal, firmly back in the present.

Paragraph 31: The outro, or payoff, neatly bring the piece full circle. It picks up the reference in the intro to Agassi being over the hill, and gives it a twist by introducing a related metaphor about climbing mountains which has the opposite meaning. Referring back to the intro in this way is a useful device when no other obvious payoff – such as reference to the subject's next match or opponent – suggests itself. It always works because it leaves the reader with the feeling of having read a carefully crafted, rounded piece that ends satisfactorily rather than merely peters out.

Opinion columns

Opinion columns are useful components of the sports pages for a number of reasons. They help to fill the space on those quiet days when there is not much live sport on which to report; they give an opportunity for the paper's best journalists to write with style and wit; they offer a platform to well-known figures from the world of sport, whose names above their columns will attract readers; they generate controversy and provoke discussion and argument among readers; and they help to keep running stories alive until the next significant development crops up. These things are particularly important now that many people get their basic information – especially about sport – from sources other than newspapers, such as radio, television, teletext, the internet and even their mobile phones.

Columnists range from those with regular weekly slots to those who write an opinion piece only when the spirit moves them or when they are specially commissioned to do so because of their unique expertise. They include former sports professionals and coaches who can bring their first-hand experience to the stories of the day, and the best sports journalists, who enliven the pages with stylish, witty, entertaining and controversial writing.

The best opinion columns combine the insights of the sports expert and the style of the professional writer. Opinion columns should be informed, but they should also be well-constructed pieces of writing. Columns can be made up of a single, longer piece or a number of shorter items.

As with most other features, an opinion column needs a peg on which it can be hung. The peg will often be a current story with an element of controversy to it – a failed drugs test, an outburst by a coach, a change to the rules of a sport – that will give the writer the opportunity to explore all sides of the issue and come down on one side or the other. Many columns are the printed equivalent of a discussion in the pub or on the way home from the game.

The most important element of a good column is controversy. The writer's opinions don't have to be popular, or even reflect the views of the paper for which he or she is writing. Some of the best columnists deliberately take unpopular views to stimulate the readers' interest and give them something to argue against. But opinions should always be based on hard facts, so careful research is essential. And an opinion column should never be used to pursue grudges.

People don't read columns primarily for information, although a good column will supply its readers with all the information they need to understand it and the arguments advanced in it. They read them for the views expressed and the quality and entertainment value of the writing. So an effective column, like any other feature, will need to grab the reader's attention from the outset and hold it through to the end. Ideally, it will also leave readers with a sense of satisfaction and encourage them to read more by the same writer the next time the column appears.

An effective column will probably need some, though not necessarily all, of the following elements:

- A peg – a recent news story with an element of controversy on which the piece is based.
- An arresting intro which will engage the readers' attention and make them want to read on (see notes on intros above).

- A witty, controversial, no-nonsense, hard hitting, style with vocabulary, grammar and sentence-length appropriate to the paper for which it is written.
- An insider's view or expert analysis of the issue, airing all sides of the argument and making comparisons with other people or events, if necessary.
- A definite stance, with arguments which justify your position.
- A recap of the story and any background detail necessary to allow readers to understand the piece. A judgement may be needed as to how much knowledge the reader can be expected to bring to the piece. If it uses a major sports story as its peg, the reader will probably be familiar with the basic detail.
- An ending which will leave readers with the feeling they have read a well-rounded and satisfying piece.

Elements of an opinion column

- Find a peg
- Write an arresting intro
- Recap the story
- Give any necessary background detail
- Make comparisons, if necessary
- Give both sides of the argument
- Reach a conclusion
- Justify it
- Write with wit, humour and style
- Be controversial
- End in a satisfying way

Example

The following is an opinion piece about women playing in men's golf tournaments. The peg is a short news item. The paragraphs are numbered for ease of reference in the discussion which follows.

News item

Former women's golf Number One Laura Davies has been invited to compete in the ANZ tournament – part of the men's golf tour – at Port Stephen in Australia.

But the sponsors' invitation has prompted Greg Norman, the Australian who twice won the Open, to call for a change in the regulations banning women from competing in men's tournaments.

There was a similar controversy when current Number One Annika Sorenstam was invited to take part in the Colonial tournament in Texas. She failed to make the cut.

Opinion piece

1 The ANZ golf tournament starts at Port Stephen today.

2 The what? And where?

3 All right, it's not the Open at St Andrew's but the world's media will be out in force. The reason is that Laura Davies is playing.

4 Yes, I know it's almost a decade since she was the female equivalent of Tiger Woods and she's since been overtaken in the pecking order of women's golf by Annika Sorenstam and – well – just about everybody else, to be honest.

5 But suddenly she's back centre-stage. Why?

6 Because she is the only woman playing in a men's tournament, and though it's now the twenty-first century – even in Port Stephen – it's caused a bit of a stir.

7 If all this is giving you a feeling of *déjà vu*, don't worry. You *have* been through it all before – when Sorenstam became the first woman to compete against men in the Colonial tournament in Texas last year.

8 Now, just when women golfers thought it was safe to go back in the water, along comes the Great White Shark (aka Aussie golfer Greg Norman, the double Open winner), who wants the regulations changed to exclude women from men's events.

9 His views will doubtless strike a chord in golf clubs around the world.

10 Poor, weak women will never compete on level terms with big, strong men is still the accepted wisdom at the nineteenth hole.

11 What's more, they'll turn up in shorts and other unsuitable items of clothing (as opposed to the chequered trousers and ridiculous baseball caps favoured by middle-aged golfers of the male persuasion).

12 Perfectly understandable views in a sport in which the only club which annually hosts a Major tournament – the Masters at Augusta, Georgia – refuses to accept female members, and the body which runs the sport in the rest of the world – the Royal and Ancient – doesn't want them either.

13 Ancient their views certainly are. It's nearly a century since the Suffragettes won the vote for women, and the world hasn't ended yet. But fair play for the fair sex on the fairways is still a long way off.

14 Women will never reach their full potential in sport until they are accepted on equal terms and the culture that surrounds most sports – even those like snooker, where physical strength is no advantage – is changed so that they feel free to get involved from an early age, like their brothers.

15 Women are not going to put in the hours of practice that is vital to success as long as they feel excluded. And if we keep giving the men a head start, they'll go on winning.

16 When women are accepted on equal terms, in sports like athletics and tennis, they can give men a good run for their money. There aren't many men who can keep up with Paula Radcliffe, and little Billy Jean King demonstrated years ago that she was more than a match for a man.

17 Of course some men can hit a golf ball further than any woman, but most of us can't hit it as far as Davies. And length off the tee is about the only area of the game where women are disadvantaged.

18 Their touch, chipping, putting and course management can all be as good as men's, and it would be easy to level the playing field, by letting them play off the front of the tees.

19 Too easy, perhaps. Because I suspect the real reason that male pros want to keep women out of men's tournaments is that so many of them are making good livings at the game even if they never make a cut. Let in the women, and there's not as much to go round for the men.

20 The result is that women golfers like Davies are being used sporadically as freak-shows by sponsors. Port Stephens is 125 miles north of Sydney and the ANZ would have attracted little publicity had she not been invited.

21 That, too, has annoyed Norman, and here he is right.

22 But the answer is not to ban women from men's tournaments. It's to let them compete and improve and to take their place alongside men in the game, at whatever level that might be.

23 That's the only sensible way to sort the men from the girls.

Discussion

Paragraph 1: The intro teases readers into wondering why an obscure golf tournament in a remote Australian town should be of interest to them. The peg has not yet been made clear.

Paragraph 2 echoes readers' concerns and gives them a stake in the piece by asking the questions they have just asked themselves. Questions are a useful way of maintaining readers' interest, encouraging them to read on to find the answers.

Paragraphs 3 and 4: The writer supplies more facts and background information without answering the questions. Readers are teased further into wondering why they should be interested in this particular woman golfer.

Paragraph 5 asks another question, and immediately releases the tension by answering it.

Paragraph 6 introduces the tone of ironic humour – it's the twenty-first century *even in Port Stephen* – that runs through the piece and defines the writer's style.

Paragraph 8 cleverly links the issue of women playing in men's tournaments to the man who wants to exclude them. The writer uses a well-known quote from the publicity for the film *Jaws* – 'Just when you thought it was safe to go back in the water' – to connect the issue to Greg Norman, the Great White Shark.

Paragraphs 9–12 marshal the arguments against women playing in men's tournament, but from a consistenly ironic perspective ('poor, weak women', 'big, strong men', 'unsuitable clothing'), and puts those views in the context of the game's governing bodies.

Paragraphs 13–15 marshal the arguments in favour of women playing, but now free from irony. They are summed up in a memorable way: 'fair play for the fair sex on the fairways is still a long way off'. Passages of striking writing like this help maintain the reader's interest.

Paragraphs 16–18 provide the justification for the conclusion the writer has reached over this issue.

Paragraph 19 further subverts the arguments for admitting women by suggesting the subtext that lies behind them.

Paragraph 22: The piece finishes with a firm opinion stated unequivocally. The reader is left in no doubt about where the writer stands on the issue.

Paragraph 23: The argument is summed up with another striking phrase that gives a neat twist to a well-known expression and rounds the piece off satisfactorily.

News features

As we have seen in the previous chapter, sport generates news stories beyond the confines of the field of play. They may concern administrators, or finance, or sports arenas, or the organisation of tournaments, or drug abuse, or a host of other things. News features look beyond the bare bones of these stories and expand on them. They may contain description, comment, analysis, background historical detail and eye-witness accounts, and make use of a broader range of sources.

The standfirst quoted above refers to a news feature about preparations for the Olympic Games in Athens. The feature would have looked at the delays in building facilities, the reasons for the delays and the likely impact on the competition, and would have quoted Olympic organisers, the Greek government, national athletics federations and individual athletes. The journalist may also have offered his or her own analysis and synthesis of the evidence gathered for the feature.

Editorials

Sport has now assumed such a central role in modern culture that some of the stories it generates are regarded as serious enough to warrant editorial comment in our newspapers. Editorials (or Leaders, or Leading Articles, as they are sometimes called) reflect the views of the newspaper and are usually carried in a column on the Leader page, with the newspaper's masthead at the top. They can be humorous if the subject allows it, but they are usually serious and reflective, looking at all sides of a story and forming an opinion based on solid argument. They do not seek to provoke controversy for its own sake, as some opinion columns do, but to represent the considered stance of the publication. They are usually written by editorial writing specialists with no BYLINE because these are the considered views of the newspaper.

Timeless features

Occasional gaps in the sporting programme create a demand for pieces that can be used to fill space when few events are taking place and when there are no major stories to provide pegs for feature writers. Because they can be used any time they are known as TIMELESS FEATURES. They may provide an opportunity to look at minority sports which do not normally command space on the sports pages, or to find unusual angles on major ones. Examples of timeless features might be a look at the lives of club mascots or at the work of the people who look after the grounds or the playing kit.

Colour pieces

Writers will sometimes be sent to sporting events not to cover the event itself but to give an impression of what it is like to be there. The features they produce are known as COLOUR PIECES, and they are often written from the perspective of the ordinary spectator rather than participant or privileged journalist. Writing a colour piece may involve travelling on the coach with the fans, drinking in a bar with them before the game, walking to the ground with them through the streets of a strange city, joining in the chanting and singing before the game, feeling the elation and the deflation with them as the action unfolds, dissecting the experience with them afterwards as they make their way home. Colour pieces concentrate on description, on eye-witness reporting, on quotation and factual detail to give the flavour of being there.

Participation features

Some of the best sports colour features are written by reporters who find out from the inside what it is like to be a sports professional, who join in the training sessions and try to do it themselves. Such pieces attempt to get beyond the surface description of sports events and try to get inside the lives of professional athletes, the training routines, the tactical talks, the treatment tables, the pain through which they have to push their bodies to succeed. They try to peer beneath the tip of the iceberg that is competition and examine the huge chunks of an athlete's life which lie below the glittering surface.

They also provide an opportunity of 'showing' readers what an athlete's life is like rather than merely 'telling' them. 'Telling' and 'showing' are important weapons in a writer's armoury, and 'showing' is the more powerful. To show someone something is the next best thing to letting them experience it for themselves. To tell someone something is to give them the information second-hand.

Example

1 'Take one of these,' says Chris Walker as we ride out of the car park, 'in case you feel the Knock.'

2 'The what?'

3 'The Knock. We sometimes call it the Bonk.'

4 'I see.'

5 One of these is a banana, and the Knock or the Bonk, according to taste, turns out to be the cyclist's equivalent of the Wall, that sudden drop in blood sugar levels that hits athletes after a couple of hours of hard physical effort. You feel the Knock quite often when you take life at an average speed of 30mph, 100 miles a day, seven days a week, 40 weeks a year.

6   Chris Walker is a professional cyclist. He's about to set off on Britain's toughest sporting event, the 14-day, 1150-mile Round Britain Race, and he's invited me along for a spot of last-minute training.

7   Dressed in black ballet tights and a technicolour jersey constructed entirely of sponsors' logos and pockets for my bananas, I am about to discover first-hand (or perhaps through a different part of my anatomy) the pains and pleasures of life in the saddle.

8   We turn left out of the car park, which is just as well, because turning right would have taken us on a 90-mile round-trip through the mountains that Chris has already made twice this week.

9   'Just a nice, steady run,' he says, but we settle instead for a more leisurely 15-mile circuit that will let me get the feel of the ten-gear, £1500 individually-tailored, hand-made bike on which Chris spends most of his working life.

10 He's a member of the Raleigh–Banana team, so called because Raleigh make bikes and high-carbohydrate bananas make them go further, releasing a steady flow of energy to the rider over a long race.

11 They make a change from jam and cheese sandwiches, the other big favourites with men on the move.

12 Chris trains up to 500 miles a week in these hills, on the roads and on mountain bikes up almost vertical slopes I would hesitate to tackle with crampons and an ice axe.

13 He has to. A professional cyclist's job security depends on performance, and performance depends on the effort you are prepared to make in training.

14 Top men like Chris make a good living as sponsored riders here and on the Continent, but the less successful pros, who could earn more for considerably less effort on a building site, are desperate to beat the big names and grab their places in the sponsored teams.

15 'We have to be on the ball all the time,' says Chris, who is 24 and in his third season as a pro. 'The pressure is always on me to do well.'

16 But the really big money comes with winning a place in a team in the Tour de France, arguably the world's greatest sporting event.

17 'I wouldn't want to be a *domestique*, one of the men the Continental teams employ just to help their top men win. I like a bit of glory,' says Chris.

18 But winning bike races depends less on individual riders than on team tactics. The riders in form will have the rest of the team working for them, helping to close up breakaways by other teams, getting them into position for bunch sprints at the end of a stage, and keeping them out of the wind.

19 The rider in the wind at the front of the race uses 30 to 40 per cent more energy than those behind him, which is why races form a *peloton*, an arrowhead formation with little wind resistance, like a great animal on the move.

20 It is a system open to jealousy and friction among a small group of riders living out of saddlebags for weeks at a time, but strife is rare.

21 'There can be a bit of elbowing and barging in a race,' says Chris. 'It has been known for people to have fights, but it is an unwritten rule that you make up straight away. You have got to ride with these blokes again, week in and week out.'

22 Each team is a mix of sprinters, like Chris, who are good on the flat stages, and climbers, who are good in the mountains. The best climbers are usually tall, light men with a good power-to-weight ratio.

23 At the foot of a hill your tall, light reporter has begun to feel the Knock. I unzip my banana. It is not a good move.

24 To begin with, eating and pedalling a bike uphill are not mutually compatible activities; secondly, it is bad tactics, and tactics are as important in cycling as pedal-power.

25 'If I made an attack on you now, you wouldn't be able to breathe with your mouth full. I would be away,' says Chris. 'You should have eaten *before* we got to the hill.

26 'Cycling is like chess on wheels. You have to use a bit of kidology, pretend you are on your last legs all the way up the hill, then shoot past the others at the last minute when there is no chance they will come back at you.'

27 Ten miles into our run, quadriceps complaining at every turn of the crank, 'on the rivet' as we *aficionados* say (nose right down on the rivet of the handlebars with fatigue), I am happy just to get to the summit.

28 But at least I have discovered why they do it: it's so good when it stops.

29 'It's mind-blowing sometimes. They say marathon running is hard. They run 26 miles perhaps four times a year. We have 100 mile stages every day for a week, and that is just one race,' says Chris.

30 'But if you can wake up every day happy to do it again, that's the difference between a winner and a loser.'

Discussion

Paragraph 1: The piece takes us straight inside the world of professional cycling by introducing us to some of the jargon the professionals, like those in any other business, use among themselves. This is also a good example of a 'dropped intro'. We are not quite sure what is going on until paragraph 6.

Paragraph 5: The physiological effects of the sport and the stark statistics of the mileage a cyclist covers each year are juxtaposed to underline how tough the life can be.

Paragraph 7: This paints a word picture of what is happening, undercut by humour to emphasise that the writer is not really part of that world.

Paragraphs 9–10: A lot of thought has gone into the style of the piece. The quote, 'Just a nice steady run', has been chosen for its irony, and the name of the racing team – Raleigh–Banana – has been cleverly deconstructed: 'Raleigh make bikes and high-carbohydrate bananas make them go further.'

Paragraphs 13–16: Having grabbed the attention of the reader in the first few paragraphs, the writer can now free-wheel for a while and throw in some analysis of the realities of a cyclist's life.

Paragraph 17: More insider talk about *domestiques*, but it is explained for the benefit of the outsider, who in this case is the reader.

Paragraph 21: Vivid quotes from the professional build on the earlier descriptions of life behind the scenes.

Paragraphs 23–25: The writer steps back into the picture to 'show' us how the professional's inside knowledge is superior to that of the amateur.

Paragraphs 26–29: The piece ends with more 'shop' jargon, more insider description and quotes, and more humour: 'I have discovered why they do it: it's so good when it stops.'

Paragraph 30: The outro, or payoff, brings us full circle with another quote from the pro – and a telling one which sums up the whole philosophy of the professional bike rider.

Exercise

Find a colleague who plays a sport with which you are not familiar. It does not have to be to professional standards. Go to a training session and join in. Talk to the other participants and find out what interests them about the sport and why they do it.

Immediately afterwards, make notes about the experience, of how it felt physically, of how difficult it was to pick up the skills, and jot down any interesting quotes you were given. Write a participatory piece using some of the techniques described in this chapter. Try to make the language you use interesting and amusing, remember that it is better to 'show' than to 'tell', and pay particular attention to the intro and outro.

If you are part of a group, read your pieces to each other and identify those sections which give the best insider's view of the sport. Also try to identify good examples of writing which 'show' us what the sport is about.

Crossover pieces

Because professional sports people are in the public eye and often highly-paid, their activities on and off the field of play are scrutinised with the same interest journalists and their audiences devote to celebrities in any other walk of life. We are interested not only in their work, but in their private lives. We want to know about their relationships, their health, their leisure activities, their clothes, their sexual misdemeanours, their gambling or drugs or drinking problems, their brushes with the law.

As a result, news stories about sports people will sometimes 'cross over' from strictly sporting topics to other areas of life. These stories often provide pegs for features about social issues. These are known as CROSSOVER PIECES.

For example, shortly before the 2002 soccer World Cup finals in Japan and South Korea, the England team captain, David Beckham, damaged the metatarsal bones in his foot. Because the World Cup is one of the biggest sporting events in the world, and Beckham was one of the highest-profile players, the story quickly expanded beyond the confines of the sports pages. For several days, news bulletins and features pages were carrying pieces by doctors and health correspondents, describing the nature of the injury, how such injuries happened and how long it might take to heal. The articles were often accompanied by drawings showing where the metatarsal bones are located. A sports story had crossed over to become a medical story.

Many crossover pieces deal with moral issues, often suggested by court cases or police investigations involving sports stars. Allegations of sexual assault made against Leicester City footballers while at a training camp in Spain, and against other Premiership players in a London hotel, prompted pieces about standards of sexual morality in modern sport. Suggestions that Australian and Indian cricketers had been involved with bookmakers produced pieces about match fixing in cricket and other sports. Allegations about the use of performance-enhancing drugs among baseball and tennis players and athletes frequently produce pieces examining the role of drugs in sport. A story about the refusal of a white South African rugby player to share a hotel room with a black team mate led to features about racism in sport.

Such pieces often demand expertise which is outside the field of the sports journalist. They are therefore often written by, or in conjunction with, specialists in other fields, such as medical or business or legal correspondents. Sports journalists are often happy to let other specialists deal with the more controversial off-field issues, to avoid souring relationships with performers they will frequently have to deal with again over sporting issues.

Exercise

Look through the sports pages of your daily newspaper and try to identify stories which lend themselves to crossover pieces. They will normally raise questions about wider social issues. Decide on the angle you would take if you were writing such a piece, and on the other specialist journalists you would collaborate with (or to whom you would hand over the story).

Keep an eye out for crossover pieces in newspapers and magazines. Because their subject matter is often of interest to a very wide readership, they will often appear in the news or features sections of newspapers rather than on the sports pages.

Summary

Sports features serve a number of important functions in newspapers and magazines. Their extended length allows journalists to deal with their subjects in greater depth. It gives them an opportunity to handle their material in a more amusing and creative way, and thus provide readers with the entertainment for which many of them say they turn to the sports pages. They also offer an opportunity for analysis and opinion, which is normally excluded from 'hard' news stories. But feature writing demands skills as disciplined as those required for reporting sports events or writing news stories. The best way of acquiring them is to study and try to imitate the techniques professional sports feature writers bring to their work.

Interviewing

Learning Objectives

- To understand the functions of a journalistic interview
- To be able to make satisfactory arrangements for conducting an interview
- To appreciate the value of research and the preparation of appropriate questions
- To understand how to select and use those parts of an interview which are appropriate to your needs
- To appreciate the importance of using quotes fairly and accurately

Sports journalism is not only about what performers do on the field of play, but what they and their coaches and administrators say off it. As with any other form of journalism, one of the most important skills is to be able to gain access to the people at the centre of the story, get them to give you their views and impressions, and present what they say clearly and accurately.

This will normally involve conducting an interview with the person or people involved, and selecting relevant quotes (and perhaps other pieces of information) for inclusion in the piece being prepared. As we have seen in earlier chapters, journalists writing features, news stories or match reports will be looking for certain kinds of information. Conducting a successful interview involves more than merely turning up with a notebook and asking the first questions which come into your head. A useful interview will involve careful preparation and a clear knowledge of what you hope it will produce. This chapter is designed to help you get the best from your interviews. (Broadcast interviews demand their own techniques, and they are dealt with more thoroughly in Chapter 9.)

Setting up the interview

The first task journalists face is to persuade prospective interviewees to talk to them. If you are setting up an interview direct with the interviewee, be polite and remember that at the precise moment you call they may have more important things to do than arrange to be interviewed by you. Explain why you want to do the interview, what the end product will be, where it is going to appear and how long the interview is likely to take. Anyone who is being asked to reveal details about their lives has a right to know these things, and if they are being asked to give up their time, they will want to know if it is going to be worthwhile.

That is not the same, however, as agreeing to allow the subject any kind of editorial control over the finished article. If they are worried about this, try to assure them what they say will be treated accurately and fairly, but resist any request to see the piece before publication. If there is no avoiding this, and getting the interview is sufficiently important, make it clear that the only changes you will be prepared to make are to errors of fact. Giving a subject the power of veto over the tone of an article or the views of the writer (or those of anyone else who is quoted in it) means that it can never be an objective piece. Some sports people (or their agents – see below) have begun asking journalists to sign written agreements giving them the right to make changes to a finished article. An interview conducted under these circumstances is rarely worth doing, and there are other ways (see below) of getting the quotes you need to write your piece.

Some interviews have to be arranged through an AGENT or press officer. Try to establish a good relationship with these people, as they are often the key to access. State which organisation you are working for, the purpose of the interview, where you would prefer to conduct the interview and whether you are taking a photographer with you. You may have to be prepared to fit into an athlete's tight schedule, so always try to give a duration for the interview. Somewhere between 30 minutes and an hour should be ample for all but the longest profile piece. You may have to make do with less, in which case preparation will become even more important (see below).

Where to conduct the interview

If you are offered the choice of venue for the interview, try to choose somewhere which will give you a better insight into the interviewee's personality, such as his or her home, or into his or her professional life, such as dressing room, training ground or stadium. People's surroundings always say something about them, and describing these surroundings in your piece will set the subject in context for the reader. You should also try to make sure that you will be free from interruptions and the presence of other people (unless you want comments from them as well) who might inhibit the interviewee's freedom to talk.

The venue you choose may depend on whether your piece is to be illustrated with pictures. The photographs will be more interesting if we see the athlete in his or her natural environment, and it is less demanding of an interviewee's time to take the photographs at the same time as the interview. It is good practice to liaise with your photographer before making the arrangements for the interview. The photographer may have a suggestion to make that you had not thought of, which could lead to a more interesting piece.

The choice of venue is particularly important for television interviews (see Chapter 9).

Rules of engagement

It is essential to establish in advance the conditions under which an interview is to take place. Most interviews are straightforward and come with no preconditions. But some interviewees or their representatives may ask to see a list of questions before being interviewed, or state that some areas of questioning are off-limits. You will need to take a judgement on the legitimacy of such requests before deciding whether to go ahead with the interview. In either case, the spontaneity of the interview will be reduced, but there may be no harm in submitting questions.

The interview process itself should offer the opportunity of getting subjects to expand on their answers, and despite the best efforts of their representatives to protect them, once they come face-to-face with a journalist, subjects are often amenable to answering follow-up questions.

Whether or not to proceed if some areas are off-limits will depend on how central those areas are to the piece you are hoping to produce. You may choose to agree if the information you will be able to get by sticking to those areas which are on-limits is essential to your article. In any event, the fact that a subject is not prepared to answer questions on a particular issue should not prevent you from covering that issue in your piece, perhaps by using other sources to throw light on it. And the fact that the subject is not prepared to discuss the issue is revealing in itself.

Unless the organisation for which you are working is paying a fee for the interview (which does not happen very often), you should avoid allowing interviewees or their agents to see and approve your copy or broadcast tape. This is close to censorship, and if it means you don't get an interview, there are other ways of obtaining information.

Informal interviews

Leading sports personalities get so many requests for interviews that they cannot possibly agree to them all. Unless you are working for a major newspaper, magazine or broadcaster, your chances of getting a face-to-face or even telephone interview with the top performers or coaches may be slim. But that should not prevent you from writing your profile. Like celebrities in any field, the top sports stars can be elusive, but they usually have to make themselves available to the media at some point. They often have to attend press conferences after events in which they have taken part as part of the contract they have with the event organisers, in whose interests it is to keep the media happy. They also make public appearances, which usually include media opportunities of some sort, in support of sponsors who are paying them for the publicity they attract. Although not as satisfactory as a one-to-one interview, these appearances offer journalists another opportunity of asking questions.

As a last resort, you may have to get what you can where you can. This may involve talking to your subjects as they come out of the players' or competitors' entrance, in the stadium car park or at the training ground. This is sometimes known as an AMBUSH INTERVIEW, though it should not be treated as a licence to behave rudely or unethically. A certain amount of unwanted attention comes with the territory for highly-paid sports people who make their living in the entertainment industry, but they should only be approached in the appropriate circumstances. Celebrities have a right to privacy, too, and it would not be appropriate to interrupt a family shopping trip or a meal in a restaurant to ask questions.

If you do decide to conduct an ambush interview, be polite but persistent, be very clear before you approach the subject about the questions you would like answers to, and be prepared to phrase them in a number of different ways. This can sometimes get you past an initial non-committal answer from someone who is not prepared for an interview.

The importance of research

In whatever circumstances your interview is conducted, you should try to do some research on the person you will be talking to and the area in which he or she operates. For instance, if the interviewee is involved in a minority sport, you may have to learn its rules and something about the person's standing within the sport. Finding out as much about your subject as possible before going to the interview not only saves time, it also helps put the interviewee in the right frame of mind. Sports people who have their own websites, who are used to being interviewed on radio and television and seeing their names in the newspapers, often have an inflated view of how much the rest of the world knows about them. If your knowledge of their careers is less than they believe it ought to be, they will be less well disposed towards you, but if you pander to their egos by taking the trouble to find out about them in advance, the interview is likely to go more smoothly.

Research is particularly important if time is short. Doing as much background research on the subject as you can before you conduct the interview means that you don't have to waste time asking basic questions. And the more you appear to know about them and their sport, the less inhibited they are likely to be about covering areas which may be less familiar or even slightly embarrassing. You should, of course, check any facts you may be doubtful of, but when time is short the important thing is to get relevant and, if possible, lively quotes from your interviewee.

Interview technique

If you have never conducted an interview before, a useful place to start is by watching people interviewing and being interviewed on television, or by listening to interviews on radio. You should do this with a critical eye and ear, and try to work out what works and what does not. You can learn a lot from watching a skilled interviewer do his or her job, but don't just listen to the interviewer and slavishly imitate the types of question they ask and the way in which they ask them. You can often learn as much by listening to the answers, working out how people respond to questions phrased in different ways and the techniques they use to avoid giving a direct answer to a question.

You can also learn from a poor interviewer: not all radio and television journalists have perfect interviewing techniques. If an interviewee is giving one-word or one-sentence answers, or if they are avoiding giving a straight answer without difficulty, ask yourself how the questions could have been phrased to produce a more forthcoming response.

Bear in mind that, when conducting interviews, print journalists are often looking for something different from broadcast journalists. Someone interviewing on radio or television may be concerned principally with bringing out the personality of the interviewee, and the structure and length of a live interview may be as important as the answers. Neither of these things is particularly important to a print journalist, as the answers are unlikely to appear in his piece in the order in which they are given, and the majority of them will not be used. The print journalist may prefer to start by gathering background information, and then trying to tease out the short, telling quotes that will liven up the article.

All interviews are different. If you have set up a leisurely meeting in someone's home or office, you can afford to take your time and conduct the interview in the style of a normal conversation. This approach tends to relax people and encourages them to talk freely. But if you only have a couple of minutes on the phone or you are trying to interview someone on the hoof while they are leaving the training ground, you need to cut to the chase at once, and be much clearer about the basic information you are after. If you then find that the interviewee is compliant and willing to talk, you can supplement your basic questions later.

Some journalists have built their reputations on spiky interview techniques, but in general it doesn't pay to be too tough or antagonistic. You will get a better reception and a better response if you are friendly and put your interviewee at ease, although you should never come across as unprofessional or inefficient. If there are tough questions to be asked, save them until the end. If the interviewee clams up or walks out of the session when faced with a difficult question, you won't have lost much. If you ask the problematic questions at the beginning, you may come away with nothing.

If you take a mobile phone with you to an interview, turn it off before the interview begins. Being interrupted by calls is discourteous to the interviewee. They will also disrupt the flow of the interview. Getting back into the rhythm again may prove difficult.

Questions

It is a good idea to make a short list of key questions in advance, just to be sure you don't miss any vital information. But don't be too specific, as this may inhibit your interviewee from giving the sort of expansive answer that will often produce the best quotes. If you have plenty of time, it is often best to begin by asking for a general view on one of the topics you want to talk about: *Tell me in your own words what happened? How do you think the game went? What are your chances tomorrow? How's the training going?*

General questions like these allow the interviewee to open up and per-haps start talking about things that had not occurred to you, and which may open up new avenues for exploration. You can always move on to specifics later, and ask supplementary questions to fill in the gaps the interviewee has not covered. This approach also allows the interviewee to feel that he or she has some control over the direction the interview is taking.

Always ask open rather than CLOSED QUESTIONS. An OPEN QUESTION is one that cannot be answered by the words 'yes' or 'no'. Don't ask: *'Was it the best moment of your life to win the Olympic gold medal?'* Instead, ask: *'How did it feel to win the Olympic gold?'* This allows the subject to describe the feeling in their own words and is much more likely to produce an interesting quote.

Unless your interviewee is being exceptionally long-winded or straying too far from the subject, you should not interrupt while he or she is answer-ing a question. The interviewee may have been about to say something interesting which an interruption will lose forever. It is better to take the opposite approach: allow the interviewee to finish, and then leave a little gap – a pregnant pause – before coming in with your next question. A con-versational hiatus of this kind feels uncomfortable and will often encour-age an interviewee to start talking again and perhaps volunteer something he or she would not otherwise have said.

Conversations are governed by informal conventions, of which a good interviewer needs to be aware. An interviewee will sometimes stop talking merely to be polite, to allow the interviewer back into the conversation. But in an interview – even a broadcast interview – the conversation should be as one-sided as possible. It is the interviewee's opinions we are interested in, not the journalist's.

Of course, interviewees will sometimes go off on their own hobby-horses. If an interview strays too far from where you want it to be, drag it back by asking a pointed question: *Can we get back to your injury problems?*

If interviewees are hostile because they don't like or trust journalists, or have had uncomfortable experiences with the media in the past, try to be reassuring. Don't risk antagonising your interviewee by defending the media too vigorously, and above all, avoid the temptation to get involved in an argument.

Notebook or recorder?

There is no point in setting up an interview unless you can make an accurate record of the replies to your questions. Until comparatively recently most journalists took shorthand notes. Now small, lightweight tape recorders, which can be placed unobtrusively on a table in front of the interviewee, are readily available and widely used. As long as the recorder does not malfunction, taping an interview is easier and more thorough, and can be less unnerving to an interviewee than seeing someone scribbling spasmodically in a notebook.

But using a recorder has some disadvantages and is not always the best solution. If the interview lasts a while, listening to it again to select the quotes you wish to use can be time-consuming, especially if you are working to a tight deadline. It is often more efficient to develop the technique (using a recorder as back-up if you wish) of selective note-taking. This involves writing down the key answers from an interview so that they can be transcribed easily afterwards. It is sensible to take down more than you think you'll need, but try to get into the habit of editing out the material you are not going to need as the interview proceeds. It makes the material much easier and quicker to handle afterwards. If you have done your research in advance, and decided on the questions you need to ask, the most important role of the journalist in an interview is to *listen*.

Use your eyes

But you should not only use your ears. You should use your eyes as well. When you come to write your piece, you will want not only to report what your interviewee has said: you will want to paint a word picture of your subject as well. We can learn a lot from people's clothes and surroundings and general attitude. Make a note of the sort of clothes interviewees are wearing, what their house is like, what sort of car they drive, what sort of pictures they have on the walls, whether their trophies and medals are on display. Details like this enable readers to deduce whether they are proud or modest, whether they live entirely for their sport or whether they have other interests.

That is why television interviews often take place in someone's sitting room or workplace. What we see at the back of the shot conveys a lot of information about the person being interviewed. In print, describing the subject's surroundings helps to set the scene and allows readers to make their own judgements about the person's lifestyle.

Telephone interviews

Interviewing someone over the telephone is quick, and therefore useful if you are working to a tight deadline. It will sometimes be the only way you can get an interview but it is rarely as satisfactory as talking to someone face to face. The telephone doesn't encourage long conversational exchanges, and because you can't see the interviewee, you are deprived of one of your senses: the opportunity to paint a word picture of your subject is lost.

Unless your phone has a recording facility, you will have to make written notes of the interview. This can be difficult, and because accuracy is important, you should not be afraid to ask interviewees to repeat themselves or slow down while they are talking. If you are right-handed, hold the phone in your left hand so you can take notes, and use something to stop your notebook sliding around the desk.

Written questions

Submitting written questions is the least satisfactory way of getting an interview, but it may be the only option open to you. Written answers tend to be flat and artificial, and – especially if the subject matter of the interview is controversial or delicate – may have been written by the subject's lawyer or public relations person. Supplementary questions are also difficult.

One way of reaching potential interviewees who might otherwise be difficult to get hold of is via e-mail. If you have (or can guess) someone's e-mail address you can often by-pass their 'minders' and reach them direct. And because e-mail is faster and less formal than most other forms of written communication, it is sometimes possible to get informal responses to questions direct from the person you want to talk to. Sending supplementary questions is quick and easy, too.

Ending interviews

Always end an interview of whatever sort by thanking interviewees for their time. It is polite, and you may want to interview them again. If it was a face-to-face interview, ask for a phone number in case there is anything you have forgotten and need to check later. Many journalists like to keep chatting after the formal interview session has ended, while they are finishing their coffee or as they are being shown out of the building. This is because the interviewee will often loosen up after the notebook or recorder has been put away, and mention something of interest that did not come out in the interview. But if you intend to use anything you hear outside the formal interview situation it is courteous to tell the interviewee this, and respect any objection he or she makes.

Writing it up

Try to transcribe the notes you made during the interview as soon as possible, while it is still fresh in your mind. Leave it a day or two and you may find them difficult to interpret, or you may forget the context in which something was said.

The act of transcription will also help you to order your thoughts and work out a structure, and maybe an intro, for your piece (which is another reason for using a notebook rather than, or as well as, a tape recorder). The same applies with broadcast interviews, where selecting the clips (see Chapter 9) you are going to use will help to determine the way in which you decide to write the script and tell the story.

Quotes help to give the flavour of the personality being interviewed, and your choice of quotes will have a major bearing on the impact of the piece. DIRECT QUOTATIONS – hearing the person's own words – make the biggest impact.

Colourful language and strong opinions should be quoted directly, rather than given as REPORTED SPEECH. Direct quotes provide immediacy and authenticity, but resist the temptation of quoting at too great a length, as this in itself can become boring. The best quotes are short, sharp and to the point.

Direct quotation means enclosing the actual words which were used between quotation marks, like this: '*Winning my first Wimbledon was the greatest moment of my life,*' said the new champion. '*I just wanted to cry and kiss that famous turf.*' The player's actual words are contained within quotation marks, as is the punctuation that belongs to them. Notice how the quote becomes weaker and less immediate if it is merely summarised in reported speech: *The new champion said winning his first Wimbledon was the greatest moment of his life, making him want to cry and kiss the turf.*

However, reported speech can be useful for condensing what someone says, or making sense of something that was not expressed particularly clearly by the interviewee.

> **Example**
>
> Question: 'How did you feel about your tackle that broke Tom Jones' leg?'
>
> Answer: 'Yeah, it was bad. But that's the way it goes sometimes in this game. The ball was there. I went for it. There was no intent.'

The answer is long-winded and not very elegantly phrased, but it can be summarised by the journalist like this:

> Reported speech: *Smith admitted the tackle was bad, but claimed he went for the ball and did not intend to break Jones' leg.*

It is important when using reported speech not to distort the meaning of what the speaker said.

Sometimes it is useful to move between direct and reported speech by inserting a short, telling direct quote into a piece of reported speech.

> **Example**
>
> *The coach said 'awful decisions' by the referee had cost his team the match.*

Remember that *direct speech* is always contained within quotation marks and written in the *present* tense. *Indirect speech* does not have quotation marks, and is written in the *past tense*.

> **Examples**
>
> 'I *am* going to complain about some of the umpire's decisions,' said the coach. The coach said he *was* going to complain about some of the umpire's decisions.
>
> 'I *will* be going for the world record in the hundred metres on Saturday', she said.
> She said she *would* be going for the world record in the hundred metres on Saturday.

Pronouns also change when reported speech is used. In this example *we* becomes *they*:

> '*We have had* the tightest defence in the league all season', said the manager.
>
> The manager said *they had had* the tightest defence in the league all season.

Moving between direct and indirect speech helps to vary the pace of an article and maintain the reader's interest. Continuous indirect speech can become boring, while continuous direct quotes often read like a verbatim report of the conversation and give the impression that the journalist has abdicated responsibility for selecting the best quotes and shaping the piece.

When attributing quotes, the word 'said' is usually adequate. It is simple and neutral. Any other word tends to seem intrusive unless there is a good reason for using it. If you are quoting extensively, it may be necessary to use alternatives such as 'commented', 'explained' or 'added' for variation. Beware of using 'loaded' attributions such as 'claimed' or 'alleged' unless there is some controversy about the facts being expressed, as these cast doubt on the validity of what the speaker is saying. Similarly, avoid words like 'admitted' or 'revealed' unless a genuine admission or revelation is involved.

Quoting fairly and accurately

As a general rule, journalists should not tamper with the quotes they have collected in an interview. In particular they should avoid trying to spice them up by putting words into people's mouths which they did not use. However, few people speak in grammatical sentences all the time, and we all add unnecessary words to buy ourselves thinking time. In such cases it is acceptable to tidy up the grammar and cut out the padding as long as the sense of the sentence is maintained.

Sometimes it is necessary for the journalist to edit what someone has said. If an interviewee makes a remark that could be defamatory, the journalist has a duty to cut it out. And sometimes people inadvertently say the opposite of what they mean, perhaps by adding or missing out the word 'not'. It is then imperative to correct them.

Exercise

Interview a friend or colleague about their favourite sports team. Make sure you have a sound background knowledge of the team's history and recent performances. Write out a short list of open-ended questions, designed to bring out firm and possibly controversial views, such as: 'Who are the strongest and weakest links in the defence?' or 'Do you think the coach is doing a good job?'

During the interview, try to take notes selectively, picking out the most powerful quotes and the most useful pieces of background information. Transcribe your notes as soon as possible after the interview, deciding which answers are strong enough to be used as direct quotes and which can be translated into reported speech. Make sure you use the correct tenses – the present tense for direct quotes, the past tense for reported speech. Decide whether any of the quotes suggest an intro for the piece. Ask the interviewee whether your transcription is a fair reflection of the interview and if not, why not.

Summary

The interview is among the most important tools at the sports journalist's disposal. Knowing how to set up an interview, to put your subject at ease, to ask the right questions in the right way and to record the answers efficiently is vital if you are to get the most from face-to-face meetings with people whose time is often scarce. If it is not possible to arrange a meeting, there are other ways of getting the information you need for your piece. But however you obtain your information, it is important that you use it with integrity, and quote your subjects fairly and accurately.

Broadcast media

Learning Objectives

- To appreciate the importance of sport to the broadcast media
- To recognise the individual qualities of print, radio, television and online media
- To identify the elements of radio and television journalism
- To be able to use the language of broadcast journalism
- To be able to write and perform scripts
- To learn the techniques of broadcast interviews
- To know how the rights to broadcast sporting events are allocated
- To understand how live sporting events are broadcast

As we have seen in Chapter 2, sport has helped to change the nature of broadcasting in recent years. It has spawned new radio stations and television channels, it is probably the major factor in the sale of satellite and cable television subscriptions, and countless websites in every developed country of the world have been built around it.

In turn, radio, television and the internet have helped to raise the profile of sports, to turn many clubs into major businesses and players and athletes into millionaires. In return for the money which the sale of rights to broadcast sporting events has brought, sports organisations have adapted to the needs of the broadcasters, particularly of television. They have changed the starting times of events to fit in with television scheduling, they stage their events on many more days of the week, and in some cases – rugby league in England being the best example – have even altered the season in which the sport is played. Television has changed the kit worn by performers – and not merely by encouraging a plethora of advertising logos. One-day cricket matches, for instance, are now played in brightly coloured suits rather than the traditional whites for the benefit of television. In some cases, the rules have been changed, too. American football games are played in short segments to meet the demands of television channels for frequent commercial breaks.

So the fortunes of sports and the broadcasters which cover them are inextricably linked. The need to build and maintain audiences is changing the way television, in particular, covers sport. Broadcasters in Britain, led by the satellite channels and Channel Four, a relative newcomer to terrestrial broadcasting, have moved on from merely pointing the camera at the action. Sports coverage – especially of lengthy events like Test match cricket – now offers much more explanation about the sport in an attempt to broaden the knowledge of viewers and maintain their interest over the longer period. The arrival of digital television now permits viewers to be 'interactive', to use their remote control buttons to tailor sports coverage to their own wishes, and choose to watch individual players or action replays at will.

Despite all this, the coverage of sport by the broadcast media remains similar to that of newspapers in many ways. When radio and television were in their infancy, most of the journalists working in these new media had come from newspapers and brought their approach to sport with them. Even today, many broadcast journalists have backgrounds in print.

Like newspapers, the broadcast media offer a combination of sports news, previews of sporting events, coverage of those events, features on sports issues and profiles of people in the sporting world. But radio, television and the internet all have their unique demands, their own advantages and limitations, which impose specific working practices and different techniques on the journalists who cover sport for them.

How the media differ

It may seem blindingly obvious how radio, television, online and print media differ from each other, but it is worth trying to look beyond the obvious, because the specific characteristics of each medium play a large part in determining how journalists working for them operate.

Print

Producing a piece of print journalism is a relatively speedy process. The information needed to write most stories or features can be gathered over the telephone, from contacts or other sources, or collated from the internet, without the journalist having to leave the office. Although reporting sporting events ideally involves being there (print journalists do sometimes report some events from television coverage), the writing process is quick, as we have seen in Chapter 5.

But production and distribution of a newspaper is a slow process, and it may be several hours, or even days, before the quickly-produced copy is read, a factor the journalist should always bear in mind when writing. Print journalism is presented in a modular format within a single package (although there may be several sections within the package). The modular format means the reader can skip from story to story or page to page quickly and easily. This in turn influences the length and style of stories, which vary from full-page features to single paragraph news items. News stories are written to a formula which allows readers to absorb the main points quickly and abandon the story at any time they wish.

Radio

Although radio is often regarded as an instant medium, its news gathering processes can be slower than those for print. Basic information can, of course, be gathered over the telephone, but putting interviews on air can take longer. Telephone interviews can be done quickly, but with a loss of sound quality, and for important stories it is often necessary for a journalist to go out with a microphone and recorder. For longer packages which require several interviews and 'actuality' sound (see below), it can take several hours to gather the necessary material. This then has to be edited, usually by the same journalist, when he or she returns to the office.

Once a story has been assembled, transmission can be very quick – most radio stations run hourly news bulletins – or even instant. But radio is a linear medium. Unlike newspapers or websites, it is not possible for the consumer to move at will between items. It is imperative, therefore, that radio journalists hold the attention of their listeners, who have notoriously short attention spans, for the duration of a bulletin. That means keeping items fairly short – (from about 20 seconds to a minute), with only the more important stories being allowed to run for longer than this. It also means cutting quickly between the various elements (voices and sounds) which make up the piece, before the listener becomes bored.

Television

Putting together a piece of television is a slow process, involving more time, effort and personnel than any other medium. Almost any piece of television journalism involves a camera crew, a reporter, and usually both, going out of the office and travelling, often long distances, to the scene of the story. They may already have spent a considerable time 'setting up' the story, making sure the people they need to interview and the things they want to film will be where they want them, when they want them. And when they get there, shooting even the simplest television story takes time. The editing process demands that sequences are shot from several angles, with CUTAWAYS (see below) to make editing easier. It can take an hour of shooting to produce a minute of television, with additional time needed for interviews.

And shooting the pictures is only the first stage in the process. A script then has to be written around the pictures, the voiceover track (if there is one) recorded, and the pictures edited into a coherent piece of television.

Transmission is also slower than radio because television channels tend to run fewer bulletins (although some satellite and cable channels now run continuous sports news programmes). Like radio, television is a linear medium, and the importance of holding the attention of the audience again dictates short, lively pieces.

Internet

Websites can combine the techniques of print, radio and television (see Chapter 10) in a single package and in a largely modular form which can be instantly updated.

Perhaps the most important difference between print and broadcast media is in the behaviour of its consumers. If newspaper readers becomes bored with a story, they turn the page: if viewers or listeners become bored, they switch off or change channels. The channel changer is the ultimate critic of bad broadcast journalism, and more than in any other sphere

Table 9.1   Comparing the media

	Print	Radio	TV	Internet
Medium	Words	Sound	Pictures	Mix
News gathering	Fast	Medium	Slow	Fast
Transmission	Slow	Fast	Medium	Fast
Style	Modular	Linear	Linear	Mix
Story length	Varies	Short/medium	Short	Varies
Format	Single package	Bulletins/ News show	Bulletins/ Magazine	Single package

of journalism, it is vital to grab the audience's attention and hold on to it. To do this, broadcast journalists must make full use of the extended and unique language radio and television put at their disposal.

The language of broadcasters

Print journalists have only words with which to work. These are sometimes supplemented by still photographs, line drawings or other images, but the language of print is the written word. Print journalists may use words in a number of ways – to write stories, headlines, STANDFIRSTS or captions – but, essentially, words are the only tools they have at their disposal.

This is not true of broadcast journalists. Words remain important but, depending on whether they work in radio, television or online, they have a number of other tools available to them which can be combined with words to make up unique, rich and complex languages. The best broadcast journalism uses this diversity of language to the full.

Radio

It may seem like stating the obvious, but radio is a sound medium. Many people who are new to radio, including experienced journalists who have previously worked in print, forget this, and produce stories which consist entirely of words, as they would for a newspaper.

Words remain the basic building blocks, of course, but the mere act of reading them into a microphone provides an opportunity to impose additional layers of meaning by the use of intonation and emphasis. The journalist's words, however, are merely the starting point for a good piece of radio journalism. The language of radio has other elements.

Radio can transport listeners to the scene of the action by using the sounds they would hear if they were there. Sound is all around us, and nowhere more than at sporting events: the roar of the crowd, the referee's whistle, the starting gun, galloping hooves, racing car engines, oars splashing in water, the sound of bat on ball, announcements over the public address system. When the sound you would hear if you were *actually* at the events is used in radio it is known as ACTUALITY SOUND.

We tend to think of radio as television without pictures, but this is not true. Radio *does* have pictures, but we create them ourselves in our mind's eye, and nothing flashes a picture up on the screen in our heads more effectively than the sound of something with which we are familiar. The best radio journalism blends actuality sound with the journalist's words. Sound is often used before we hear any words as a means of setting the scene.

We have already learned that holding the attention of the listener in the linear medium of radio is vital. An effective way of doing this is to offer the listener fresh sounds at frequent intervals. In addition to the journalist's voice and actuality sound, radio pieces can ring the changes in a number of other ways.

Interviews are essential to most sports stories, and clips of interviews with one or more of the people involved in the story not only give listeners the opportunity of hearing what they sound like, and therefore forming an opinion about them as people, but also add variety to the sounds we are hearing. VOX POPS with fans can be used in a similar way.

Another option open to the sports broadcaster is to inject interest and drama into a piece by using clips from commentaries. The excitement generated by the best commentators at climactic moments in sporting events will immediately change the tone and pace of a radio piece, and help produce more pictures in the mind.

Music, too, is part of the language of radio. Sports fans often invent and sing their own songs, which can be used to good effect by journalists. And many sports lend themselves to musical interpretation, whether through the words of a pop song or the tune or rhythms of a classical piece. Music can be used for emphasis at appropriate points, or simply used unobtrusively underneath the words to create a mood. Listeners who might otherwise lose interest in radio items have been known to stick with them just to listen to their favourite music.

Radio elements checklist

✓ actuality sound
✓ journalist's voice
✓ interview clips
✓ commentary clips
✓ vox pops
✓ music

Television

Television is a picture-led medium and professional sport, which depends for its existence on spectators, is ideally suited to television. Moving pictures convey the action as it happens, but they also provide the key element in television reportage. The quality of the pictures available to a television journalist normally determines the importance attached to a story, and even whether the story is used at all. With sport, of course, getting hold of dramatic pictures to illustrate a story is rarely a problem. However, pictures provide only one element in the language of television.

Television uses many of the elements of radio journalism: actuality sound (known in television as NATSOF, natural sound on film), a journalist's voice over pictures, interview clips, commentary clips, vox pops and music. But the language of television is even more varied and complex than that of radio. In addition to contemporaneous moving pictures, television can also use still photographs, archive material, captions and signs to help tell its stories, and because it engages two of our senses – sight and hearing – it is capable of delivering information through both at the same time. The secret of good television journalism is to use pictures, words, sound, and sometimes music, together and in harmony, to squeeze as much information as possible into every moment of screen time.

While a journalist is telling us something in a VOICEOVER (v/o) we can also be seeing action or perhaps gathering additional information from captions or signage. These additional elements can be used by journalists to provide information that otherwise would have to be included in their voice-overs. A good television script uses not only words, but also pictures and other elements in unison, as we shall see below.

Television elements checklist

✓ moving pictures
✓ words
✓ stills
✓ archive material
✓ NATSOF
✓ interview clips
✓ vox pops
✓ commentary
✓ captions
✓ signage
✓ music

Internet

Because websites can offer a hybrid of print and audio and video clips, they can use a combination of all the above elements (see Chapter 10).

Inside radio and television sports departments

Radio and television companies organise their sports coverage in different ways, depending on their size and local circumstances. Sport forms an integral part of most broadcast news bulletins, and many channels employ specialist reporters to provide sports news coverage. Sometimes they will be part of a bigger sports department which also makes feature programmes and provides OB (OUTSIDE BROADCAST) coverage.

Many companies, however, particularly in television, use independent production companies to provide feature and OB outside broadcast material. Because of the specialised equipment and expertise involved, it is often more cost-effective to contract such productions out to companies which specialise in sport. For the same reason, most broadcasters use freelance commentators and expert analysts.

Sports news

The amount of airtime devoted to sports news on radio and television varies from short slots in general news bulletins or news magazine programmes to dedicated sports news channels providing continuous, rolling coverage.

Although the rights to cover most major sporting events are now sold to individual broadcasters, this does not preclude other broadcasters from providing news coverage before and after the event. Clubs and organisations are anxious to maximise their pre-event publicity to generate interest in their events and fill their stadiums. Similarly, broadcasters who own the rights to an event can expect bigger audiences if it is plugged in advance on rival channels. Pre-event press conferences and interviews with players and coaches are, therefore, usually open to all broadcast media, though some of them may choose not to publicise events being shown on competing channels.

After the event, reciprocal NEWS ACCESS agreements often allow television broadcasters who do not own the rights to show clips of the action on their news programmes.

In recent years, the design of websites has had an important influence on the way television sports news is presented, especially on dedicated sports news channels and in 'results service' programmes. Although live presenters are still used to introduce news stories and packages, their images on screen now tend to be surrounded by text. In the manner of websites, the viewer is bombarded with continuously changing information in sidebars and in crawlers along the bottom of the screen, a development driven by a growing demand for sports statistics and for regular and immediate scores and results updates.

Story structure

Whereas most stories written for print follow a classic structure, as we have seen in Chapter 6, the format in which a broadcast news story is presented will vary according to the importance of the story, the time available to produce it and the elements with which the journalist has to work.

Television

News stories in television tend to fall into one of four categories.

Camera read

The simplest television news story is known as a CAMERA READ. The bulletin presenter, who is in vision throughout, reads the copy from the AUTOCUE. Camera reads are written to get breaking stories on air quickly, or when no pictures are available to accompany the story.

> **Example**
>
> *Bulletin reader*: We've just heard that the former Leeds United and Wales footballer John Charles has died at the age of 72. Charles scored 42 goals in one season for Leeds, which still stands as a club record. He later moved to the Italian club Juventus for a record transfer fee.

Underlay

If pictures are available, shot specifically for the purpose or taken from the library of tapes which all television stations keep, they can be screened to illustrate the story the presenter is reading. This type of story is called an

UNDERLAY. The presenter remains in vision while reading the link to the story. Pictures are then run under the presenter's voice as the story continues. The pictures which are available will dictate the way the story is written.

Example

Link: The former Leeds United and Wales footballer John Charles has died at the age of 72.

V/o (Bulletin reader's voice over pictures)

It was goals like this that earned Charles the reputation of one of the greatest footballers who ever lived. He scored 42 goals in a season for Leeds, and later moved to the Italian club Juventus for a record transfer fee.

Upsound

If an interview or interviews are available, clips from them can be run on the end of an underlay, turning it into an UPSOUND. What the interviewees say in their clips will influence the way the preceding script is written.

Example

Bulletin reader: The world of football has been paying tribute to John Charles, the former Leeds United and Wales footballer who has died at the age of 72.

V/o

The centre forward who scored 42 goals in a season for Leeds was taken ill on a visit to Italy and underwent surgery for a blood clot in his leg. He was flown back to England in a private jet by his former club Juventus, but died this morning in a Wakefield hospital. Charles was never cautioned or sent off in his career, and was known as the Gentle Giant.

Interview clip (Wales manager, Mark Hughes)

'I was always struck by his humility whenever I met him, yet he was the greatest player ever to wear the Welsh shirt. He will be sorely missed.'

Package

An important or complex story will usually be presented as a PACKAGE. This involves a reporter bringing together on tape a number of elements, usually including voiceovers and interview clips. Packages may also include vox pops, a PIECE TO CAMERA by the reporter, archive material, still pictures, NATSOF and music. The bulletin presenter reads a link to introduce the pre-recorded tape which has been compiled by another journalist. Each of the elements is kept short – usually a maximum of 20 seconds – to hold the viewer's attention.

Example

Link: John Charles, one of the greatest soccer players of his age, has died. Leeds United's record goalscorer became the most expensive player of his era when he was transferred to the Italian club Juventus. This report from Jim Smith.

Package (Jim Smith's voice over today's pictures of players and fans observing a minute's silence)

A silent tribute to a gentle man. Players and fans show their respect for a footballing legend ahead of today's Manchester United/Leeds match.

Vox pops (short clips of fans)

'He was the greatest player I ever saw in a Leeds shirt.'

'He was a lovely man. I never saw him commit a deliberate foul.'

'He had everything – strength, speed, a great header of the ball.'

V/o (archive footage of Charles during his playing career)

John Charles was just 17 when he moved from his native Swansea to Yorkshire, and it was goals like this that brought him to the attention of the entire football world.

Interview clip (Jimmy Armfield, former Leeds manager)

'He was different. His balance was good – he was strong and that is why he had this wonderful leap. It wasn't just his height that made him good. He had a terrific leap.'

V/o (archive shots of Charles playing for Juventus and Wales)

He became one of the first British footballers to play in Italy, moving to Juventus for a record fee. Charles was capped by Wales while still in his teens and played in the World Cup finals.

Interview clip (Mark Hughes, Wales manager)

'I was always struck by his humility whenever I met him, yet he was the greatest player ever to wear the Welsh shirt. He will be sorely missed.'

V/o (Library footage of Charles speaking at a dinner)

In retirement, Charles toured the after-dinner circuit raising money for charity. He was taken ill on a visit to Italy.

(Recent still photograph)

Never cautioned, never sent off, he was known as 'The Gentle Giant'. John Charles died this morning.

Discussion

Notice how the package moves quickly from element to element, and from action shots to talking heads, to maintain the interest of the viewer. Mixing packages with upsounds and underlays within a bulletin also helps to maintain the viewer's interest.

Exercise

Write a television package about 90 second long using the following newspaper story as your source. Scripts are normally read at about three words a second, but using all the elements of television language available to you will help you cram a lot of information into a minute and a half.

Assume you can film whatever you wish, and interview whoever you wish. Set out your script in the same way as the one above, indicating where each element begins, and describing the pictures which will accompany the voiceovers. You should try to make an impact with your opening shots (or sounds, if you are writing a radio script) to grab the audience's attention.

First, write a link to introduce the story. Write the script for your package, including the wording of any interview clips and vox pops you are using. List the pictures you intend to use in brackets above the text they will illustrate. This will help you see how the elements you intend to use will fit together. You should use captions to give the names and positions of interviewees. This means you will not have to name them in your voiceovers. Similarly, locations can be identified by shots of signs or buildings.

News story

England's *cricketers arrived in Jamaica today at the start of their tour of the West Indies.*

They will be trying to win a Test series in the Caribbean for the first time since 1968.

Exercise continued

The West Indies have just returned from a tour of South Africa, where they were soundly beaten, so this may be England's best chance for decades of ending that dismal run.

The Windies once terrified the opposition with fast bowlers like Courtney Walsh and Curtly Ambrose. Now they depend on their batsmen, especially captain Brian Lara, who is still one of the world's best.

England captain Michael Vaughan is hoping to improve on their recent defeats in Sri Lanka, and they will be boosted by fast bowler Simon Jones, who returns to the Test side for the first time since he damaged knee ligaments in an horrific incident while fielding against Australia in Brisbane nearly 18 months ago.

Suggested answer

Link: England's cricketers began their tour of the West Indies today, trying to win a Test series there for the first time since 1968. Jane Jones is with them.

Package script
(Calypso music beneath the entire package)
NATSOF (original commentary over archive pictures of 1968 victory, sound gives way to voiceover, but archive pictures continue underneath)
'And that's the winning run – England have won a famous victory...'

V/o
The Beatles were top of the pops, Harold Wilson was Prime Minister and the Americans had just put a man on the moon

(shot changes to close-up of moon in daytime sky, camera pulls out to reveal Caribbean beach with children playing cricket)
but since then England have been beaten by generations of West Indian cricketers. Bowlers like these
(quick shots of West Indian fast bowlers dismissing England batsmen)
made the Windies the world's top team. Not any more. They've just been beaten in South Africa
(shot of South Africa match)
but they've still got one of the world's best batsmen.
(Establishing shot *of Brian Lara batting in the nets*)
(Interview clip with Lara)
'People have started to write us off, but playing here on our own soil we will be very hard to beat.'
(Shots of sugar cane being cut)

V/o
England are relying on their own crop of fast bowlers to prove him wrong. And life can only get sweeter for one of them.

(Continued)

Exercise continued

(Archive shots, with NATSOF commentary, of Simon Jones sustaining injury in Australia)
'Oh, and that is a dreadful injury'
(Shots of Jones and other England players shopping in Jamaican market)

V/o
But Jones is back in business, and top of his shopping list are a few West Indies wickets.
(Shots of England captain Michael Vaughan bowling to local kids on beach)
(Interview with Vaughan)
Interview clip
(Shot of Vaughan bowling out one of the kids)

V/o
England's chances of winning here are the brightest for decades, but one thing's for sure – it won't be this easy.

Discussion

The television package uses most of the resources of the language of the medium. Notice how the link is almost identical to the newspaper intro. The reporter's name-check stresses that she is there with the team, which adds authority to the piece.

The calypso music sets the scene and holds the package together, while the script is shaped by the pictures the reporter uses. Starting with black and white archive footage of the last England victory is a quick way to show that it was a different era, and the voiceover (which complements, rather than refers directly to the pictures) underlines this.

Cutting from a reference to a man on the moon to a shot of the moon itself provides a smooth link to the present, and the pull-out shot of the beach is a simple way to establish that we are in the Caribbean. The shots of children playing cricket there underline the differences between the two cultures and suggest that this is how all West Indian cricketers begin.

Because almost all professional sports events are now filmed, archive material is one of the most useful tools for a television sports journalist. It is almost always possible to find shots of the people or events they require. These should, however, be interspersed with newly-shot material where possible. In this piece, shots of the market and sugar cane plantation provide local flavour and added interest for the viewer, and the voiceover subtly weaves them into the cricket narrative.

The piece ends satisfactorily by bringing us full circle, with a shot of an English cricketer beating a West Indian, but with an amusing twist. The beach cricket shots also take us back to the start of the package, which has used many of the elements of television language to convey a lot of information in a short space of time.

Radio

Radio bulletins are also made up of a similar mix of stories which are roughly equivalent to those in television. The simplest is a COPY ITEM read by the newsreader – the equivalent of a camera read on television. If more information is available, a reporter may be asked to write a VOICEPIECE, a free-standing story introduced by the bulletin presenter by means of a cue, which is the radio equivalent of a link. If interview clips are available, these can be attached to the end of a copy item or voicepiece – the radio equivalent of an upsound.

As in television, an important or complex story will be presented as a package if the required elements are available. Radio packages closely follow the style of their television equivalents (see above). They will normally include voiceovers and interview clips, and may also include vox pops, clips of match commentary, archive material, actuality sound and music.

Exercise

Compile a radio package on the cricket story dealt with above, identifying any actuality sound or other elements you will use.

Other options

Both radio and television have other options available to them for varying and improving their sports news coverage. Packages are often used as the basis for a studio discussion, with guests invited in to comment on the subject of the story.

Packages can be given greater immediacy with a LIVE or AS-LIVE introduction by a reporter at the scene. Standing a reporter outside a stadium gives the impression that he or she is on the spot to cover the story as it is unfolding. When reporters introduce and end ('top and tail') their pieces

Table 9.2 Types of story

Radio	TV
Copy item – read by bulletin reader	Camera read
Voicepiece – read by reporter	Underlay
Copy item or voicepiece with clip	Upsound
Package – mix of reporter and clips	Package
Studio guest/interview – often off back of package	
Lives/as-lives	
Cue (same as a newspaper intro)	Link

in this way, the packages are known as DOUGHNUTS, because the package fills the hole in the middle.

If a story is just breaking and no package is available, the same effect can be achieved by doing a TWO-WAY INTERVIEW with the reporter at the scene or by getting the reporter to do a live interview there with an expert who can comment on the story.

If no means of sending live pictures from a location is available, the same effect can be achieved by recording a piece as if it were live and sending the tape back to the studios. Such pieces are known as as-lives.

Performing scripts

In broadcasting, it is not enough to produce sharp, informative, entertaining scripts, although all these things are important. Scripts must be written in a way that makes them easy to read. This will often mean writing short, simple sentences with no sub-clauses.

Broadcasting is a performance and the way in which a journalist reads a script on air influences the audience's perception of the story. Scripts should be read with confidence and authority (and occasionally with wit or charm or solemnity). This is easier to do if you are performing your own material, because you can write it in a way you will find easy to read. Most of us find some words or phrases difficult to pronounce. It is a good idea to read each sentence out loud after you have written it to make sure you can get your tongue round it easily and smoothly. Read the whole script out loud when you have finished it and before you attempt to record it. Change it, if necessary, to make it more comfortable to read – such as rephrasing a sentence or choosing an alternative word. And always rehearse your performance before recording the script or reading it live.

Scripts should be performed in a way that enhances their meaning for the listener. This means that the more important words should be emphasised (see below). Try to avoid a monotonous and unvaried delivery or you will lose the listener's attention. It is often a good idea to emphasise the first word, as this grabs the listener's attention.

Don't be afraid to change a script written by someone else (providing you don't alter the sense of it) if you are uncomfortable with it, as no two people have the same reading style. Bulletin readers always read through the whole bulletin before they go on air, and change any words or sentences with which they feel uncomfortable.

Exercise

Go through the package you have written and underline the key words you need to emphasise when you record it. Aim to vary the pitch and tone of your voice, hitting the emphasised words harder.

Now perform your script and get colleagues to offer constructive criticism, or record it and criticise yourself. Repeat the exercise and see whether you can improve your delivery. Always listen carefully to the way professional journalists deliver their scripts and try to learn from them.

Performing in vision

Television journalists sometimes perform in vision as well as recording voiceovers for their packages. If you are doing a piece to camera, try to make that interesting, too. Watching a reporter walk through an appropriate location – the pits at a motor racing track, for instance, or among the weights and exercise bikes in a gym – is much more interesting and informative than seeing the journalist standing still in the same location. The changing background gives the viewer a much better feel for the atmosphere. Even more effective is to demonstrate to the camera what you are talking about: deliver part of your report while skiing down a section of the slalom course, or from behind the wheel of a Formula 1 or rally car.

Broadcast interviews

The interview is an important ingredient of almost any form of broadcast sports journalism. It is a vital element in upsounds and packages, and in the build up to or aftermath of live or recorded highlights coverage of events. Many of the guidelines for newspaper interviews (see Chapter 8) apply equally to broadcast interviews. However, it is fairly easy for a print journalist to select random sentences or even phrases from the dullest interview and produce an interesting piece. For a broadcast interview to be effective, on the other hand, it is crucial that the interviewee should sound and look interesting. It is important, therefore, for the interviewer to coax an interesting performance out of the interviewee, especially if the interview is live and there is no scope for editing.

Setting up an interview

It can be easier to persuade sports personalities to give one-to-one interviews to radio or television than to the print media. They know that what they say cannot be distorted (although it can be used selectively). Appearing on radio or television appeals to the egos of many people, and those who have been involved in sport at a senior level will be used to the broadcast media. They are unlikely to be nervous of microphones or television cameras.

Against that must be set the additional demands broadcasters frequently impose on them. It is often necessary to persuade interviewees to come into a studio or to go to a specific location which will provide a suitable backdrop for the interview. In such cases, journalists should always be prepared to provide taxis or other forms of transport if necessary, and to make sure they do not waste the time of their interviewees by keeping them waiting.

Interview technique

Choosing the location for an interview should be the first consideration. A suitable background (or appropriate background sounds) help to set the mood. On radio, the sound of bookmakers shouting the odds will transport the listener to the racetrack. On television, interviewing an ice hockey coach on the rink or a rower in front of the boat shed has the same effect. Similarly, what the interviewee is wearing – a track suit or team shirt – helps to provide the right context.

The growing importance of sponsorship in sport means that some interviewees will insist on doing interviews in front of boards which contain the names and logos of their sponsors. Many broadcasters now accept this as inevitable, but overt advertising conflicts with the guidelines of some broadcast organisations. It may be necessary to ask an interviewee to remove a cap or other item of clothing which displays commercial branding, or to get the camera operator to frame the shot so that it is not visible.

No matter how experienced your interviewee (and many managers and coaches do dozens of radio and television interviews every week) it is important to put them at ease before the interview begins. A joke off-camera or before the recorder is switched on will break the ice, relax the interviewee and establish a comfortable relationship with the interviewer. This is particularly important if the prime aim of the interview is to bring out the personality of the interviewee.

Most radio interviews are one-to-one, but television interviews may involve several people (a journalist, a camera operator, a sound recordist and sometimes a director or producer). This can make some interviewees nervous, although this is less frequently a problem than it once was. Television crews have reduced in size in recent years. It is now usual to have just a reporter and a camera operator, and some television companies have begun using one-person crews – video-journalists or VJs. If an interviewee is intimidated by the size of the crew, the numbers can be reduced by letting the journalist handle the microphone.

Another method of relaxing television interviewees is to try to get them to ignore the camera. In any event, interviewees should never stare into the camera. Instead, they should look slightly off-camera, at the interviewer. This gives viewers the impression that they are eavesdropping on a conversation. The easiest way of achieving this is to tell the interviewee: 'Ignore the camera and just talk to me.'

Most broadcast interviews are pre-recorded, and in many cases the journalist will be interested only in a brief SOUNDBITE for use as part of a package. In such cases it is important to try to get the most appropriate form of words, expressed in a lively or concise way.

The interviewer should listen carefully to the way answers are phrased. If they are not lively enough, or contain too many ums and errs, or the language used is too complex, the interviewer should try to find a different way of asking the question, perhaps at a later stage in the interview, when the interviewee has relaxed a little. This will often produce a different and perhaps more usable version of the answer. In the last resort, perhaps if the person has made two related points in different answers which will be difficult to edit together, he or she could be asked to repeat them in a single sentence. But interviewers should always avoid putting words in people's mouths.

Some people can be animated and articulate and even difficult to shut up before the camera or recorder is switched on, and then give one-word or single-sentence answers when the interview begins. It is sometimes helpful to tell people in advance what you are going to ask them, and explain the purpose of the interview to them. Indeed, you should always do so if they ask. Interviews are not intended to catch people out but to help them express their views clearly. However, it rarely pays to rehearse a broadcast interview or spend a long time chatting informally about the subject matter before you begin. This tends to make interviewees feel they have already answered your questions, and so they are rarely as open or forthcoming in the real interview.

Always try to use OPEN QUESTIONS, which cannot be answered by a simple yes or no. Try to avoid anticipating the interviewee's likely views in your question (*You must be delighted with the result?*) because this invites them merely to agree with you.

It is important that the interviewer should sound confident and well-informed. It is a good idea to prepare questions in advance. You will not have time (especially if your interview is live) to try to remember questions you have forgotten, so write them down if necessary.

It is a good idea to start with a general question (*What's your view of the game?*) and ask specific questions as follow-ups if they have not already been covered in an earlier answer. If you are not to lose the attention of your audience, you should not allow answers to continue for too long – 20 or 30 seconds is often enough. Don't interrupt too often, but be prepared to do so if the answers to your questions are too expansive, stray from the subject or are just plain boring.

If an interview is live, you will be working to a strict time limit. Tell your interviewee in advance how long the interview will last, and agree on a pre-arranged signal you will use when you want it to end. Try to shape the interview so that you cover all the points you want to within the time available.

Exercise

Get a fellow student or colleague to read reports of a game or event and play the role of a competitor or coach in an interview. Prepare your questions and record your interview, on camera if possible. Play it back and listen to or watch it critically. If you do not have access to recording equipment, conduct a series of interviews as a group. Listen to and watch the interviews of your colleagues and offer constructive feedback.

You should always watch or listen to the interviews conducted by professional journalists on radio or television critically, and try to learn from them. With packages, listen to the interview clips that have been used and ask yourself how they have helped the reporter to tell the story.

Covering events

The big advantage broadcasters (especially television broadcasters) have over the print media is that they can take their audiences direct to events.

They can cover sporting action live, or broadcast it after the event, in its entirety or as HIGHLIGHTS. But their access to events will normally depend on whether they have bought the rights from the people (normally a sports governing body, but sometimes individual clubs or promoters) who own them.

Rights

The rights to a sporting event will normally be sold to the highest bidder, although a broadcasting organisation which can offer more exposure for the sport, or a higher standard of coverage, may be preferred. Individual events will often be included in a wider package which will give the same broadcaster access to all the games in a particular league or cup competition, or series, for instance, or all the races at a particular track. Rights are normally sold for periods of several years, which makes it cost-effective for broadcasters to establish the expensive infrastructure required to cover sports events live.

Sports often maximise their rights income by selling rights in a number of countries (although pictures will normally be provided by a single broadcaster), secondary rights to show highlights packages, pay-per-view games and radio rights.

Live broadcasts

Because broadcasters pay a lot of money for sporting rights, they want to get as much value from them as possible. Live events (usually known as outside broadcasts or OBs) are now typically broadcast as part of an extended package which sandwiches the action between pre- and post-match slots. To brand their programmes and give a taste of the excitement to come, broadcasters often spend a lot of money on an opening graphics sequence before the presenter introduces the programme. The build-up to the event typically involves discussion between expert guests (often current or former players or coaches) and features or news packages on the players or teams involved. The event itself may be followed by post-match interviews, expert analysis and a highlights package of other games in the same competition. It will often end with a sequence of the key incidents set to music. Again, the priority is to vary the content to maintain the interest of the audience.

Broadcast coverage, therefore, follows a similar pattern to that of print journalism discussed in Chapter 5 – build-up, preview, event coverage, inquest – but condensed into a much narrower time-frame, which will often be a single programme.

An outside broadcast of a sporting event is a complex technical and logistical operation which requires a great deal of planning, the mobilisation of expensive equipment and contributions from professionals in a wide range of disciplines. For that reason they are often carried out by specialist companies contracted to the broadcasters who own the principal rights to the event. Because televised sport is now a global industry, the company covering the event may also be providing a 'feed' of its pictures to a number of other domestic and foreign broadcasters, who will arrange their own commentary and analysis.

Outside broadcasts

Radio outside broadcasts are relatively simple affairs, often involving a single journalist, perhaps accompanied by a summariser and a technician, using a permanent line linked to the studio. A live television outside broadcast, on the other hand, is a major technical and logistical operation. The biggest sporting events, such as the Olympic Games, can involve scores of cameras and journalists working from dozens of different locations over a period of several weeks. But even one-off events involve large numbers of people and a great deal of sophisticated equipment.

The exact set-up for a live outside broadcast will depend on the nature of the sport being covered, but the approach is usually similar. This is how a live soccer match might be covered.

Cameras

The principal coverage will be provided by two fixed cameras placed on the television gantry, which is usually suspended from the roof of the main stand of the stadium, level with the half-way line. One camera provides wide shots of the playing area; the other provides close-ups.

There will be additional cameras at the side of the pitch, to provide tight close-ups of the players, the coaches and substitutes on the bench, and of the crowd. These are useful for goal celebrations, when players are being treated for injuries, and for shots of the reactions of the crowd and coaches to key incidents. At least one will be a roaming camera, known as a STEADICAM. These are attached to their operators by a frame, which allows them to move up and down the touchline to get closer to an incident.

There will be a camera behind and slightly to the side of each goal, to record goals and goalmouth incidents, and to provide replays from a different angle from the gantry cameras. There may also be cameras midway between goals and halfway line, principally to cover offside decisions. There may also be a camera on a crane, or even attached to a balloon suspended above the stadium, to provide aerial shots.

All the cameras are situated on the same side of the pitch, to avoid confusing viewers about the direction in which teams are playing. The camera operators follow instructions issued by the director. They can also hear the match commentary.

Commentators and analysts

The commentary team will normally have a high vantage point on the halfway line. They, too, are in contact with the director. The presenter and analysts providing pre- and post-match comment will normally be in a separate studio or box.

Director and technicians

The pictures are controlled from a scanner truck which is normally parked outside the stadium. Inside are a series of television monitors which show the pictures being shot by each camera. The director selects which of these to screen at any given moment, and asks camera operators to get specific shots. Sports coverage normally consists of a mix of wide, medium and close shots, intercut quite quickly. It is the responsibility of the director to make sure this is done smoothly and unobtrusively, and that shots of key moments, preferably from more than one angle, are always available.

All the pictures are recorded on a series of machines controlled by a replay technician whose job is to provide instant action replays when requested to do so by the director. The crew will also include a sound engineer and other technicians.

Events being covered specifically for inclusion in highlights packages will normally be taped by a single camera operator, usually working from a gantry high above the arena, which gives a good, uninterrupted view of the action. The operator will switch between wide shots, medium shots and close-ups, as the action dictates.

Because highlights sequences often have to be edited quickly, it is essential that the camera operator keeps an accurate LOG of the key moments in the action. Television tapes are time-coded in hours, minutes and seconds, and the log gives the times at which goals, near-misses, injuries, interesting close-ups and EDIT POINTS, such as shots of crowd reaction which can be used as cutaways, occur. This allows editors who have the task of reducing,

Figure 9.1 Set-up for major outside broadcast

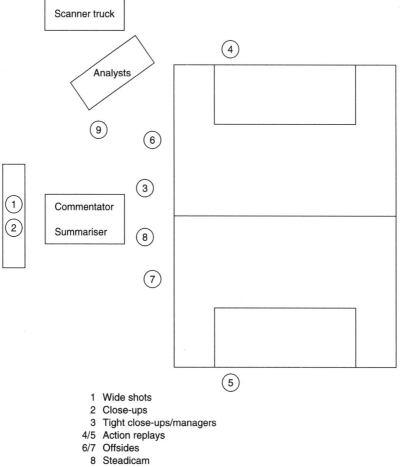

1 Wide shots
2 Close-ups
3 Tight close-ups/managers
4/5 Action replays
6/7 Offsides
8 Steadicam
9 Crane camera

say, a 90-minute soccer match to two minutes of airtime, to find quickly the sequences they need from the RUSHES – the unedited tapes.

Tape log

Dayton v Exfield

00.08.20   Dayton hit post
00.11.40   Exfield good chance
00.17.00   Robins goal 1–0

00.22.10   Exfield shot over
00.34.50   Dayton header wide
00.42.10   Jameson goal 1–1
00.47.50   Exfield free kick and shot saved
00.56.00   Dayton good shot saved
01.01.30   Dayton cross and chance missed
01.07.10   Smith goal 1–2
01.10.20   Exfield penalty claim
01.19.10   Dayton run and shot saved
01.26.20   Jones goal 2–2

Commentary

The skills of which viewers and listeners are most aware when sport is being broadcast are those of the journalists, commentators and expert summarisers who describe and explain the action. They require the same in-depth knowledge of their sports as their colleagues in print journalism, but their skills and working practices are often different.

Most print journalists covering a sporting event work on their own, but broadcast journalists almost always work as part of a team. This may include fellow commentators and summarisers as well as a director and technicians. For long events such as cricket and tennis matches, they may work in shifts of an hour or so, sharing commentary with half a dozen others. It is essential to establish a good working relationship with other members of the team.

Although sports broadcasters are often regarded as having glamorous jobs, their work can involve travelling long distances, working long hours, arriving at an event early and leaving late. If the job is to be done well, it can also involve hours of preparation.

Preparation

Broadcasters who are covering events live must have all the information they require at their fingertips – and preferably inside their heads. Live commentary demands instant reaction, and often there is no time to refer to notes.

It is essential for commentators to recognise the players and competitors taking part in the event. Many now wear their numbers and names on their shirts, of course, but it is not always possible to see them in the thick of the action. In some sports they don't have them, so commentators must be able to identify people by sight. If unfamiliar performers are involved, they will study videos or team photographs before the event, but even faces can be indistinct at the opposite end of a sports field. Many commentators try to find ways of identifying people at a glance – the player wearing white boots, the one with his shirt outside his shorts, the fat, bald one or the tall, thin one.

Identifying people is the basic requirement, but commentary will often demand more than that. If a performer does something of note, it may be necessary to talk about them at some length, so background information about each of them is also necessary. Most commentators make notes on each player or competitor, with details of how many goals or runs they have scored, how many appearances they have made, their disciplinary records, international appearances, other teams they have played for, and so on.

Commentators must also have the information necessary to put the event into context. They must be aware of the significance of the result for both teams, the results of any previous games between them, the sequences of victories or defeats, the consequences for coaches or managers of victory or defeat.

Exercise

Choose a sporting event which is to be televised and prepare to do a commentary on it. You will need to recognise the competitors who are expected to take part and to make notes on them. You will also need to research the information you will need to put the event in context. Use some of the sources outlined in Chapter 4. When you have made your notes, read them through and try to memorise as much of the information as possible.

On air

Commentary teams are typically made up of professional journalists, whose basic skills are with words, and summarisers, who are often former players or coaches, chosen for their knowledge of the game and tactics. The journalists, however, also need to have expert knowledge of the sports they are covering and the summarisers should be articulate: not all former sports people are.

Covering a sporting event live is different from most other forms of broadcast journalism. It consists largely of unscripted talk. Audiences who are used to listening to carefully scripted material will expect the same high standards. Waffle will not do.

Although the action itself will often be strong enough to hold the interest of the audience, regular changes of voice within the commentary team also stop audiences becoming bored. The best commentaries often feel as if the listener is eavesdropping on a conversation between two keen and knowledgeable fans. But radio and television commentary pose different challenges.

Radio

Because radio audiences can't see what is happening, the main function of commentators is to describe the event to the listeners, to allow them to picture what is happening in their minds. In addition to a talent for vivid description, they should be able to criticise performances and tactics and be prepared to fill gaps in the action with background material and analysis. Silence is not an option in radio: it suggests to the listener there has been a break in transmission.

The best radio commentary simulates the excitement a fan may experience at the event, and lively descriptions of key moments can be used again to recreate that excitement in post-match reports.

Television

Because television viewers can see the action taking place before them, commentary serves a slightly different function. It is sometimes best to let the action speak for itself, with the commentator merely applying a touch to the rudder at times, by naming the players on the ball or providing background information that will increase the audience's understanding.

That does not mean that the preparation need be any less thorough, because television viewers can see if the commentator gets something wrong. And because sporting events are often viewed collectively, in pubs and bars, viewers are more likely to point out errors and air their criticisms. The best way to study commentary is to listen to professional commentators, analyse their performances and try to copy those which work best. There is time to develop your own distinctive style after you have learned to do it well by imitating the best.

Dangers of live broadcasts

Live and instantaneous coverage of sporting events imposes special responsibilities on the journalists and summarisers involved. Print journalists, even when working to the tightest of deadlines, have a little time to think about the effects of what they are writing, but radio or television commentators may have only a split second. Sporting events have strong potential for controversial or difficult moments, off the field as well as on it: crowd violence, racist chants, the appearance of streakers, serious injuries to competitors and even, in the most extreme cases, disasters like those at Hillsborough football stadium in Sheffield when nearly a hundred spectators were crushed to death, or the fatal fire at Bradford City soccer ground. Journalists reporting live must always be aware that friends and relatives of those involved will be watching and listening.

Exercise

Now watch the broadcast for which you have done your preparation. Watch it with the sound turned off, giving your own commentary on the action. Record the coverage and watch it again, this time with the sound turned on. Look out for ways in which the professional commentary differs from your own.

Post-match interviews

Because post-event interviews have to be fitted into a tight broadcasting schedule, it is preferable that they are arranged before the event and that the interviewees know precisely when they will be interviewed and where the interviews will take place. Most major sports stadiums have a routine for post-event interviews, with a dedicated interview room, or facilities to conduct interviews in the tunnel leading from the dressing rooms to the arena, or at the side of the pitch.

Some broadcasters also like to conduct interviews with coaches or competitors not currently involved in the action during the event itself. Such interviews help to fill pauses in play or explain key moments, such as significant injuries to competitors, or tactical changes such as substitutions. They usually occur during breaks such as stoppages for injury, changes of end at tennis or badminton, the fall of wickets at cricket or while players are walking to the next hole on a golf course. It is essential that potential interviewees are aware of and agree to this in advance, and that they know the interviews are likely to be brief.

Summary

Sports journalists working in broadcasting share many of the objectives of their colleagues working in print, and must approach their tasks with the same commitment to thorough research and an equal depth of background knowledge. They must also be able to take advantage of the additional tools that broadcasting offers them. Successful broadcast sports journalists need to be able to make good use of the more complex language at their disposal while working as part of a team which includes many other disciplines and within the limitations imposed on them by the technology with which they work.

Online publishing

One of the most important developments in sports journalism in recent
years has been the growth of ONLINE publishing, or websites on the internet. Websites have provided thousands of new outlets for sports journalists, created many new jobs and offer new ways of satisfying the growing
thirst for sporting information. Because websites are easy to set up and

relatively cheap to service and maintain, the growth has been rapid. Almost every sports club and governing body now has its own site, many of them employing professional journalists. The web now supports sites operated by everyone from commercial and public service media organisations, through sporting organisations and individual athletes, to fans. Not surprisingly, the quality of sporting websites is equally variable.

Media websites

The best sites are usually those set up by existing communications organisations such as newspapers and broadcasting companies. These include the BBC and the *Guardian* in Britain, the *New York Times* and *Washington Post* in the USA, in Australia the *Melbourne Age* and *The Australian*, the *Times of India* and many others. These sites provide not only alternative (and often free) access to material produced for the newspapers or broadcasters which own them, but often additional material produced specifically for their websites. This ranges from reports, news, features, columns and statistics to chat rooms and other interactive facilities and (an invaluable reference source for other journalists) access to much of the material they have published in previous months and years, which is known as the ARCHIVE.

They often employ specialist teams of journalists to service their website, either writing their own copy, or turning copy produced for print or broadcast into material suitable for online consumption.

The growth of the web has also spawned new companies specialising in online sports journalism. These sites (see Appendix 1) sometimes cover a single sport, and sometimes range over many. They are usually funded by advertising, although some also offer subscription services.

Official sports websites

The biggest – and therefore the wealthiest – sporting organisations also tend to have excellent websites. They recognise the commercial and public relations value of the internet, and are willing to spend the money necessary to make their sites professional and useful, and therefore attractive to their fans. They often employ journalists to provide editorial material, but users of these sites should always bear in mind that they exist primarily to promote the interests (often commercial) of a sport or a club. The editorial content may therefore be written more in accordance with principles of public relations than of independent and balanced journalism. Material on them should be treated with the same care as a press release produced by any organisation seeking to maintain and improve its public image and commercial viability.

Such websites usually offer news stories, features, reports, press releases and statistical and historical information, but there is more to them than journalism. Their main function is often to sell merchandise or to promote other products such as subscriptions to television and radio channels. But as with the older media, it is editorial content – the breaking news, the background features, etc. – which draws users to these sites.

The best of them, such as those of Manchester United or the New York Yankees, are almost as good as media sites. They often provide alternative angles on their own stories by reproducing what the media and others in the sport are saying on an issue.

Unofficial sites

For every official club website, there may be dozens of websites set up by fans – the online equivalent of FANZINES. These are often of poor quality and may contain libellous material but can provide a useful guide to what fans are thinking about controversial issues within sports organisations.

Online journalism

Perhaps the main advantage online journalism offers over other forms is that it eliminates the fixed news deadline. A website can be updated at any time, and technology is available that can deliver BREAKING STORIES direct to people's desktops. Websites are therefore attractive to users who want the latest sports news as it occurs, or who want to read reports of sporting events as they happen. In addition, sports organisations often choose to release information online first, to attract fans to their websites and to make sure that they set the agenda by writing the story from their own angle.

Internet journalism still has much in common with other forms of journalism. It demands good writing, accuracy, impact and balance. But there are important differences, many of them determined by the way in which internet journalism is consumed, which is normally via a computer screen.

The shape of a computer screen, its relatively small size compared with a newspaper page, the availability of additional elements such as sound and video clips, and the need to allow users to navigate their way round the site, dictate the way in which information is presented online. The roles occupied by page designers and sub-editors in print journalism take on even greater importance on websites. A web page can accommodate only a relatively small amount of information, so website users have to be directed simply and quickly to other pages where they can get the information they want. The task of the web designer is to get as much information as possible on a computer screen, without creating clutter and confusion. The space available for editorial content is limited not only by the size of the screen, but also because each page must contain navigational aids and sometimes advertising.

Editorial space takes second place to user-friendliness on a good website. Journalists, therefore, have to work within the constraints imposed on them by the site design. This often means finding new ways of presenting information so that it can be consumed easily on screen. Online journalists have combined some of the elements of print journalism, such as words, pictures and graphics, with elements from the broadcast media, such as SOUNDBITES and VIDEO CLIPS, to create a new form of journalism suited to a new medium.

A report which would appear in a newspaper as a single piece of copy may be split into a number of elements for a website. The basic facts will still be presented by means of a headline and paragraphs of copy, but background information may be displayed as factfiles in SIDEBARS, and quotes made available direct from the speaker by means of an audio or video clip.

Example

The following story was written for the sports pages of a newspaper. The italicised sections could be displayed as FACTFILES on a website.

Waugh hits a high note in swansong

Steve Waugh, the world's most capped cricketer, brought his 18-year Test match career to a close with an innings of 80 that saved the match and the series against India.

At the end of his 168th and final test, a record fifth-day crowd of 27,000 at the Sydney Cricket Ground cheered Waugh as he was chaired round his home arena by his team mates.

With his 33rd Test match century in sight, his innings ended when he was caught on the boundary by Sachin Tendulkar off Anil Kumble's bowling. But the 38-year-old had already ensured that Australia would rescue the fourth and final Test to tie the series at one victory apiece.

'It shows that after 168 Tests you can still lose the plot under pressure,' said Waugh afterwards.

Without his contribution, India might have won a series on Australian soil for the first time. Australia needed an unprecedented 443 in the final innings to win, and the match ended with them on 357 for six.

Waugh's dismissal brought to an end one of the greatest international careers in cricket history, in which he captained both Australia's Test and one-day sides.

He came in with his side under pressure at 170 for three, and hit 15 boundaries *to take his total in Tests since his debut 18 years ago to 10,927 at an average of more than 51. As a Test bowler he took 92 wickets at an average of 37.*

He also played 325 one-day internationals, scoring 7,569 runs at an average of more than 52, and taking 195 wickets.

'I felt tranquil out there,' he said. 'It's only a game, after all, and perhaps it took me to the final innings to realise that.'

'This is as good as it gets,' he added. 'I'll never forget it. I saw the faces in the crowd and their reaction. The whole game was an amazing experience and I can't thank the crowd enough.'

India's captain Sourav Ganguly was disappointed to see victory snatched from his grasp after a match in which *his side scored their highest ever total, Tendulkar made his highest Test score of 241 not out and Kumble took 12 wickets in the match. But he was full of praise for his opposite number. 'A lot of players, including me, have looked up to you for your attitude,' he told Waugh.*

Website version

This is how the same story might be presented on a website:

Waugh quits on a high

Steve Waugh, the world's most capped cricketer, brought his 18-year Test career to a close with an innings of 80 that saved the match and the series against India.

A record fifth-day crowd at the Sydney Cricket Ground cheered Waugh after he rescued the fourth and final Test to tie the series.

Without his contribution, India might have won a series on Australian soil for the first time.

Australia needed an unprecedented 443 in the final innings to win, and ended on 357 for six.

Waugh came in with his side under pressure at 170 for three, and hit 15 boundaries, and the match was safe when he was caught on the boundary by Sachin Tendulkar off Anil Kumble's bowling.

It brought to an end one of the greatest international careers in cricket history.

The quotes could be displayed as a separate story:

What they said

Australian captain Steve Waugh: 'This is as good as it gets, I'll never forget it. I saw the faces in the crowd and their reaction. The whole game was an amazing experience and I can't thank the crowd enough.'

'I felt tranquil out there. It's only a game, after all, and perhaps it took me to the final innings to realise that. (My dismissal) shows that after 168 Tests you can still lose the plot under pressure.'

Indian captain Sourav Ganguly: 'A lot of players, including me, have looked up to (Steve) for (his) attitude.'

Sidebar 1

The Waugh years

Age: 38

Test caps: 168

Test runs: 10,927

Average: 51

Highest score: 200

Test 100s: 32

Wickets: 92

One-day caps: 325

Runs: 7,569

Average: 52

Wickets: 195

Highest score: 120 not out

Sidebar 2

Match records

India's highest total: 705–7

Highest total against Australia in Australia

Test best scores for Tendulkar (241 not out), Katich (125) and Patel (62)

Anil Kumble's 12 wickets his best outside India

Attendance (27,056) highest for fifth day at Sydney Cricket Ground

Total attendance (189,989) record for five-day test at SCG

In addition, the quotes (and coverage of Waugh's dismissal and his reception by the crowd) could be carried as audio or video clips, or both.

All the information which has been italicised in the print version has been dealt with separately for the online version. Factfiles, because they display information concisely, can contain additional information to that covered in a single report.

Online sports coverage

The content of web sports pages reflects that of newspapers and the broadcast media. The difference lies in speed of delivery and presentation.

Sports reporting

Sports reporting online is possible while an event is taking place, just as it is on radio and television. Indeed, some websites offer live commentary and even visual coverage, though restrictions over rights apply to online journalists just as they do in radio and television. But websites are free to provide regularly updated running written copy and still photographs of the action as it is happening, as well as considered reports when the event has finished. Websites can keep their users in touch with an event moment by moment by refreshing the site at regular intervals or whenever there is a noteworthy incident. With the various codes of football, for example, a site can be refreshed whenever there is a score, while tennis reports can be updated point by point or game by game, and cricket reports ball by ball or over by over. The journalistic technique involved is similar to that employed by journalists working for evening sports papers, who dictate copy over open phone lines, often straight from their heads, whenever something significant happens.

Some sites also provide a service of updates – often a condensed version of what appears on the site itself – delivered direct to people's desktops. Journalists servicing websites are expected to provide considered reports when the event is over. Because of the constraints already discussed, these will often be more tightly-written than for a newspaper, and quotes may be added later, or displayed separately in a sidebar or as a REACTION STORY.

Exercise

Using a video of a match, write running copy for a website, providing a short paragraph of one or two sentences every ten minutes. If there is a lot of interesting action, this limit can be extended, as the availability of space is more flexible on a website than in print.

At the end of the match, turn your copy into a short, considered report, concentrating only on the most important aspects. Follow this up with a separate piece containing after-match quotes.

News

News can also be covered fast on a website. Breaking stories will either replace older stories on the home page or be flagged up there by CRAWLERS and a link to the story. Breaking stories may often be little more than a paragraph in the first instance, with the story being updated and expanded as it develops.

Features and profiles

These also work best online if they are broken down into easily read sections. This is sometimes done by means of newspaper-style CROSSHEADS, but often by dividing the feature into several elements. Quotes, for instance, can be lifted out and presented in a question-and-answer format, with life and career details contained in a sidebar. Again, the key lies in design and presentation.

Some sites do run features of similar length to those found in the print media, and many newspapers make the contents of their print versions available on the web. But long pieces on a website can deter reader because they are difficult to read across the wide measure of a computer screen, and if they are condensed into newspaper-style column widths, a great deal of scrolling is necessary to read them. Ideally, features written for print should be rewritten for the web and presented in an easily absorbed format.

Exercise

Select a feature or a profile from a newspaper and turn it into a piece suitable for a website. Reduce the narrative to its essentials and present statistics and background information in a sidebar. Present quotes either in a free-standing question-and-answer format or as audio clips. You may also need a separate section on what others have to say about the subject of the piece, and a picture or even video clip of the subject in action.

Style

For pieces written for web pages, therefore, style should generally be tight, simple and factual. The format does not offer much scope for florid writing, even in features.

Statistics

These are ideally suited to sports websites because they can be quickly and regularly updated, and the space available for them is virtually unlimited.

Archives

Archives are an important element of many websites for the same reason. It means you can get anything you want just by typing in key words.

Interactive features

These are also available on many sports websites. They give fans the opportunity to have their say about the latest sports news stories and join in the debates over controversial issues, often by means of chatrooms which allow users to talk to each other online. Some websites also make sports personalities or journalists available online to answer users' questions. Many also offer a service of results, score updates and reports direct to mobile phones, as well as updates, daily messages or headlines direct to subscribers' computer screens at work or at home.

The influence of the web

As we have seen in Chapter 9, websites have had an important influence on television sports presentation. Although sports news channels and sports report and results programmes use live presenters or ANCHORS to deliver information, they have begun to borrow tools and design features from websites to increase the amount of information they are able to deliver at any one time. Their screens now resemble websites, offering constantly changing information in crawlers across the bottom, and frequently updated information in sidebars. They are also heavily reliant on statistics such as fixtures, league tables and score updates.

The interactivity of websites is also being reflected in the broadcast media, by radio phone-ins and text messages to radio and television programmes. The print media, too, now provide much more space for sports statistics, break up sports news stories and features with sidebars and graphics, and use more pictures in more creative ways.

The web as research tool

Although there is a sense in which the internet has revolutionised publishing, it has complemented and influenced, rather than replaced, existing media. Because it offers instantly available information from a wide range of organisations that can be accessed from anywhere, one of its principal uses for journalists is as a research tool.

The easiest way to find information online is to use a search engine such as Google, Yahoo, Lycos or Ask Jeeves. Call up the Home Page, type your keyword or words into the Search box, and let the search engine do the rest. It is advisable, however, to try to define your search as narrowly as possible, or the response may overwhelm you. A search for sites relating to popular organisations such as Manchester United or the New York Yankees may throw up pages of sites. In addition to many well-organised and informative sites, there is a lot of junk out there. One way of refining your search is to request only official sites; another is to choose to search for sites only in your own country, or in the country in which the organisation you are looking for is based, rather than worldwide.

Cutting and pasting information from the internet is easy, but it also presents hazards. Websites are covered by the same copyright legislation as printed or broadcast material, and you should beware of infringing that copyright (see Appendix 3). You should also be wary of plagiarism. You must not pass off someone else's work as your own, and neither should you let what someone else has written get in the way of producing your own distinctive piece of journalism in your own style. If you use information from anything other than a primary source, such as a club website or an individual athlete's own site, you need to check its accuracy just as you would from any other media source.

Researching a story on the net will often involve visiting more that one site to gather together the ingredients. For instance, if a player is rumoured to be moving from one club to another, the websites of the clubs involved will probably offer their official view on the story, and the player's own site or that of his agent may have something to say. Sometimes the information found there will be conflicting, but it can still form the basis for a story.

The internet has also made it more difficult for people to hide from journalists. There are times – for instance, if they have failed a drugs test or have been involved in some scandal away from the arena – when sports people would prefer to keep a low profile. The internet offers additional ways of tracking people down, through online telephone directories and easily searchable registers which will provide addresses in response to a search for a name. Journalists can now also use e-mail as a way of reaching someone for a quote when it is difficult to get a personal interview or reach someone by phone. Most people read their e-mails and a reply takes only seconds. An e-mail interview can sometimes be useful, though it is no substitute for speaking to someone direct.

Summary

The rapid growth of online journalism has been led by established media organisations. Most major sporting organisations have set up their own websites with a mix of information and commercial objectives. New methods of presentation have been developed for the web, and these are now being adapted by the established media. One of the major advantages of the web for sports journalists is as a quick and easily accessible source of information.

Appendix 1

Getting a job

Journalism is regarded by many as an exciting, even glamorous, occupation and the competition to get into it is intense. Most media organisations receive far more applications for jobs than they can fill, and many would-be journalists are inevitably disappointed. But the media sector in most developed countries – and sports journalism in particular – has been expanding, and opportunities do arise for people with talent, enthusiasm and perseverance.

What employers are looking for

New entrants – whether they are journalists or photographers – normally have to start by learning the whole range of journalistic skills. That means they will be working as general news reporters or as part of a team of photographers. Employers will therefore expect applicants to demonstrate a wide range of interests, not merely in sport.

They will be looking for a good knowledge of current affairs, both national and local; an interest in people, places and events; the ability to write simple prose, with a sound understanding of grammar, spelling and punctuation; a willingness to work unsocial hours; calmness under pressure and an ability to meet deadlines; and the determination and persistence to track down a story.

Career paths

Most journalists start by getting jobs as trainees in newspapers, radio or television, or by enrolling on pre-entry training courses at colleges or universities. They are normally expected to work as general news reporters and opportunities for sports journalism may be limited at first. It may be a couple of years before there is an opportunity to specialise in sport. Those who do make it to the sports department will often be asked to specialise in one or two sports, and to cover the affairs of one or more clubs. Many sports journalists stay with the same organisation all their working lives, but others progress from weekly to daily newspapers, and some cross over into broadcasting. Only the very best secure staff jobs on national or regional newspapers, or on national radio or television.

Training

In Britain, around 40 per cent of journalists start by training on a local news-paper, under the terms of a training contract. There they receive on-the-job training with senior journalists, supplemented by BLOCK-RELEASE to courses on which they can study for a professional qualification. Some of the bigger newspaper and broadcasting companies operate their own training schemes. Places on these schemes are sometimes advertised in newspapers and the trade press. Competition for these places is always very strong.

Many universities and colleges now run degree courses in journalism, some of which incorporate a professional qualification. Journalism schools have been in operation in the USA since the early twentieth century. It was the 1960s or later before they were established in Britain, where the National Council for the Training of Journalists (NCTJ) is the union and industry body which co-ordinates training. Many colleges train students for the NCTJ certificate, which is the standard journalism qualification in Britain. Entry to such courses may involve passing an aptitude test designed to establish whether potential students have the qualities necessary to become a successful journalist.

Minimum educational qualifications are usually required to gain employ-ment as a journalist or entry to a training course. In Britain, the minimum job entry requirements are five GCSEs (General Certificate of Secondary Education) at A, B or C grades, or the equivalent. One of these should be English language. It is unusual, however, for entrants to be taken on without at least two Advanced level GCSEs, and journalism is rapidly becoming a graduate profession. More than 60 per cent of recruits are now university graduates.

Some students on pre-entry training courses are sponsored by prospec-tive employers, but the majority pay their own way. Many universities also offer post-graduate diplomas for students with a first degree who wish to acquire journalism skills. Courses normally cover the entire range of journalistic skills, including law, public affairs, newspaper and broadcast journalism, though some offer options in sports journalism. Brighton University in the United Kingdom introduced the first degree course in sports journalism in 2003, combining sport studies and media studies and a period of work experience.

Press photography courses are also available, which teach news values alongside photographic skills. Courses are also available in photo-journalism, which combines photography with reporting. As well as an interest in photography, the qualities required for acceptance on these courses are energy, commitment, personality, an enquiring mind and an eye for a 'different' picture. Some universities run courses in broadcast journalism, and there are college courses in magazine journalism which include news and feature writing, production and design.

For British college courses the minimum requirement is usually two A level passes, though universities may ask for three passes at high grades. Most colleges only give places to people who have some work experience in the field and who are therefore sure that the job is the right one for them.

Work experience

Getting a job, a traineeship or even a place on a journalism course is difficult, but your prospects will be enhanced if you can show a strong commitment to journalism. The best way to do that is by gaining as much work experience as possible on newspapers, in radio or in television.

To get a work experience placement you should write to a number of local newspapers or broadcasting organisations explaining why you want to become a journalist or press photographer, what qualities you think you would bring to the job, and asking if you can work in the newsroom for a few days. Applications for work experience reach their height in the summer months, and you may increase your chances of being offered a placement if you avoid June, July or August. You will not be paid, but getting a foot inside the newsroom door is the best way to make contacts and hear about any job opportunities that come along. Many jobs in journalism are not advertised, but go to people whose work an editor knows and can trust. Some editors will take on – or at least publish the work of – people who are keen and good at the job, even if they have no formal qualifications.

The best way to get your name in front of employers who may be seeking to take on staff is to compile a portfolio of your work. In the end, employers are interested in what you can do. You may have to start small, by getting stories and features published in weekly newspapers, or in Saturday afternoon sports papers, which are often willing to take freelance pieces on minor sports to help fill their pages in advance of the day's big-game action. You may not be paid for them, but the cuttings in your portfolio will be invaluable.

Freelancing

Some freelances start by offering sports editors reports on minor league matches and expand into profiles of players once their work is known and their judgement about what makes a good feature is accepted. It may be necessary to persuade the sports editor that there is a lot of interest in your sport at that level. If you can become an expert in your own small field, the sports editor may start calling you, and once you have established the quality of your work, you may be offered bigger assignments, and eventually a job on the paper.

When you have built up a small portfolio, you should compile a CV listing your qualifications and experience. Most editors do not need to advertise for junior staff, but keep the details of likely candidates handy, so it is important to get your CV into as many places as possible. You should also ask to go in to the newsroom and talk to the sports editor or someone else on the sports desk. Get them to show you around and explain what they do. Enthusiasm counts for a lot with people who are looking to hire staff.

Even if a staff job does not materialise, freelance experience with local newspapers can lead to bigger things. National and regional newspapers employ few staff sports writers, but rely heavily on freelances to cover events at weekends and in the evenings. They are always looking for new writers, and will often be willing to give an opportunity to someone who can show a track record of producing competent work at local level. The growth of local and specialist sport radio stations and television sports results services is also providing fresh opportunities for freelance sports journalists.

Working as a freelance has its advantages. You can work from home and you can turn down jobs if you feel like a day off – although if you do that too often, people will stop calling. It has its disadvantages, too. Some freelances work long hours because they cannot afford to turn work down. You also have to sell your work to sports editors, to chase up your fees and expenses from some employers, and you have no job security and no access to office politics.

But freelancing gives you the opportunity of working for more than one employer, and often in more than one medium. Many freelances will cover an event for both radio and newspapers. Most large media organisations have their own freelance rates of pay. In Britain, the National Union of Journalists (NUJ) has a list of minimum freelance rates.

Whether they are freelances or staff writers, most sports writers specialise in one particular area. Only the top writers can cherry pick across the world of sport. One fruitful area for freelances is to offer TIMELESS PIECES which can be used to fill space on the sports pages when there is little action to report. Another is the 'crossover' piece, in which expertise in other areas is used to throw light on current issues in the world of sport. Examples include fashion (what the top sports people are wearing), business (the share prices of clubs, their merchandising activities, clubs going into receivership), medicine (injuries to high-profile performers, the use of drugs), and celebrity reporting (the social lives of sports people).

Useful books

Benn's UK Media Directory (annually) and Willing's *Press Guide* will provide the names and addresses of British newspapers for those seeking jobs as trainee journalists.

Useful websites

www.smarterwork.com – for writers seeking commissions
www.honk.co.uk/fleetstreet – from job hunting to payments
www.brighton.ac.uk – details of sport journalism degree course
www.nctj.com – details of journalism and photographers' training courses in Britain

Appendix 2

The sports journalist's tool kit

This is some of the equipment you will need to work as a sports journalist:

Personal computer and printer – the basic equipment for writing articles and storing information electronically. It should have access to the internet, which is vital for research, and should offer an e-mail facility, which is useful for communicating with sports desks and for filing copy.

Laptop computer – useful for writing reports at sports events and for filing copy via a modem and telephone line. Most laptops now give internet access and e-mail facilities.

Mobile phone – vital for communicating with the sports desk while working at events, and useful for telephoning copy if no land line is available.

Notebook – use a small spiral bound reporters notebook that slips easily into the pocket and with pages that flip over easily. This is useful when taking notes at speed. Never write on the backs of envelopes or odd scraps of paper, which can easily be lost. Notebooks should always be kept tidily, with your name and telephone number (in case you lose it) and the date the notebook was begun on the cover. You should also date each of your entries, so that you can refer back to notes easily. The names of people who are providing you with information should be written clearly alongside the appropriate notes.

Contacts book – choose a small, hard-covered book which can be slipped into the pocket. It should be divided alphabetically so that you can easily find the details of the person you want to talk to. Enter the telephone numbers (home, work and mobile) and postal and e-mail addresses of all your contacts – even those you rarely use, because one day you may need them. Try to keep it up to date, as people change addresses and telephone numbers (especially mobiles) frequently.

Stopwatch – useful for recording the times at which goals are scored (but always rely on official time-keeping at athletics meetings and other racing events).

Binoculars – handy for getting close to the action at an event. Press boxes can be situated some distance away. Choose a small, light pair which is easy to carry around, preferably with a case which can be slipped into a pocket or bag, or attached to your belt.

Shorthand – the ability to write quickly and accurately is extremely useful for print journalists, particularly at press conferences and in interviews. It allows quotes to be taken down quickly and accurately, and cuts out the need to play back a tape. The National Council for the Training of Journalists requires a minimum speed of 100 words per minute shorthand. Pitmans (which was invented in the nineteenth century but is still the best and most thorough system) and Teeline (which was devised in the twentieth century specifically for journalists) are the most popular. Some journalists devise their own systems, usually based on omitting vowels from words and reducing common words to single letters. Thus *the* become *t* and *would* becomes *wd*. Most provincial newspapers will demand good shorthand from applicants.

Tape recorders – small, hand-held tape recorders can be useful as a back-up to written notes and for recording interviews in difficult situations, such as in a media scrum outside a dressing room or in the car park of a stadium. If you use a recorder for interviews, always ask the interviewee whether he or she minds the conversation being recorded. Some people may be intimidated by a tape recorder. Whenever possible, you should also take written notes in case of a mechanical problem, and because these are usually quicker to transcribe.

Yearbooks – these are produced for most major sports and give details of the leading clubs and their players, together with the governing bodies. They often also include biographies of leading figures and records of past competitions. The best known is probably *Wisden*, the cricket almanac.

Filing cabinet – a great deal of sports information can now be stored electronically, but much of it still arrives in paper form, especially at sporting events. A filing cabinet is useful for storing cuttings and information handed out by sports organisations. Many sports journalists also choose to keep their own records.

Transport – sports journalists need to be highly mobile. Access to a car and the ability to drive is almost essential (although some sports journalists do travel by public transport).

Other tools

Before going to an event, sports journalists should always make sure they have caught up with the latest developments by finding out what is being said about it in the media. This means they should read previews in the newspapers and listen to radio sports preview programmes on the way to the events. When they arrive, they should always remember to collect an official programme and team sheet.

Before attempting to cover a sport with which you are not familiar, make sure that you know the rules, at least. There is usually a website (see below) which can help.

Health issues

The tools a journalist uses can lead to health problems unless used sensibly. Long periods using a keyboard can lead to Repetitive Strain Injury (RSI), which usually makes itself felt as damage to the tendons in the wrists or arms. Using a computer screen can damage the eyes. Have your eyes checked regularly if you work at a VDU screen or on a laptop computer for long periods. There are also potential health risks from the use of mobile phones, though these are currently unproven. Try to keep calls short and use a land line when possible. Some sports events can be dangerous and it is advisable to make the appropriate health and safety checks before going to cover them. Steer clear of dangerous places at car rallies and race meetings.

Appendix 3

Copyright

Journalists own the copyright in their own work unless they are directly employed by someone else to produce it. The copyright in an employee's creations is automatically assigned to the employer, but if work is commissioned from you as a freelance, you retain the copyright unless there is a contract to the contrary. Because you are self-employed it is your own, so make sure you don't sign it away.

All written work, sound recording, film and broadcast is protected by copyright. There is no copyright on ideas, but copyright protection in the UK and many other countries applies automatically if the work exists physically. This applies even if it is still in the form of a manuscript or computer program.

For work originating in the European Union, copyright lasts for 70 years after the death of the author of written, dramatic, musical or artistic work. Sound recordings, broadcasts and cable programmes are protected for 50 years. In other countries, the period is that granted by the country of origin of the work.

Copyright can be bought, sold or otherwise transferred, and copyright owners can license others to use their work while retaining ownership of the copyright. You should approach the copyright owner for permission to use material.

In certain circumstances, however, permission is not needed. Limited use of work is permitted for research, private study, criticism, review and reporting current events. Publication of excerpts, such as quotes, requires an acknowledgement.

Copyright applies on the internet as it does to paper. Material may not be posted on a website without consent. Many websites give details about how the material they contain may be used. Permission should always be obtained before establishing a link to another website.

Useful websites

www.intellectual-property.gov.uk – UK Patent Office
www.wipo.org – World Intellectual Property Organisation

Appendix 4

Sports books and films

Books

The popularity of sport has spawned thousands of books, and they are currently being published faster than ever. Many of them are the memoirs of famous sports personalities or – thanks to the success of Nick Hornby's *Fever Pitch* (see below) – the accounts of obsessive fans. The former (even if they are 'ghosted' by professional authors) are often not well-written and tend to rehash already familiar successes. The latter can often be self-indulgent and tedious unless you happen to share the author's obsession.

However, the literature of sport does contain some excellent volumes, many of them written by journalists rather than participants or administrators. The following is a selection of the best.

Sports journalism anthologies

The Picador Book of Sports Writing, edited by Nick Coleman and Nick Hornby (Picador, 1996) – selection of pieces from journalists and other writers, covering a wide range of sports (but with something of an obsession with the boxer Muhammad Ali).

The Norton Book of Sports, edited by George Plimpton (Norton and Co., 1992) – an American writer's selection of sports pieces.

American Football

Paper Lion, Confessions of a Last-string Quarterback, George Plimpton (Deutsch, 1968) – participation journalism from the American writer better known for editing the *Paris Review* interviews.

Baseball

Out of My League, George Plimpton (Deutsch, 1961) – more participation.

The Boys of Summer, Roger Kahn (HarperCollins, 1972) – a classic history of baseball and the Brooklyn Dodgers.

Boxing

The Fight, Norman Mailer (Penguin, 1975) – the American novelist's account of the 'Rumble in the Jungle', the world heavyweight title fight between Muhammad Ali and George Foreman in Zaïre.

Cricket

Cardus on Cricket, Neville Cardus (Souvenir Press, 1977) – an anthology of pieces by the acknowledged master of cricket writing.

Beyond a Boundary, CLR James (Serpent's Tail, 1963) – philosophical reflections on cricket in the West Indies and England, widely regarded as one of the best books ever written about any sport.

The Willow Wand: Some Cricket Myths Explored, Derek Birley (Sportspages, 1979) – another philosophical look at the summer game and those who have played it and written about it.

Hell for Leather, Robert Winder (Victor Gollancz, 1996) – a thoughtful account of the cricket World Cup staged in India.

Cape Summer, Alan Ross (Michael Joseph, 1957) – the poet and journalist's account of an England tour of South Africa.

Golf

The Bogey Man, George Plimpton (Deutsch, 1969) – a month on the Professional Golfers' Association (PGA) tour in America.

Ice Hockey

Open Net, George Plimpton (Deutsch, 1985) – yet more participation.

Motor Racing

The Death of Ayrton Senna, Richard Williams (Viking, 2000) – uses the Brazilian driver as a peg for a wide-ranging examination of Formula 1.

Rugby League

At the George, Geoffrey Moorhouse (Sceptre, 1989) – a classic account of the birth of Rugby League (at the George Inn of the title in Huddersfield), the author growing up with the game in northern England and watching it in Australia and New Zealand.

Rugby Union

Muddied Oafs: The Last Days of Rugger, Richard Beard (Yellow Jersey Press, 2003) – a wide-ranging and stylishly quirky look at the way the game has changed since it went professional.

Soccer

Fever Pitch, Nick Hornby (Victor Gollancz, 1992) – a well-observed account of a fan's obsession with Arsenal, which spawned a host of imitators.

All Played Out: The Full Story of Italia 90, Pete Davies (William Heinemann, 1990) – a detailed account of the World Cup finals, on and off the pitch.

Swimming

Haunts of the Black Masseur: The Swimmer as Hero, Charles Sprawson (Random House, 2000) – an intelligent history of swimming.

Fiction

Fiction writers have not often been attracted to sport, although some of the world's greatest novelists and playwrights – Charles Dickens, James

Joyce, Samuel Beckett and Harold Pinter – have written about cricket. The following have written more recently about other sports.

This Sporting Life, David Storey (Longmans, Green, 1960) – a 'kitchen sink' school novel about the life and loves of a rugby league player in the 1960s, based partly on the author's career as a Leeds player.

Own Goals and *Goodnight Vienna*, Phil Andrews (both Hodder and Stoughton, 1999 and 2000) – soccer-based thrillers using the financial problems of Premier League clubs and the pressures facing the England manager as backgrounds.

Films

Despite its in-built drama, sport has not been particularly well served by the cinema. Hollywood is the main producer of feature films in the West, but American sports do not travel well and the most successful have been based on sports with a wider appeal, such as boxing.

Features

This Sporting Life (1963), directed by Lindsay Anderson and based on David Storey's novel (see above), is one of the best sports-based films ever made. Action scenes were shot at Wakefield Trinity's Belle Vue ground.

Raging Bull (1980) is Martin Scorsese's ringside melodrama, based on the life of middleweight boxer Jake La Motta.

Chariots of Fire (1981) is David Puttnam's accomplished account of a Scotsman and a Jew running for Britain in the 1924 Paris Olympics.

Documentaries

Olympiad 1936, directed by Leni Riefenstahl, records the 1936 Berlin Olympics and is beautifully filmed. It has often been imitated since (though not the Nazi propaganda).

Appendix 5

Legal and ethical issues

Journalists and the law

Like all other journalists, those who specialise in sport must abide by the laws of the country in which they operate and in which their work is published or broadcast. Sports journalists will not find themselves constrained by legal considerations as often as crime correspondents or court reporters, but they cannot afford to be complacent about legal issues.

There will be occasions – when writing about sports people who have been accused of criminal offences or of drug misuse or some other misdemeanour, for instance – when a sports writer will need to be aware of the laws of defamation and contempt.

Defamation involves writing or broadcasting something you cannot prove which could expose the subject to hatred, ridicule or contempt, or the loss of business or professional standing. Sports people have been known to sue newspapers which have accused them of match-fixing, for instance. And don't forget that any quotes or interview clips you use from other people could be libellous. If you have any doubts at all, don't use them.

Contempt of court involves writing or broadcasting something which may unfairly influence court proceedings. For instance, the trials of the Leeds United footballers Lee Bowyer and Jonathan Woodgate were halted after a newspaper published an interview with a relative of the man they were alleged to have assaulted.

Sports journalists must also be aware of the laws of copyright and those covering data protection.

Of course, the law on these and other issues that affect journalists differs from country to country. For instance, laws on what you can publish before and during legal proceedings are less inhibiting in the USA than in Britain and many other countries. Even in the United Kingdom, the law in England and Wales is different from that in Scotland. It is not, therefore, possible to give detailed guidance here. Instead, you should make sure you are familiar with the law in the country in which you are working. In many countries, there are useful reference works written especially for journalists. In Britain, the main reference work is *McNae's Essential Law for Journalists*, edited by LCJ McNae, T Welsh and W Greenwood (OUP, 17th edition, 2003).

The best way to avoid legal difficulties is to check all your facts scrupulously, and never make assumptions or jump to conclusions. If in doubt, consult the legal department of the organisation for which you are working.

Ethics

In addition to legal constraints, sports journalists should also ensure that their behaviour and work conforms to the ethical standards expected of all journalists. Most major print and broadcasting organisations, as well as media regulating bodies in many countries, have their own Codes of Conduct. Staff and contributors are expected to follow them, and they are often written into their terms of employment.

They deal with issues such as fairness, the correction of mistakes, dealing with people who are experiencing grief and trauma, offensive language, plagiarism, privacy, race and gender issues, the protection of sources and the use of subterfuge to gather information. They also deal with the personal conduct of journalists, such as conflicts of interest (when writing about a team you support or an athlete with whom you have a relationship, for instance) and the acceptance of payment or gifts from the people about whom you are writing.

You should study carefully the Code of Conduct of the organisation for whom you are working, or of one of the media regulating bodies in the country in which you are working. The Code of Practice of the British Press Complaints Commission (www.pcc.org.uk) is a useful statement of ethical behaviour for journalists.

You will find the following checklist useful in dealing with some of the ethical issues you may encounter as a sports journalist.

Checklist

✓ Were the methods I used to gather my information honest, legal and transparent?
✓ Have I respected the privacy of the subject and others?
✓ If not, is my intrusion in the public interest? Why?
✓ Is my piece balanced, fair, honest, accurate and objective?
✓ Does it display prejudice because of race, gender, age or disability?
✓ Does it reinforce race or gender stereotypes or ageism or disabled issues?

✓ Could it cause distress to the subject or his or her family or friends?
✓ Have I been honest about my sources, even if I can't name them?
✓ Is the language I have used likely to offend a reasonable person?
✓ Have I infringed anyone's copyright?
✓ Have I reproduced anyone else's work without attribution?
✓ Has my objectivity been compromised by financial inducements or gifts?
✓ Are any photographs which have been digitally altered or enhanced clearly labelled as such?

Key Terms

Actuality sound   natural sound effects, such as the roar of a crowd or galloping hooves, used in radio to help listeners picture the scene

Agent   a sports person's representative, who conducts wage negotiations and sponsorship and transfer deals. The agent may also speak on behalf of the athlete and deal with interview requests

Ambush interview   an interview conducted when subjects are approached in a public place or on their doorstep

Anchor   a presenter on a television or radio programme who reads reports and introduces items

Angle   the point of view from which a feature is written

Archive   previously-used material which can be accessed via a website

As-live   a piece which appears to be live, even though it was shot some time earlier

Autocue   device which allows television bulletin presenters to read the text of scripts from the camera lens

Block release   a period of time during which a trainee is released from his or her job to attend a training course

Breaking story   a story appearing for the first time

Byline   name of the journalist *by* whom a story has been written

Camera read   television news item without pictures, but with presenter in vision

Catchline   name given to a piece of copy to distinguish it from others

Closed questions   questions which anticipate the answer or which are capable of being answered by a single word, for example: 'You must have been happy with your performance?'

Colour piece   a lively, descriptive piece, sometimes opinionated, funny or impressionistic, rather than a straight news report

Contact   someone willing to provide information to a journalist

Contacts book   list of contacts, with home and mobile telephone numbers and e-mail addresses

Copy text of a story or feature produced by a journalist (from which a compositor once *copied* the printed version)

Copytaker person who keys in copy telephoned in by journalists working away from the office

Copy item radio news item read from script by bulletin presenter

Copy tasting assessing the relative value of a story and deciding its position on a page or bulletin

Crawler moving text, usually along the top or bottom of the screen

Crosshead a sub-heading, often a single word, in a newspaper column or other text, used to break up the text and make it easier to read

Crossover piece feature on a general topic which uses a sports story as its 'peg'

Cutaways shots which allow an editor to move seamlessly from one sequence of action to another sequence which may have taken place much later in real time, for example, shots of the crowd or of coaches watching the action

Deadline latest time by which copy should be received, or edition must go to press

Diary contains information about events the sports desk may wish to cover

Direct quotations the actual words used by the interviewee, enclosed in quotation marks, for example: 'I think I played very well this afternoon.' They are always in the present tense.

Doughnut package 'topped and tailed' by the reporter from a relevant location

Edit points points at which a tape editor needs to move from one part of the action to another, usually by using a cutaway

Embargo a fixed time before which information supplied to journalists should not be published

Establishing shot a shot of the interviewee, preferably involved in the sport he or she represents, shown immediately before a clip of interview, to establish the person's identity in the viewers' minds

Estimate same as prospects (see below)

Exclusive a story to which no other news organisation yet has access

Factfile a column of facts accompanying a story

Fanzine unofficial magazine giving a platform for the views of fans, who may also operate unofficial websites

Feature a longer and more detailed piece of writing providing background information about people or events

Filing   sending copy from an event to the sports desk, usually by means of laptop computer, e-mail or telephone

Follow-up   a story which expands on an earlier story

Freelance   self-employed, as opposed to staff, journalist. May have contracts with one or more media organisations

Hard copy   a story on paper rather than in a computer

Highlights   condensed version of a sporting event, focusing on the key moments

Intro   the first paragraph, or introduction, to a report or story, often providing a brief summary of what follows

Laptop   portable computer used by sports writers in the field, from which copy can be filed via a modem and telephone line to the sports desk

Live   a piece of television or radio filmed or broadcast as it happens

Log   a list of key moments, with the times at which they can be found on the tape

NATSOF   Natural Sound On Film (the television equivalent of actuality sound)

News access   agreement allowing television broadcasters who do not own the rights to use action clips on news programmes

OB (outside broadcast)   Coverage (usually live) of a sporting event from the location at which it is taking place

Off the record   information which may help a journalist understand a story, but which is not for publication

On the record   information which can be published without restriction and attributed to the informant

Online   available via the internet

Open questions   questions which demand a considered answer and which cannot be answered with the words 'yes' or 'no', for example: 'How do you feel about your performance?'

Opinion piece   column expressing the writer's views on a controversial issue

Outro   opposite of 'Intro'; final paragraph which rounds off a piece

Package   television news item compiled by a reporter and consisting of several elements, such as voiceovers and clips of interviews

Payoff *see* Outro

Peg the basic event (often a news story) around which a feature is written

Piece to camera a segment of television package delivered with the reporter in vision

Press conference a meeting called by an individual or organisation to provide journalists with information and allow them to ask questions

Press release information provided by an individual or organisation to the media for publication

Profile a biographical piece about an individual

Prospects a list of stories and features that are expected to be available on a specific day

Reaction story a story which contains responses to an earlier story

Reported speech the interviewee's words are summarised by the reporter, with no quotation marks, for example: He said he thought he played very well. Reported speech is also known as an indirect quotation and is always in the past tense.

Running copy story or report filed in a series of 'takes'

Running story a story which develops over time and generates regular follow-up stories

Rushes unedited tape of action, or of shots filmed for a documentary or a news item

Sidebar a box alongside an online story containing additional information

Soundbite brief clip (usually between 10 and 30 seconds) from an interview for inclusion in a package

Standfirst introductory paragraph which explains what the feature is about and usually includes the writer's byline

Steadicam camera attached to the operator by a frame, which allows him or her to move easily and get close to the action

Stringer freelance journalist hired by the day to cover specific events

Style book guide to the organisation's preferred spelling, grammar and punctuation

Sub-editor an office-based journalist who corrects factual, grammatical and spelling errors in reporters' copy, cuts or extends it to fill the space allocated and writes the headline

Take a segment of copy filed as part of a 'running' story

Timeless pieces stories or features which can be used at any time to fill space when there is little live action to report

Two-way interview dialogue between bulletin presenter and reporter

Unattributable information which may be published, but not attributed publicly to the person who supplied it

Underlay television news item read by bulletin presenter while appropriate pictures are screened

Upsound as underlay (see above), followed by clip(s) of interview(s)

Video clip a short extract from television coverage or an interview

Voiceover reporter's words over television pictures

Voicepiece radio script read by reporter, but introduced by bulletin presenter

Vox pops from the Latin *vox populi* (voice of the people), these are short interview clips with ordinary people, such as sports fans, which are used to add interest and variety to radio and television packages

Website online source of information about an individual or organisation; can be found by typing the name of club, athlete or governing body into a search engine such as Google, Yahoo or Lycos

Wires copy provided to the media by news agencies, so called because it was originally sent by wire, though it has been available online since the 1980s. Most countries have their national wire services. In the United Kingdom most sports news is provided by the Press Association, though there are other specialist sports wire services

Bibliography

Adams, S. (2001) *Interviewing for Journalists*. London: Routledge.

Beaman, J. (2000) *Interviewing for Radio*. London: Routledge.

Benn's Media UK 2004 (2004) Tonbridge: CMP Information.

Bourdieu, P. (1998) *On Television and Journalism*. London: Pluto.

Boyd, A. (2001) *Broadcast Journalism* (5th edition). Oxford: Focal Press.

Briggs, A. and Cobley, P. (eds) (2002) *The Media: an introduction* (2nd edition). Harlow: Longman.

Bromley, M. (forthcoming) *Online Journalism*. London: Sage.

Coleman, N. and Hornby, N. (1996) *The Picador Book of Sportswriting*. London: Picador.

Featherstone, S. and Pape, S. (2005) *Newspaper Journalism*. London: Sage.

Fleming, C. (2002) *The Radio Handbook*. London: Routledge.

Fleming, C. (forthcoming) *Introduction to Journalism*. London: Sage.

Frost, C. (2000) *Media Ethics and Self-regulation*. Harlow: Longman.

Harcup, T. (2003) *Journalism: principles and practice*. London: Sage.

Harris, G. and Spark, D. (1997) *Practical Newspaper Reporting*. Oxford: Focal Press.

Hennessey, B. (1997) *Writing Feature Articles*. Oxford: Focal Press.

Hicks, W. (1998) *English for Journalists*. London: Routledge.

Hicks, W. (1999) *Writing for Journalists*. London: Routledge.

Hodgson, F.W. (1996) *Modern Newspaper Practice*. Oxford: Focal Press.

Holland, P. (2000) *The Television Handbook* (2nd edition). London: Routledge.

Keeble, R. (2001) *Ethics for Journalists*. London: Routledge.

Keeble, R. (ed.) (2001) *The Newspapers Handbook*. London: Routledge.

McNae, L.C.J., Welsh, T. and Greenwood, W. (2003) *McNae's Essential Law for Journalists* (17th edition). Oxford: Oxford University Press.

McNair, B. (2003) *News and Journalism in the UK*. London: Routledge.

Pavlik, J.V. (2001) *Journalism and New Media*. New York: Columbia University Press.

Plimpton, G. (1992) *The Norton Book of Sports*. New York: W.W. Norton.

Quinn, S. (2001) *Digital Sub-editing and Design*. Oxford: Focal Press.

Randall, D. (2000) *The Universal Journalist*. London: Pluto.

Sanders, K. (2003) *Ethics and Journalism*. London: Sage.

Sheridan Burns, L. (2002) *Understanding Journalism*. London: Sage.

Ward, M. (2002) *Journalism Online*. Oxford: Focal Press.

Whannel, G. (1992) *Fields in Vision: television sport and cultural transformation*. London: Routledge.

Hollis, N. (ed.) (1999) *Willing's Press Guide UK*. Teddington: Hollis Publishing.

Index

SCHOOLING IN AMERICA:

Scapegoat and Salvation

SCHOOLING IN AMERICA:
Scapegoat and Salvation

Seymour B. Sarason

THE FREE PRESS
A Division of Macmillan, Inc.
NEW YORK

Collier Macmillan Publishers
LONDON

The Free Press
A Division of Macmillan, Inc.
866 Third Avenue, New York, N.Y. 10022

Collier Macmillan Canada, Inc.

Printed in the United States of America

printing number

1 2 3 4 5 6 7 8 9 10

Library of Congress Cataloging in Publication Data

Sarason, Seymour Bernard
    Schooling in America.

    Includes index.
    1. Non-formal education — United States. 2. Public schools — United States. I. Title.
LC45.4.S27 1983   371'.04   83-47506
ISBN 0-02-929050-3

Epigraph cited in C.P. Snow, *The Search*. New York: Curtis Brown, Ltd. Copyright © by C.P. Snow, 1934, 1958, pp. 22–23. Reprinted by permission.

Quotation cited in text is reprinted by permission of the publishers from Harlan Lane, *The Wild Boy of Aveyron*. Cambridge, Mass.: Harvard University Press, Copyright © by Harlan Lane 1976, pp. 3–6.

Dedication

To Julie
who, in ways unknown and unknowable to her,
was in part responsible for this book.

It was a long time before I understood Luard. I had to go to two universities, to listen to the educational theorists, to examine in university scholarships myself, before I fully realized why he had lost heart and made his lessons so conventionally arid. Indignantly I discovered the mixture of vested interests, muddled thinking and memory of their own past that had made men adhere to the "logical" method of teaching science. "If you want to interest your pupils," I remember someone telling me as I was pleading for a gleam of something to catch boys' imaginations, "you can put them in the position of the original discoverer." Put them in the position of the original discoverer! The pedagogic nonsense of it all! When you think of the chances and stumbling, the flashes of insight and the sheer mistakes, that have gone to every discovery since science began! And then to expect to teach in that way. "The real method of teaching science apart from the frills," the man went on, "is to go from the observations to the conclusions. Start with simple experiments, note your deductions from them, and don't worry them with the new-fangled stuff. It's the way of experience, Miles, it's the logical way, and you can't do better than that." The logical way. They might as well teach French by starting with an agglutinative language like Eskimo and follow the logical changes in language through the Basque down to the European tongues. They might as well teach Biblical history by making the boys spend forty years in Sinai.

And this pedantry goes on when there is every chance of rousing a child's enjoyment, from stars to motor-cars, from atoms to the lives of birds. When I think of the conspiracy of dullness in which these exciting years are wrapped, I no longer wonder at the drab routine the Middle Ages made of Aristotle: I wonder instead that they kept him so fresh and clear.

C.P. SNOW,
The Search

CONTENTS

PREFACE

FROM THE TIME I finished graduate school in 1942 I have been associated with public schools in diverse roles. A fair amount of my writing has been about schools, particularly *The Culture of the School and the Problem of Change*, published in 1971. In 1979-1980, while preparing the second edition of that book, I came, much to my surprise, to see that I was overlooking the "axiom" that education best occurs in classrooms in school buildings. Why had that axiom remained unformulated in my mind, as well as in that of almost everyone else? What if that axiom were invalid? I gave thought to raising these questions in that book, but the discussion just did not fit. Also, there was that still, small voice that said: wait awhile, give it more thought, let it germinate. I knew that my thinking was taking me in directions for which my past activities were no sure guide. I also knew that the book I had to write would be too personal to be scholarly; in other words, I had to work the ideas through in my own mind to my satisfaction.

I really should not have been surprised by my discovery because in recent years I had become both fascinated and absorbed by the nature, origins, and consequences of our world view, a view that socialization insures will not have to be learned in any conscious sense and that possesses us far more than we possess it. That interest first received expression in my book *Work, Aging, and Social Change: Professionals and the One Life–One Career Imperative* (1977) and was central to a later book, *Psychology Misdirected* (1981). If I came to see the significance of world views and the axioms without which they make no sense, I was unable to generalize to education what I was thinking and learning until I was well along on the second edition of *The Culture of the School and the Problem of Change*. As I point out in the present volume, flushing out one's world view and putting it into words are extraordinarily difficult tasks and, at best, we succeed only partially. We do far better when we attempt to analyze the world views that dominated past eras.

I am grateful to a number of people in universities and schools who took time seriously to respond to the question: what if it were illegal to teach subject matter in a classroom in a school? Their answers were instructive and encouraging. It was fascinating for us to let our imaginations go, unhampered by the usual imagery of the bounded classroom in the bounded school.

I am enduringly grateful to Yale's Institute of Social and Policy Studies for providing the ambience and means to think, work, and write. Among the most helpful features of that ambience is the person of Grace Petro: a most delightful and supportive individual, who happens also to be a superb secretary.

SEYMOUR B. SARASON
New Haven, Connecticut

SCHOOLING IN AMERICA:

Scapegoat and Salvation

1

THE ARGUMENT
IN SUMMARY

THIS BOOK MARSHALLS CONSIDERATIONS about schools leading to conclusions that some readers will find strange; others, unpalatable; and others, impractical. A few may find them liberating and helpful. And yet it is safe to assume that every reader is dissatisfied with schools, albeit in varying degrees, ranging from mild disapproval to vitriolic disdain to a call for their demise. Perhaps the most frequent reactions are puzzlement and frustration about the failure of efforts to improve schools; i.e., we conclude that something is wrong somewhere when, instead of getting better, schools appear to be impervious to improvement and may, in fact, be worse than they were. The explanations have been many, as have been recommendations for new efforts, but no one seems at all confident that what is proposed will be effective. Following the 1960s, when the substance, structure, and goals of schooling were center stage in our society, educational debates noticeably subsided, except in relation to certain civil rights issues that got reflected in legislation or were consequences of court decisions. I refer specifically to issues concerning racial segregation and the rights of handicapped children to an education in the least restrictive environment.

Today there are signs that schooling may be returning to the societal agenda because of the perception that "scientific illiteracy" has reached proportions endangering our economic stability and military security. The scientists are upset, the Department of Defense is worried, and presidential speeches written by advisors in the Department of Education predict a gloomy future if remedial action is not taken. A large part of the problem is seen as deriving from errors of omission and commission by the schools. Our society has always looked upon schools as a vehicle for secular salvation, which, when this goal is obviously not being reached by our youth, leads people to scapegoat schools. The current conversations (they are hardly discussions, let alone debates) reflect this ambivalence. One facet of these conversations I find truly astounding: the failure to realize that everything being said and proposed was said, proposed, and acted upon earlier as a reaction to the narcissistic wound experienced by our society when the Soviet Union orbited the first sputnik in 1957. I am forced to the conclusion that as a societal problem scientific illiteracy is far less serious than the ahistorical stance.

The arguments I advance in this book cast past and present discussions of schooling in a distinctive light. By using the adjective "distinctive" I do not wish to appear blithely to arrogate merit to my conclusions; rather, I am signaling that my perspective is remarkable for its absence in matters educational. I am not the first to offer this perspective, but I do think I have marshalled the arguments in a new way. Let me very briefly summarize the major points I raise:

1. Schools as we have traditionally known them have been, are, and will be uninteresting places.

2. Responding to the changes wrought or reinforced by World War II, the generations born after the war assimilated a

world view that made the world of classroom and school frustratingly unrelated to the "real world." For these generations, curious and interested in that real world, exposed to that world through new mass media and new means for quick travel, and prompted by their elders to explore that world, the chasm that has always existed between the inside and the outside of schools became wider and, from the standpoint of students, unbridgeable.

3. As the post–World War II decades succeeded each other, the ability of schools to engender and sustain student interest, especially in junior high and high schools, steadily decreased. "Let's make schools interesting" became the basis for a new industry stimulated and subsidized by federal, state, and local policies and monies.

4. The efforts, by no means minuscule in scope and budget, to improve schools were based on an axiom as potent as it was unverbalized: *education best takes place in classrooms in school buildings*. That axiom, embedded in a world view that is millennia old, could be neither formulated nor challenged. It so riveted attention on the physically and socially isolated school building as to preclude recognition that the axiom was both unfounded and self-defeating.

5. More than ever before, schools in the post–World War II era sought ways to give young people experience outside schools that spoke directly to student curiosity and needs. These programs, varying considerably in their intellectual-educational thrust, justification, and quality, were "add-ons" to the curriculum and were hardly related, if at all, to core subject matter. In the main, these were programs for students for whom core subject matter seemed inappropriate or too difficult. Nobody worried that those for whom core subjects were considered appropriate continued to experience the classroom as a boring place and to regard the learning of subject matter as labor and not work.

6. Can traditional subject matter be assimilated more quickly and have more sustained and productive consequences outside schools in contexts in which the substance and structure

of subject matter are manifest in their need and meaningful in their employment? What if it were illegal to teach math or science or biology in a classroom in a school? Where and how would you teach these subjects? If you start with such questions, unimprisoned by the imagery of a classroom and a school; unhampered by the artificial, arbitrary separations between theory and practice, on the one hand, and between them and the contexts from which they are derived, on the other hand; if you take seriously what anecdote after anecdote describe when students are exposed to subject matter in contexts in which it is both necessary and practical—once you begin to be liberated from a world view in which is embedded a picture of where and how schooling "should" take place, you begin to understand why efforts to improve schools are doomed.

7. If education can better take place outside the traditional classroom in the traditional school, what do we *do*? How do we *do* it? Isn't this notion wildly impractical? These are productive and fair questions *only* if you have concluded that schools cannot be interesting, intellectually stimulating places and that alternative educational settings must be seriously considered. The millennia-old view has such a hold on our minds that when it is challenged we retreat to what is familiar to us. The fact is that there are many ways to answer these questions.

That is the skeleton outline of my argument. It is not one that stems from a particular social, political, or economic orientation and it is not one that assigns blame to any special group. As I make clear in the following chapters, however much various groups of critics differ from each other and however much they collectively differ from professional educators (who are not unanimous either in their views or in their responses to critics), they all agree that education best takes place in bounded classrooms and schools. Whether challenges to this axiom will gain currency I cannot say. When you consider how long it took for world views about men and women, races, old people, and handicapped people to begin to change—for new views to gain currency to the point that new actions and roles were first imaginable and then possible — you cannot expect that my proposals will have a different fate.

This book is about an axiom in a world view. It is not a call for action, not because I am opposed to action but because in this instance I would define action as appropriate only if those to be affected by it had worked through the turmoil associated with giving up an old stance and adopting a new one. It is a turmoil that I experienced when, after decades of thinking and writing about schools and of being involved in undertakings related to them, I came to realize that like everybody else I had not flushed out and confronted certain axioms in my world view. After I took this step, I began to ask specialists (especially in the sciences) how their subject matters could be taught outside the classroom. I was encouraged by the ease with which they generated possibilities and, in a number of instances, by their accounts of how they had done just that with middle or high school students. And yet the significance of what they had done, the contrast between what they described and what bothered them about the traditional classroom, had not propelled them to challenge in any way the millennia-old axiom about where schooling should take place.

This book is an attempt to state and examine a particular axiom. It is not my purpose to look into how and why our schools came to have the structural, organizational, and physical features they do. Nor do I discuss why our schools have different career consequences for different groups of students. These are important issues, of course, and have engendered heated debates. For my purposes, however, discussion of these issues would divert attention away from the ever increasing gulf between the worlds inside and outside schools. As I have said, this gulf, which has always been with us, dramatically widened after World War II and, therefore, requires special scrutiny.

This book is not a polemic and it does not contain a blueprint. What we call a "blueprint" has to be seen as one in a series of blueprints all of which were preceded by sketches, a form of "playing around" with the ideas and problems initiated by the need to create something. To the extent that the rationale for the blueprint is understood and accepted by those with a vested interest in the final outcome, that outcome stands a chance of achieving desired goals. The major purpose of this book is to put forward the argument that a particular axiom about education requires serious challenge. If this argument gains currency, one may then hope that different people in different places will engage in a sketching process from which will emerge the foundation for appropriate action. A blueprint, whether for a building or an institutional change, has a concreteness that too frequently facilitates rejection: either the plan strikes one as strange or, as is sometimes the case, it gets a quick acceptance that deprives one of both the benefits of the sketching process and the chance to gain understanding and acceptance from those who will be affected by implementing the blueprint. So, if this book does not provide a blueprint, it is because the substance of the issues has hardly been glimpsed. I do not derogate those with different views or those who will make short shrift of my position. In this particular arena *argumentum ad hominems* may be titillating but they are a distraction from the fact that what is at issue is the nature of our world view, a problem in cultural change and social-intellectual history, not in a narrow psychology.

The stakes are high and they go far beyond scientific illiteracy. Indeed, I do not consider it at all encouraging that current talk about schooling derives from concerns that, however important, have the effect of narrowing both the scope of the problem and the range of its possible solutions. In science, the significance of a contribution is in part proportional to how much it renders previous contributions obsolete. In the arena of societies and their major institutions, contributions are significant if they illuminate how what appears to be an obsolete past is nevertheless present and, precisely because it is unobtrusive, profoundly influential. Improving schools is, unfortunately but inevitably, not a matter of social engineering. When a major societal institution like schools appears unamenable to change, when more people than ever before are unperturbed by the suggestion that we should cut our losses and do as little as possible, when puzzlement about past failures degenerates into apathy, the red lights should start flashing to warn us that we may be taking something for granted that deserves our closest attention.

TWO MAJOR CRITICISMS OF EDUCATORS

WHEN YOU READ the history of criticism of our public schools, two themes emerge that seem to contradict each other. The first theme is that school personnel (or that abstraction called the "school system") are rigid and resistant to needed change. The picture this theme conjures up is that of a top-heavy, complex administrative hierarchy that spends its time either erecting roadblocks to change and innovation or transforming the goals of change to bulwark its own agenda. When the epithet "bureaucracy" is hurled at the administration, it is for the purpose of blame and not mere description. Years ago I asked an executive of a large foundation how he would go about changing the New Haven schools. He answered, with practically no reaction time, "The first thing I would do would be to figure out a way to get all of the school principals to a two-year meeting in Mexico City." In singling out principals for scorn and blame, he was adopting a more narrow target than other critics, who would prefer not a meeting but a convention in Mexico City that would accommodate the entire bureaucracy. Then there are, of course, critics who, although they do not find school administrators an attractive lot, take aim at teachers, whom they regard as unimaginative, change-killing creatures who at best are educational equivalents of military police and at worst are destroyers of any spark of creativity or curiosity in their pupils. With rare exceptions, adherents of this first theme do not in their public utterances or publications express themselves as openly as my words suggest. The theme is cloaked in a rhetoric that bears kinship to the language of diplomacy, in which "a frank exchange of views" translates into "a heated discussion" and "areas of agreement were reached" means "the parties agreed to disagree on many things." But in private conversation these adherents can employ very picturesque language to express their disdain and despair.

Among the most articulate proponents of the first theme have been university people. It is not happenstance that the field of education is very low on the university prestige ladder. This has to do less with any commerce some of these critics have had with schools or school personnel than with the belief that school personnel value techniques more than substance for one or all of several reasons: their substantive education has been incomplete, they are not among the most intelligent people, and they insulate themselves from sources of new ideas such as scholarship and research. These critics sound very much like Professor Henry Higgins, in *My Fair Lady*, who, after castigating women for various defects in their makeup, says pleadingly: "Why can't a woman be more like a man?" I should hasten to point out that among these university critics are people in schools of education. Indeed, it is my impression that the more prestigious the school of education the more its faculty are numbered among the proponents of the first theme.

The most blanket indictment of our schools has come from spokespeople for racial and ethnic minorities. These critics, unlike others I have mentioned, almost never distinguish between levels in the school hierarchy. They tend to see the whole educational system as a victim of the poison of prejudice. The problem is not one of changing the administrative structure or eradicating the evils of bureaucracy. The problem is one of substituting one kind of personnel for another. Of course they indict bureaucracy per se, but in principle they are criticizing the ethnic and racial composition of the bureaucracy. Their criticism is similar to that of Marxists who see the schools as part of a socioeconomic-political system and ideology helping to maintain class oppression and discrimination. They do not seem to quarrel with the school structure or to question the need for some kind of bureaucratic organization; rather, they object to the implicit and explicit ideology that powers the school system and guarantees inequality of opportunity and results. Strictly speaking, neither Marxist nor social-ethnic critics should be viewed as proponents of the first theme, which at its core contains an indictment of bureaucratic structure—its dynamic of growth and power, its insulation from new ideas, and its wondrous capacity to frustrate change and innovation. When articulated, it is a core most applicable to urban school systems. When these critics look elsewhere, another part of the core is revealed: educators are an intellectually and educationally inferior group.

Let us now turn to the second theme, which, on the surface at least, appears at variance with the first. The second theme states that school personnel have been mindlessly receptive to the fads and fashions of the day. Far from being rigid opponents of new ideas, school personnel have accepted myriad theories and practices without much basis in research, common sense, or the traditions of public schooling. The picture these critics conjure up is that of school personnel searching nervously in the marketplace of ideas for bargains that would allow them to present themselves as keeping up with the fashions of the day. In the minds of some the picture is that of passive, dependent, defenseless people who are easy targets for the sales-people of educational panaceas. Look at the following list:

values clarification
team teaching
open classrooms
division of the school day into shorter and more modules
ungraded classrooms
promotion according to age or social maturity
ungraded report cards (rewarding effort as much as per-
    formance)
homogeneous classrooms
heterogeneous classrooms
behavior modification
reduced homework
contract teaching
decentralization
peer counseling
management by objectives
affective education
the new math, biology, physics, and social studies
curricula for social problem-solving skills
curricula for sex education
curricula for career education
curricula for drug education
curricula for driver education
curricula for teaching creativity
curricula for affective education
reading method A, B, C, etc.
sensitivity training, group dynamics

Each item is shorthand for a rationale or practice that has been introduced into some—often many—schools in the past three decades and has been the subject of criticism. It is a very abbre-viated list, and those with a knowledge of educational history will see that some of the items are modern variants of old issues.

Whatever the era, one has no difficulty finding critics of schools' introduction of "newfangled" ideas. One does not have to be a professional educator — or a professional of any sort — to know that today's "back-to-basics" movement is, among other things, an explicit reaction to many of the items listed above. The phrase "back to basics" can be translated "away from frills and untested ideas." If, the argument goes, the schools had not been seduced into introducing all kinds of changes, there would have been no need for a back-to-basics pendulum swing.

What do the two themes have in common? The most obvious commonality is a derogation of school personnel. At its most offensive, this position indicts both the intelligence and the intentions of school personnel. At its least offensive, it credits them with good intentions but indicts them for extremely poor judgment. The second commonality is a variant of the maxim that "war is too important to be left to the generals": societal institutions like schools are too important to be left to the educators. The third commonality, very closely related to the second, is that what happens in schools is fateful not only for pupils as individuals but also for society as a whole. In this respect, educators, of course, completely agree with their critics.

Indeed, the agreement is so general and deep that reports suggesting that schooling has far less of an effect than is commonly assumed are greeted with staring disbelief. This agreement is powered by the view that schools make a difference and *should* make a difference. So, to the suggestion that schools may have less of an effect than we think, the reply is that we have to insure that they come to have a large effect. This stance is not based on the belief that schools are important but that they are absolutely essential. The justifications for schools are many and diverse, but they all share the axiom that schooling, like oxygen, is a necessity. Without schooling, the *individual* is, so to speak, a dead duck.

In point of historical fact, this axiom was preceded as a basis for action by another: schooling is absolutely essential if this *society* is to be true to its traditions and place in the world. Although justification for public education in terms of societal and national interests has always been in the picture, education was not in the foreground in terms of policy and action because education was considered a local and family affair into which the federal government should not intrude. World War II and its consequences changed all that, and public education came to be seen as too important to the nation's interests for schooling to remain a local affair.

It was not fortuitous that one of the most important pieces of federal legislation in this period was called the National Defense Education Act. As had never happened before, education was catapulted onto the national agenda. Generally speaking, this was viewed by critics and educators, albeit for different reasons, as a positive step. Educators, especially those in our urban centers, viewed the federal role as a drowning person would a lifeline from a rescue vessel. They saw in the federal government a means for them to do better for more people what they had been doing. Put another way, the educators diagnosed the problem as one of woefully inadequate resources, not one of innovation or fundamental change. The critics, most of whom were in the universities, had traced the problem to inadequate personnel who were insulated from the larger society, the world of ideas, and the educational implications of the scientific revolution.

We are told that the narcissistic wound we experienced when the Soviet Union put up the first sputnik was the stimulus to a massively expanded and rapidly accelerating federal role in education. That is true, but this explanation should not obscure two facts: the critics of our schools had been building up a head of steam for some time and the aim of federal programs was not only to support schools in a financial sense but also to change them.

The stage was set for a battle between the schools and their critics, and on that stage got acted out the drama we call the Great Debate of the 1950s and 1960s, with reruns and rewrites up to today. The word "debate" is a euphemism when one considers the level of vitriol and the substance and size of the stakes involved. Whatever else its consequences, that donnybrook served to broadcast the two themes I described earlier. Although the two themes were, historically speaking, by no means new, they were now embedded in the context of national interests. Of course, concern for what happened to pupils as individuals continued to suffuse the rhetoric about the significance of schooling, but a not so subtle shift in focus had occurred in that the perceived quality of education, like that of the military establishment, was seen as vital to this country's role, status, and influence in the world — or, more correctly, as vital to the preservation of this country's leadership. So, as never before, comparisons began to be made between the quality and emphases of our schools and those of other countries. And, it seemed, we suffered by the comparisons.

Commonalities aside, how contradictory are the two themes? That is not a question to tickle the imagination or to indulge speculation. If taken seriously, and they have been, these themes suggest different courses of action and levels of optimism (pessimism might be more appropriate). Some people would argue that the themes are not contradictory because the frantic responsiveness of school personnel to educational fads and fashions is more apparent than real; i.e., "innovations" are chosen precisely because they in no way threaten the administrative and power structure of schools. That is to say, the educational bureaucracies possess a wisdom that permits them to appear forward-looking and creative without intending any real change. Far from being unreflectively responsive, these personnel know how, so to speak, to roll with the punches. It may come as a surprise to some that perhaps the largest single group of adherents to this view are classroom teachers, who, as the proletariat in the school hierarchy, see their administrative superiors as people who justify their existence by dreaming up ideas that oppress and annoy teachers. As one teacher in an urban system said to me about "downtown", "God forbid they

should come up with something that requires *them* to change."
School administrators are quite aware of how they are regarded
by many teachers and their response, ironically, reflects the
core of the first theme: they argue that teachers tend to be unimaginative and resistant to change. But in the past two decades the response of administrators has included an additional
feature that, again ironically, evokes one of the themes,
namely, that teacher unions have become a major obstacle to
the innovative intentions of administrators. And if one were to
look at our schools from the vantage point of the superintendent or the board of education, the rigidities of a plethora of unions (e.g., principals, custodial staff, and cafeteria workers)
make real educational change extraordinarily difficult.

The more one examines the theme that indicts bureaucratic size and structure—the ways in which the bureaucracy
socializes its occupants to maintain both size and structure—
and the more one looks into the distribution of, and the constraints on, power vis-à-vis diverse groups within the system, the
more persuasive the theme seems to become. I asked the superintendent of schools in a rather large urban area to respond to
the validity of the two themes. Her reply (paraphrased) went
something like this:

> I really feel that the theme that describes school personnel as
> relatively unintelligent, unimaginative, and poorly educated is
> a distraction from the main issue. From my standpoint, if over-
> night you could get rid of all current personnel and put in their
> places whomever you consider to be bright, creative, and well
> educated, you would in a rather short period of time find them
> being criticized the way current school personnel are. What-
> ever the reasons may be, we have school systems that have tra-
> ditions and structures that are obstacles to any real change.
> Don't kid yourself: administrators are under constant pressure
> to improve things and they know that most of the time they are
> pushing a new idea less because they are convinced that it is a

good idea and more because they have to do *something*. Yes, we latch on too quickly to a new idea and we too frequently promote it as the latest version of revealed truth. What is the alternative? To sit in your office and do nothing?

Let us not accept too readily the argument that the responsiveness of school personnel to new ideas, programs, and practices is both unreflective and insincere. Certainly the argument has merit. But there are two points that should not be glossed over. The first is that not all efforts at change have studiously avoided diluting the negative consequences of stultifying structure and the arrogation of power. Community participation, alternative schools, decentralization, and teacher participation in policy decisions are efforts that cannot be considered as more shadow than substance. I am quite aware that far more often than not school personnel have been resistant to the goals of these efforts. I also know about several instances in which school personnel actively subverted such efforts. The point that should not be neglected is that in some instances these efforts have been initiated and nurtured by school personnel. The second point—related to, but going far beyond, the first—can be put this way: I have never come across a recommendation made by a serious critic of our schools that has not been implemented in some school. And what I find even more interesting is that these schools are always near other schools whose personnel assert that what the former are doing cannot be done or should not be done.

These atypical instances are not explainable by the laws of chance and they do not confirm either of the themes we have been discussing. What, then, is their significance? Let me hasten to say that in asking this quesiton I in no way intend to suggest that the answer, like a polio or flu vaccine, could be injected into schools elsewhere (that is something the critics from without and the "agents of change" from within schools have never understood). There are two parts to the answer. The first is obvious: apparently, it is possible to bring about marked alterations in school structure and power distribution even though the system has the characteristics critics describe. The second is that people in or related to innovative schools have come to share a set of *ideas* that in the most explicit way asserts that (1) the traditional basis governing relationships and decisionmaking in the schools is inimical to all participants; (2) there must be forums for discussion that encourage articulation of the views of different constituencies; (3) the substance of these discussions should be taken into account by those bearing legal responsibility for making decisions; (4) if the previous guidelines are consistently followed, everyone will feel more worthy; and (5) in this situation, the educational performance of pupils will improve. These statements are sociopolitical in the same sense that our Constitution was a sociopolitical reaction to perceived inadequacies in the Articles of Confederation. Just as in the Constitutional Convention the central issue was how to distribute power to prevent its abuse, these assertions reflect concern with the allocation of authority. I italicized the word "ideas" in order to indicate that the assertions that followed it were not only statements of values but also sophisticated maps of how one goes from here to there. One cannot, of course, account for these schools on the basis of ideas and maps alone. What I am emphasizing here are not ideas in general but ideas whose substance speaks directly to the themes I have described. There are critics who would view these ideas as another instance in which school personnel are distracted from their "real" purpose: to educate children. One would hope that these critics would at least recognize that the people in these schools are bright, imaginative individuals capable of a vision alternative to that guiding the present.

But, critics could query, Are you not clutching at straws? Are you not trying to be hopeful in the face of overwhelming evidence substantiating the themes? Are not these instances exceptions that prove the rule? As will become apparent in later chapters, I have serious reservations about these atypical instances as answers to problems on the educational scene.* I have employed these instances primarily to illustrate what can happen when people arrive at and take seriously a drastically different picture of what our schools can be — not a picture containing gimmicks or fads, or preserving completely intact the structure and culture of the traditional school, or (most important for my later purposes) describing education as a process that is the sole responsibility of educators. In short, these are instances in which people, for whatever reasons, have sought to free themselves from traditional conceptions. If I emphasize this point it is as prologue to another point. The adherents of each or both themes have essentially given up believing that our schools are capable of being changed or improved. They were far more hopeful ten or twenty years ago but today they can generate no hope. If they feel hopeless, it is not because they think their diagnoses are at fault. On the contrary, they are more convinced than ever before that their diagnoses are correct: there is something about the quality of school personnel and the structural-administrative features of schools that defeats the purposes of education.

One cannot blithely dismiss the possibility that the critics are correct. Elsewhere I have brought together evidence that certainly is consistent with their criticisms (Sarason, 1982). But if one uses this evidence, one has to conclude that when it comes to ideas that will change and improve schools, neither the educators nor the outside critics come up smelling roses. As good an example as any is the comprehensive criticisms that were directed at schools because of their outmoded curricula in math, science, and social studies. It was a barrage of criticism that was powered by a lot of federal money. The educational policymakers in Washington (in both the legislative and the ex-

*I refer specifically to the absence of evidence that in these schools alterations in the allocation of decisionmaking power have led to improved educational performance. I am in complete agreement with the rationale for these alterations on the basis of political principle, but it mystifies me why people think that political principles affect anything in the classroom.

ecutive branch) reflected the views of—indeed, supported—the outside critics. These critics were eminent people, not ones who got caught up in fads and fashions. And if they were listened to, it was not only because they were deservedly eminent but also because they clearly recognized that what was at stake was the quality of our educational system, as well as the centrality of that system to the role and power of this country in a perilous world. There was then, as there is now, complete agreement between critics and school personnel on this point. Memories are short and, therefore, we have to be reminded that school personnel, generally speaking, were very receptive to what these curriculum critics were saying, and this receptivity was facilitated by the fact that the critics were not expostulating from their armchairs but were offering concrete and detailed revisions of the curriculum. School personnel could not be accused of being unreceptive to change. And unless you believe that these curriculum critics were only a notch above snake oil salesmen, you cannot accuse educators of mindlessly reacting to fads and fashions.

How do the critics explain the failure of their ideas and efforts to improve performance in schools? They could say that the schools poorly implemented the new curricula. Somehow, explanation in terms of hapless implementation on a national basis is not persuasive. Certainly, as I have discussed elsewhere, hapless implementation was an important factor, but in using such an explanation the critics would be hoist with their own petard: they were as ignorant of the problems of implementation as were the school people (Sarason, 1982). The critics could resort to a second explanation: they vastly underestimated the educational and intellectual inadequacies of school personnel, meaning teachers. Like the first explanation, this one also cuts two ways because if the critics are right, one has to ask of them: why were you so ignorant of these inadequacies? Indeed, one might be tempted to say that the ignorance of the critics approached the unethical. How bad and harmful must a diagnosis be before you indict the competence of the diagnostician? The second explanation also runs absolutely counter to my personal experience — more correctly, to that of my wife (Esther) and I both. In 1969 she did the first observational study of the teaching of the new math, shortly after it was implemented in a local school system. She came to know and observe many math teachers, and in the course of my own work in many schools I had met and talked with scores of math teachers. To explain the failure of the new math in terms of the inferior intellect of math teachers is to compound error with snobbishness.

What the critics have been unable to do is to examine the possibility that there may be something radically wrong in their diagnoses and prescriptions. This is not to say that there are no important and valid elements in their diagnoses but to suggest that they may be guilty of that of which they accuse school personnel: inability to accept responsibility for failure and avoidance of the question of what is being taken for granted that should not be taken for granted. When an institution appears over time to be resistant to change *and* improvement from within and without, with money and without money, the effort sometimes powered by passionate sincerity and sometimes by the needs of image making; when critics and school personnel are licking their wounds, hardly able to generate energy to re-enter the fray, left only with the hope that the passage of time will somehow bring improvements, does this not suggest that both critics and educators share some blind spots — that there is something in their basic assumptions that they are unable to identify and whose silent existence is part of the explanation for the present malaise and impasse? In raising this possibility I am not suggesting that identifying and confronting these assumptions will disperse the confusion or lead to a peace treaty among the combatants, allowing us all to move together to the improvement of education. On the contrary, it is a characteristic of widely held but unarticulated assumptions that they serve the purpose of defining and bulwarking individual and societal perceptions of what is right, natural, and proper. These assumptions are not learned in the sense that we learn to drive a car, but they are absorbed by us, become part of us, in the course of our socialization. So, for example, up until relatively recently (by the clock of history) males and females did not have to think about what a woman was, what roles she should play, and where she would play them. These were not issues to be examined, not because people were told not to examine them but because the socialization process put them beyond the realm of questioning. When rare individuals did consciously articulate and challenge what seemed right, natural, and proper, they and their horrified critics got a glimpse of how the structure and rationale of the society needed the traditional view of women—i.e., that the oxen of many people and institutions would indeed be gored if these unexamined issues began to be taken seriously and, God forbid, accepted.

No society is truly comprehensible without taking into account its unverbalized axioms. The problem is that to the extent that socialization is effective, it largely prevent us from taking distance from self and society to ferret out these silent but powerful axioms. The fascination of history lies in the fact that one can look at past eras relatively unencumbered by the world views of those eras and ferret out their silent axioms—that part of the world view without which it makes no sense. But to do that for the era of which we are a part is a task that, at best, we can do only partially. What makes the task at all conceivable are societal issues, like education, that confuse us by their seeming intractability. In regard to education we are at a point that should force us to examine what we have taken for granted. But in starting such an examination we have to recognize that the process will have all of the characteristics of what Murray Levine, a colleague, so felicitously described as problem creation through problem solution. When silent axioms are given voice, the decibel level of discourse quickly escalates as their implications for change are discerned. We then realize that these axioms are windows through which to see our society, but boarded windows.

In this chapter I have discussed two of the major themes running through the critical literature on schooling. It should now be apparent that although I think that neither theme is without merit, I do not believe that the way they describe the issues and the remedial actions to which they have led has been productive. Put differently, these themes have obscured the possibility that critics and school personnel share too many silent axioms — they have too much of a conceptual and ideological stake in the way things are — to expect that whatever happens will satisfy anyone. I am not calling down a plague on both their houses. I respect the seriousness with which critics and school personnel have approached the issues. Before we try to fathom the role of silent axioms, it is advisable, indeed necessary, to look into why it is so difficult to take distance from the way things are. This we shall do by taking up in the next chapter two related questions. First, why are school personnel viewed ambivalently, disparagingly, or even hostilely by so many segments of our society? Second, why is it so difficult for observers of the educational scene to recognize that their observations and conclusions are determined by the socioeconomic niche they occupy?

THE SOURCES
OF CRITICISM

CRITICISM OF, AND DISDAIN for, public school personnel are not new social phenomena and do not require deep explanation. After all, when parents send their children for a good part of the day, for a large part of the year, over the course of many years to be under the control of adults who are unrelated to the family, strong differences of opinion, conflict, and controversy are likely to arise. And it should not be surprising if those in conflict come to belittle each other. Parents expect that teachers will be adequate to, and effective with, their children, but they are often unaware that precisely these expectations are held by all other parents. In short, a teacher is expected both to be equally effective with all children and to like all children to the same degree. What is surprising is that these expectations are shared by school personnel, especially school administrators, who would look askance at any teacher who said, "There are some children in my class whom I do not like and with whom I am not effective." These expectations are so much a part of the school culture that teachers, who know that they are not effective with certain children, may come to feel guilty and inadequate because they know they are not effective with all children. Teaching may be the only profession for which we have such expectations. I can think of no other teaching-helping group from whom we expect so much wisdom, detachment, and adaptability. Although it is a glimpse of the obvious to say that parents are not equally effective with their own children, and many parents (at least in the confessional or the psychotherapist's office) confess to not liking each of their offspring to the same degree, they nevertheless expect teachers to be better approximations of perfection. The unrealistic expectations that lead to marital discord and divorce are similar to those that often characterize teacher-parent relationships.

The one unassailable experience shared by parents and teachers is that they were once pupils. And among the different attitudes and memories they may have about their sustained experience as pupils none is more central than the role of power in the classroom, the school, and the school system. They remember well that as pupils they had little or no power and that they were required to conform to the rules laid down by powerful adults. Even when these retrospections are more positively than negatively toned, the fact of inequality in the allocation and uses of power is not denied. And when they are more negatively than positively toned, their contents always center around the perceived need to conform to those who possessed more power. I have never met an adult, regardless of how positive his or her memories of pupil life may be, who could not relate many instances of resenting the consequences of perceived powerlessness. Such resentment becomes more clear in an adult's memory as he or she describes instances from the later years in school. It is in these years that one's understanding of the role and rule of power is enlarged beyond individual teachers to include a complicated organization. One becomes aware that much of what teachers do or do not do is somehow a function of power wielded by people remote from the classroom.

There is an irony here, one that has been analyzed and described by a political science colleague, Edward Pauly (1982). As one might expect from a political scientist, Pauly looked at the classroom (and the school and school system) in terms of the uses and allocation of power. Among the many points he made, several are relevant here. The first is that parents, pupils, and school personnel accept the norm that school personnel *should* have power and control. The second point is that from the standpoint of school personnel pupils have a good deal of power, actual and potential. That is, of course, not obvious, but Pauly made a very compelling case for the argument that central to the phenomenology of school personnel is the need to control, blunt, or channel the power of pupils to defeat the purposes of teachers and others. It is a struggle that waxes and wanes and results in subtle (and often not so subtle) compromises and adjustments. And when this setting does not seem to generate a struggle, it is not for lack of power but for other reasons that Pauly discussed. The third point is that the role of power in the classroom, as perceived both by pupils and by teachers, is never independent of their perceptions of how power is viewed and employed by others in the school — by other teachers and pupils and by administrators. When I present Pauly's argument to teachers, their initial, unreflective response is a mix of hesitant rejection and "it rings a bell," followed by "of course, he's right." We have been socialized to think (and to hope) that schools are oases of peace in which learning proceeds uncontaminated by the role and rule of power. So, when we observe a classroom that seems to be out of control and we fault the teacher, we gloss over the fact that we have observed an extreme instance of a "normal" process of mutual adjustment to relationships of power. And by faulting the teacher we sustain the myth of pupil powerlessness when, in fact, it explodes the myth. Similarly, when we observe a classroom in which teachers and pupils seem relaxed, happy, and productive, we blithely take satisfaction in the confirmation of our belief that the classroom is no place for power. Such a picture says far more about our hopes than it does about reality.

This discussion should help to illuminate the fact that it is in the nature of the culture of the schools to engender in pupils and staff a tremendous resentment and hostility. This can be expressed in myriad ways: in this way and for that reason by X, and in that way and for that reason by Y, and so forth. Moreover, these negative attitudes can exist side by side with and even be far stronger than positive ones. This reservoir, comprised of unique experiences of unique individuals, ordinarily remains unfocused, uncoalesced into a social force or movement. It takes events and changes in the larger society to give shape and direction to the contents of that reservoir. What had been a reservoir of unique events in unique individuals comes to appear to be a unity of experiences shared by highly similar people. The strength of the disdain that large segments of the population have for school personnel is in part a function of that ever present reservoir—but only in part. No psychology of individuals is able to explain widely held critical views of schools or the periodicity with which these appear. Their appearance is not random but always in some relation to changes external to the school.

It is not necessary for me even to summarize the historical relationships between social change and cries for changing the schools. Cremin's *Transformation of the School* (1961) and Doris's chapters in Sarason and Doris's *Educational Handicap, Public Policy, and Social Change* (1979) provide material that amply confirms the thesis. Let me very briefly look into the post–World War II era. There are different ways in which one can label and describe issues that have been controversial in our society in terms of their substance, their diagnosis, or their resolution. Race, poverty, health, gender, international status, and religion are labels that can be employed. Some would say that any list would be egregiously incomplete that did not include intergenerational conflict. Here, at least, I am indifferent to the aesthetics or appropriateness of labels. Describe the post–World War II era any way you wish and there would be no problem in demonstrating that each label refers to an array of national events and actions from which came criticisms of what schools were or were not doing: schools are racist; they help oppress poor people; they neglect the study of health; they encourage stereotyping of males and females; they are harmful to this country's maintenance of its intellectual and scientific leadership; they are godless; and on and on. In the post-World War II era, every major societal institution was under attack either for being silent on many of these issues or for being on the "wrong" side. But none rivaled public education in the number of issues for which it was assigned some degree of blame. And, it has to be added, only the schools have continued to be the object of criticism and disdain from scores of groups in our society. This sustained barrage cannot be explained, except in part, by the reservoir of resentment I described earlier. To explain a widespread social phenomenon in purely psychological terms would be to trivialize it. Far more than psychology is at play.

Early in our society, the schools were given a major role to play in determining the individual's development. Different groups had different reasons for giving so much importance to schooling. Some saw it as essential for socializing immigrants and protecting the existing social fabric from foreign ideologies. Some saw it as a way to foster "good citizenship." Others saw it as essential for vocational choice and training. And some saw the public schools as screening devices to select those capable of higher education and of taking positions of leadership in the public and private sectors. And then there were some—by no means organized, powerful, or articulate—who saw schooling as providing food for the mind; i.e., the tools and substance of thinking without which life has a dim luster and with which one stands a chance of being liberated from tradition and superstition. There were other reasons, depending on which era one chooses, but they all rested on the belief that schooling is important and necessary. Moreover, people had experienced schooling, they thought they understood schools and school personnel, and most of them had loved ones in schools. Schools were and are visible structures whose personnel are both visible and, in a legal sense, accountable to the community. In many communities, people elect members of the board of education, and whether they vote or not they know that schools are financed largely by local taxes. Unlike the Congress, the presidency, or the state legislatures, schools stand in a very direct relationship to local communities. Citizens can walk into schools or attend meetings of the board of education; similarly, if you insist on seeing the principal, or your child's teacher, or the superintendent of schools, your request will be granted. Schools are "there," or in people's "here and now," in a way not true of any other community agency and, comparatively speaking, people feel powerful in relation to schools. To put it in terms of the perception of school personnel: schools are fragile, vulnerable institutions dependent on the understanding and goodwill of local citizens. Schools are salient not in terms of certain abstract values and goals but becasue so many people are affected daily by what goes on in schools.

Precisely because society expects so much and so many different results from schooling, criticism of schools tends to be sustained and varied. Ordinarily the criticism is muted and unorganized, but when there are sea-swell changes in the society, criticisms become stronger and more focused. To expect otherwise is vastly to misunderstand the importance given to schooling. Not only do we expect a great deal of schools but also we require them continually to enlarge their scope. That is why criticism addresses both errors of commission and errors of omission. We expect so much from the schools that when they fall short of the mark, the conclusion is that whatever they are doing they are doing poorly. And expecting so much from schools permits some to criticize schools because they did not anticipate certain problems or failed to introduce new programs and activities. As one religiously devout teacher explained with wry humor, "The criticisms make absolutely no sense unless you see that underneath them all is the belief in schools as salvation for the child, family, country, and world.

We are a country of salvation seekers and we decided that schooling was the best way to be saved. And who can live with the possibility that *that* road to salvation may be taking us nowhere?" This teacher was articulating something explicit in the early colonial period: schooling was necessary to insure that people could read and follow the Bible, thereby becoming able to steer their lives over the road to salvation. Over the course of time the definition of salvation has changed—and the religious concept of salvation has faded from the educational scene—but the importance attached to religious salvation subtly became attached to salvation in the secular world. The schools are still seen as vehicles for the salvation of the individual, the community, and the nation. Secular salvation, however defined, was not thinkable without schooling, good schooling. There was no argument about this, in the abstract at least. If there was no argument, there was also no disposition to inquire into the possibility that as a vehicle for secular salvation the public schools, would, for diverse reasons, be unable to save all its celebrants and when that would be discovered the schools would be vigorously criticized.

Few countries have been as persistently optimistic about what schools can do as our country has been. By no means is that optimism restricted to schools. We have always been a land of great expectations and, in the minds of most people, of limitless resources and opportunities. And whatever justifications for schooling and compulsory education were advanced, they always contained the goal of making more opportunities available to more people. That people could be saved seemed obvious; that schools could help save them also seemed obvious.

A song that was popular during World War II, "We Did It Before and We Can Do It Again," captures in its title the American attitude in the face of adversity and disappointment—a war the outcome of which is uncertain (as in the first two years of World War II), an economic depression, becoming Avis to the Soviet Union's Hertz in the race to space, or schools that fall markedly short of their goals. All that is required is to make the right diagnosis and create a strong national resolve: the problem will be licked. Prejudice, poverty, child abuse, cancer, heart attacks, smoking, mental illness, and inadequate schools—there is no reason in principle or in our history why these ailments cannot be overcome. So, when in the case of educational problems our schools do not respond to efforts to improve them, the collective anger is strong. I think it is true today, for the first time in our history, that more than a few people (within and without the schools) believe that the public schools will not "make it" and that alternatives will have to be tried. There are limits to national optimism and, according to some people, the schools have exceeded them. And then there are those who do not advocate scrapping our school system but who believe that it really makes no difference whether schools receive more or fewer resources than in the past: the outcome will be the same in either case. The two themes I discussed in the previous chapter—themes that have for long dominated debate about changing and improving schools—have to share the limelight with two new, related themes: there is no point trying to change the schools and let's scrap the public schools as we have known them. Whether these two themes will gain more adherents among citizens and lawmakers I cannot say. What I am attempting to do is to understand the substance of criticism about schools and the psychological, political, sociohistorical, and ideological factors contributing to the unusual strength of this criticism.

Let us now turn to an issue that pinpoints a specific source of criticism at the same time that it illuminates a general ambivalence on the part of society toward teachers. More specifically, it is an issue that has long been a subject for debate in the university, although it is an issue that antedates the modern university, but took on sharp form in it.

The idea that those who take or are given responsibility for educating young people should successfully traverse a program in pedagogy is based on an assumption: mastery of subject matter (e.g., math or English) is no guarantee that it will be taught in ways that permit students to assimilate it. This assumption is relatively recent, having taken hold in the nineteenth century, when different strands of intellectual and sociopolitical history converged to give that assumption the status of a silent axiom. The first of these strands was the questioning of the belief that children are little adults. Once that belief was challenged, the question became: if children are not small versions of adults, what distinguishes their intellectual functioning and its development? This question was never raised in a social vacuum but always in relation to practical needs of time and place, i.e., in terms of improving the results of education for those few for whom education was then deemed appropriate. A second strand was one contained in the socioeconomic-political upheavals ushered in by that panoply of phenomena known as the Renaissance. In its most simple and brief form that strand can be put as a question: what is man capable of knowing, inventing, and controlling? This question reflected the recognition that man's view of, and place in, the world had changed. The pursuit of knowledge, unencumbered by religious dogma and increasingly threatening to that dogma, was part of a changing conception of freedom in the political and social arena. Whether through revolutions, civil wars, or wars of nationalism, class lines were undergoing change and blurring, one result of which was that the need or demand for literacy (and more) increased. That need or demand could be met informally by individuals who by either reputation or special circumstance could fill the role of teacher. But as a result of the American and French revolutions and an absolute increase in the human population, the numbers who sought an education increased exponentially, faster than the rate at which people could be informally drafted into the teaching-tutoring role. The location, selection, and training of would-be teachers had come to require a formal institutional solution.

Aspects of these two strands are contained in an experiment that took place in France at the end of the eighteenth century. That this event took place in France shortly after the revolution is not surprising, just as it is not surprising that the experiment aroused general interest and controversy. After all, what was at stake here were the issues of man's perfectibility and the degree to which society shapes the human organism from birth on—questions that were always present in the complex of forces and events that constituted the French Revolution. The experiment was conceived and conducted by Jean-Marc Itard, with the collaboration of a female teacher; this story has been recently published as *The Wild Boy of Aveyron* (Lane, 1976). Victor, a twelve or thirteen year old, had been spied several times in 1797 either fleeing through the woods or searching for acorns and roots. He was captured in 1798, put on public display, but managed to escape. Over the next year or so, the wild boy was seen from time to time foraging for food. On July 25, 1799, three hunters spotted him in the woods, gave chase, and captured him. He was entrusted to the care of a solicitous old widow. The boy again escaped, but he was recaptured in January 1800. How Itard came to Victor, what he did with him and how he interpreted the results, the sociopolitical ideologies that caused Itard and Victor to be centers of attention, and the way the experiment influenced the course of educational practice and theory—rarely has a single case drawn so much discussion over such a long period of time. No one has described the significance of the experiment and explained why it continues to grip us better than Lane:*

> The Luxembourg Gardens are an island of calm, of lawns, gravel paths, fountains, and statues, in the heart of left-bank Paris. On a summer's day in 1800, two young Frenchmen from the provinces met there for the first time and joined together their lives and futures. Although neither could have said so, each was engaged in a search whose success required the other.

*This passage from Lane is included also because it raises issues directly relevant to the moral basis for education, an area I take up in the final chapter. How do we and how might we decide what we owe children and what they owe society?

The first young man was well but not elegantly dressed in a long coat, drawn in at the waist, with full lapels. His curly hair fell in locks over a slanting forehead; his aquiline nose extended the plane almost as far as his jutting chin. Tightly drawn wide lips and large, dark brown eyes completed the Mediterranean features, set off by a broad white collar that rose funnel-like from his frilly white shirt. Jean-Marc Gaspard Itard was twenty-six and had just become a doctor. He had left the barren village at the foot of the French Alps where he was raised and had come to Paris in search of a place for himself in the new social order that had emerged from the chaos of the Revolution. Paris at this time was vibrant: painting, theater, music, and literature were flourishing, abetted by the glittering salons of the very rich, the rendezvous of the intellectual and social elite. Medicine was surging ahead; it had become possible to protect people against disease by giving them some of the disease itself, although no one really knew why. One of Itard's teachers, Philippe Pinel, had just written the first book on psychiatric diagnosis, and had dramatically ordered inmates of the city's insane asylums to be unchained. The first anthropological society was formed, while expeditions returned with the flora, fauna, and inhabitants of Africa, Indonesia, and the New World, to the delight and fascination of naturalists, anatomists, and, above all, philosophers. Itard had left the relative isolation of the provinces in search of this excitement of senses and mind, to share in it, even to contribute to it if he could. His alliance with the strange boy rocking back and forth in front of him would surely bring him public attention; it might admit him to the ranks of the great doctors and philosophers of his time, or it might destroy his career right at its beginning.

The boy was twelve or thirteen years old, but only four-and-a-half feet tall. Light-complexioned, his face was spotted with traces of smallpox and marked with several small scars, on his eyebrow, on his chin, on both cheeks. Like Itard, he had dark deepset eyes, long eyelashes, chestnut brown hair, and a long pointed nose; unlike Itard, the boy's hair was straight, his chin receding, his face round and childlike. His head jutted forward on a long graceful neck, which was disfigured by a thick scar slashed across his voice box. He was clothed only in a loose-fitting gray robe resembling a nightshirt, belted with a large leather strap. The boy said nothing; he appeared to be deaf. He gazed distantly across the open spaces of the gardens, without focusing on Itard, or, for that matter, on anything else. That same day, he had ended a grueling week-long journey. By order of the Minister of the Interior, Napoleon Bonaparte's brother, Lucien, the boy had come to Paris from a forest region in the province of Aveyron in southern France. This journey was the latest development in his search, which began a year before when he clambered out of the forests, worked his way across an elevated plateau in the bitterest winter in recent memory, and entered a farmhouse on the edge of a hamlet. He exchanged the freedom and isolation of his life in the forests of Aveyron, where he had run wild, for captivity and the company of men in society. He came without a name, so he was called the Wild Boy of Aveyron.

Perhaps Itard knew better than the savants of his time, who expected to see in the boy the incarnation of Rousseau's "noble savage," man in the pure state of nature; perhaps he did not. What he saw, he wrote later, was "a disgustingly dirty child affected with spasmodic movements, and often convulsions, who swayed back and forth ceaselessly like certain animals in a zoo, who bit and scratched those who opposed him, who showed no affection for those who took care of him; and who was, in short, indifferent to everything and attentive to nothing." The society of the eighteenth century had held both young men at bay, depriving the first of the best it had to offer, depriving the second of everything. Itard sought to master the ultimate skills of his culture — trained observation, persuasive language, social grace — the boy, their rudiments. So be it: they would help each other. Educating the boy would be a test of the new science of mental medicine and a proof of philosophy's new empiricist theory of knowledge. It would give still more justification for social reform by showing how utterly man depends on society for all that he is and can be. If the effort succeeded, the nineteenth century would give them their proper place, where the eighteenth had not.

Much more than a century later, nearly two, I sat in the Luxembourg Gardens and wondered about the two young men who had met there. Off to my left, the National Institute for Deaf-Mutes, where Itard had taken the wild boy to live and to learn. There, in his efforts to train him, Itard created a whole new approach to education, centered on the pupil, closely adapted to his developing needs and abilities, seconded by instructional devices—an approach we have accepted so thoroughly as our ideal that we scarcely imagine any other or credit anyone with its discovery. Behind me, the Sorbonne, where Itard had defended the possibility of educating the boy against the judgment of the great philosophers and doctors of the time, who contended that the boy was left in the wild because he was an idiot, not an idiot because he was left in the wild. Behind me, and farther north, the Academy of Medicine, where Itard read his historic reports on methods for teaching the deaf and the retarded to speak—methods he had developed with the wild boy. In front of me and to the south, the Hospital for Incurables, where Itard's student, Edouard Seguin, set out to prove that idiots were educable, contrary to unanimous medical opinion, where George Sumner came to see Itard's methods in action, bringing them back to America to start the education of the retarded there; where, finally, Maria Montessori came, to end by extending Itard's methods to the education of the normal preschool child as well as the handicapped.

Thinking of these places close at hand, where the drama of Dr. Itard and the wild boy took place, shaping the lives of countless children up through my own time, imagining the excitement of another time when men affirmed, "Yes, the deaf can speak, the retarded can learn," when they believed that the only sure limit to a child's knowledge is his society's ignorance, when they were convinced, as I am, of the perfectibility of man — thinking of these times and places one summer afternoon in the Luxembourg Gardens, I decided to begin my own search, to find Itard and the wild boy. (Pp. 3–6)

There is one feature of this case that is obvious but requires emphasis. It was taken for granted that the validation of theories about the nature of man would require the development, among other things, of pedagogical methods and practices. What was required were not teachers in general but teachers who could devise teaching methods consistent with the picture of man contained in the theoretical rationale. When you read about the degree to which Itard agonized over how to reach Victor, how he experimented with different ways of stimulating, rewarding, and punishing the boy, how he struggled with a conception of the learning process, you are witnessing the emergence of a teaching methodology. In short, many people shared Itard's **theory** or **ideology** but very few of them could have practiced what they preached in the way that Itard did. Knowledge of a problem and the most passionate commitment to one's task are no guarantee that one's actions will have the desired consequences. Between theory and knowledge, on the one hand, and productive practice, on the other, stretches a mined obstacle course. The assumption that mastery of subject matter is no guarantee that you can help others learn is not an invention of educators. If that idea took hold in the nineteenth century and took organized shape in the form of teacher training institutes and normal schools — centering around the ideas of such educational philosophers as Comenius, Bell, Lancaster, Pestalozzi, Rousseau, and Seguin — it had very little to do with the worship of technique and much to do with the question of how to deal with the mass education of heterogeneous populations for whom education was deemed necessary and by the end of the century made compulsory.

The same point could be illustrated by the work and writings of a Frenchman from the end of the nineteenth century.

Alfred Binet was no worshiper of technique but rather someone with curiosity about an amazing number of human problems and about the way in which knowledge scientifically gained about these problems could inform methods to deal with them. To gain knowledge and to apply it were his goals. In her biography of Binet, Wolf (1973) documented why he had more to do than anyone else with starting the field of experimental pedagogy. How to translate knowledge into tactics and strategies appropriate to the needs and characteristics of children *and* to the nature and constraints of the classroom was one of Binet's central interests. And that interest has to be seen in the context of Binet's criticisms of Parisian schools, the criticisms of a scientist and a social activist (Sarason, 1981). Of direct relevance to our discussion is Binet's reaction to James's *Talks To Teachers* (1899). As Wolf put it:

> He had long been a great admirer of the American psychologist-philosopher, but now he was evidently ruffled by James's harsh criticisms of his own attempt to apply scientific psychology to pedagogy. ". . . all the useful facts from that discipline could," James asserted, "be held in the palm of one hand." Furthermore, Binet thought himself the target of James's lengthy objections to "teaching teachers how to undertake scientific research." "One is not made into a good teacher by knowing psychological facts," James declared. Binet took issue with both viewpoints: there was evidence of "useful applications" far beyond the capacity of any palm to hold, and, while readily admitting that he himself would have difficulty in directing a class, it did not follow that because knowledge does not make a good teacher, it is therefore useless, or even dangerous, for a teacher to have it! (P. 311)

I must add that I cannot read Binet without being in awe of how much he knew about children, teachers, and classrooms—the same reaction I have when I read Dewey. But when I read James on education I always wonder whether in his adult years he ever was in a classroom or school. I say this not because James included anything in his lectures to teachers with which I disagree. What he did, in that captivating Jamesian style, was to state a number of principles that make for productive learning. But one does not know what these principles might look like when applied by a teacher facing (in those days) thirty, forty, or more children in the classroom. What James can be faulted for is not the absence of "how to do it" but rather the absence of "how to think about how to do it." Is part of the explanation in the following quotation, the language of which is so sparkling?

> The difference between an interesting and a tedious teacher consists in little more than the inventiveness by which the one is able to mediate these associations and connections, and in the dullness in discovering such transitions which the other shows. One teacher's mind will fairly coruscate with points of connection between the new lesson and the circumstances of the children's other experience. Anecdotes and reminiscences will abound in her talk; and the shuttle of interest will shoot backward and forward, weaving the new and the old together in a lively and entertaining way. Another teacher has no such inventive fertility, and his lesson will always be a dead and heavy thing. This is the psychological meaning of the Herbartian principle of "preparation" for each lesson, and of correlating the new with the old. It is the psychological meaning of that whole method of concentration in studies of which you have been recently hearing so much. When the geography and English and history and arithmetic simultaneously make cross-references to one another, you get an interesting set of processes all along the line. (James, 1902, pp. 96–97)

James seems to be saying, in contrast to the educational philosophies of the day, that some teachers "have it" and others do not and one cannot expect those differences to be appreciably lessened by exposure to pedagogical strategies and techniques.

James, of course, would not have questioned the need to master subject matter. What he questioned is the value of any formal pedagogical preparation beyond that mastery. *Productive teaching requires more than a knowledge of subject matter —* that assumption James apparently rejected. He did, of course, as his lectures demonstrate, clearly believe that teachers need to understand psychological principles, another type of subject matter. In this view, mastery of subject matter, plus knowledge of psychological principles, make for the good teacher *if* that teacher has an inventive mind.

In colleges and universities, programs for the preparation of teachers are based on the assumption that more than mastery of subject matter and psychological principles is necessary if the teacher is to enable children to assimilate subject matter. Let me put the assumption more generally: *any* teacher with students of *any* age needs to know more than subject matter. So, for example, if you are a psychologist who knows all there is to know about abnormal psychology, besides which you know all there is to know about general psychology, it does not follow that you will teach abnormal psychology in ways that are productive for your students. That assumption, without which schools of education lose their reason for existence, is rejected by the oldest and most prestigious part of the university: the faculty of arts and sciences. In that part of the university, mastery of subject matter is assumed to insure effective teaching. That assumption is in direct contradiction to that which undergirds schools of education. This contradiction sheds a lot of light on why in the university the school of education is looked upon with disdain and its faculty considered to be second-rate minds who spend their time teaching methods and gimmicks instead of making sure that students are thoroughly steeped in the subject matter they will teach in schools. Almost every criticism of public schools that I discussed in the previous chapter has been made of the school of education by other parts of the university. And, it should be noted and be no occasion for surprise, university critics, predictably articulate, are always in the forefront of those seeking to improve the schools. This is not an exclusively American phenomenon. In 1964, the highpoint in England for building new universities, Daiches edited a book entitled *The Idea of a New University. An Experiment in Sussex*. Most of the book examined the innovative purposes and goals of different departments and schools. Let us listen to the opening paragraph in the chapter on the school of education:

> The attitude towards education in English universities makes an intriguing and also an odd story, whose history might be well worth studying in detail as a sociological phenomenon. This is not the place for the history of the matter, but it is relevant to note, at the outset, that the ice is cracking—indeed, since the Second World War, there has been a considerable thaw. The McNair Report of 1944, which proposed the establishment of Schools of Education and the acceptance by universities of a major responsibility for the training of teachers, marked a big advance—even if one has to add that the universities failed to implement the full scheme and contented themselves with adopting the modified responsibility represented by institutes of education (the University of Cambridge has to this day refused to incorporate the Institute of Education in the University). To accept the idea of training teachers, however, is a fairly easy way out: to offer certificates, even diplomas of education, is not to admit education to any very important degree of academic respectability. Virtually all universities, with the exception of Keele, have continued to exclude education from undergraduate courses, arguing that education is not really a subject, and even if it is that it is not a discipline.
>
> As a result, the assertion has in most instances become the fact. Departments of Education, with their responsibility for providing a one-year postgraduate course for the training of teachers, have not looked much like "genuine" university departments. (Ford, 1964, p. 135)

There are university critics and there are university critics. No one was as articulate as John Dewey in criticizing schools and their personnel. A particularly clear example is his presidential address ("Psychology and Social Practice") to the American Psychological Association in 1899. That address, however, has to be seen in the context of two facts: first, Dewey came to the University of Chicago because he could head up a program in psychology *and* education; second, in 1896 he created the Laboratory School, in which he tested his ideas about children, classrooms, teaching strategies, and teacher training. Consistent with his way of thinking, Dewey had to experience the situation he criticized. His criticisms were never ad hominem because he understood that if schools and teachers left much to be desired, this lack said less about them and more about social-intellectual history. As I have discussed elsewhere, psychology and the social sciences in the university did not know how to deal with Dewey's interest in education (Sarason, 1981). They were content to view that interest as an aberration or fall from grace away from pure research and scholarship to applications. So, today, psychology categorizes Dewey not as the towering psychologist he was but as an educator. To the rest of the university that pejorative judgment is further confirmed by giving him another label: philosopher. (And if the reader would like another example, quite juicy in its details of the status of education in the university, I recommend Cherniss's 1972 study of the creation and demise of Yale's department of education.)

There is one other source of the criticism and disdain directed at the schools: the preponderance of teachers in this country has always been female. It is beyond my purpose to go into detail about the myriad reasons for the dependent, intellectually, socially, and vocationally restricted roles of women in this country. Suffice it to say, whatever the basis for the respect that women did enjoy in the past, it did not contain a positive judgment about women's conceptual, analytic abilities. It was not that men thought that women should not be in certain roles but that women *could not* live up to what those roles required: whatever culturally sanctioned and supported activities in which women acquitted themselves well, even superbly, obviously did not require abilities in short supply among women.

And that included teaching, which was seen as an extension of the role of women in the family. In the case of a woman who was unmarried or was married but had no children, it was "natural" for her to give expression to her motherly inclinations and her "high moral sensitivity" (higher, that is, than that of men, who had to deal with a cruel and complex world) through teaching the young.

Welcomed as a way to tame and socialize children — to transform young ignoble savages into well-behaved little men or women (or dutiful soldiers who, in Dewey's phrase, would follow their "military commanders") — teaching was seen as a pouring in, an engineeringlike feat that provided food for the mind and stamped in and reinforced, conveyorlike, the right habits of thinking. It is hard to say how much of the low status of the teacher derived from this conception of what was or should be involved in teaching and how much from the status of women. If the position of women has changed somewhat in the post-World War II era, this development has not altered the conception that teaching is similar to, but a notch above, what the animal trainer does. That may strike the reader as an unwarranted and unseemly comparison, quite unfair to a public that places such importance on the role of teacher. This is but one of many instances in which we give importance to a role at the same time that we belittle those who are in it, the kind of contradiction that is explainable more by sociocultural history and ideology than by the strange workings of intrapsychic dynamics. When Dewey suggested that public school teachers should be remunerated at the same level as university professors, it was not because he was hostile to university professors and wanted to ingratiate himself with school teachers; it was because he had come to an understanding of the teaching process and relationship that made it impossible to maintain the dichotomy between "lower" and "higher" education. One was not easier than the other and one was not more important than the other. If society rewarded one more than the other, this disparity said more about culture and social history than about the demands of the process.

I have mentioned only a few of the sources of criticism and disdain of schools and school personnel. The story is far more complicated than the discussion suggests. For example, one could write at length about how these criticisms and disdain have influenced the self-selection process in regard to who goes into teaching, the hiring criteria employed by schools and communities, and the day-to-day work of school personnel. This is an assimilative process the consequences of which produce a degree of commonality in attitude between school personnel and their critics. If school personnel did not to a significant degree see themselves as their critics have seen them, we should have cause for wonder. I have presented enough of the issues to turn to another point: the difficulties one encounters (must encounter) in trying to take distance from the particular perspective from which one ordinarily sees schools and education.

Let me start with a recent experience. The occasion was a meeting to explore ways by which a liberal arts college could forge mutually beneficial relationships with the private and public sectors. It was, of course, not fortuitous that the meeting was taking place at a time of a severe economic recession, when a liberal arts education was not a passport to a job. At the meeting were representatives of large corporations, public utilities, labor unions, and governmental agencies, as well as faculty and administrators of the college. It was a freewheeling discussion and several themes soon emerged. The first theme was that a liberal arts education was either irrelevant or somewhat antithetical to the world of work, as that world was perceived by its representatives. It would be a mistake to characterize those who articulated this theme as crassly anti-intellectual or anti–liberal arts. To paraphrase their position: "Given the skills our work settings require, liberal arts majors have nothing to offer us. They do not have the skills, but they do have high expectations. They have been poorly counseled about the relationship, or lack of one, between their major and the job market." There was no suggestion that the college should change in any fundamental way the substance of liberal arts majors but rather add to them, especially in regard to science and technology. A second theme emerged from descriptions of efforts by large corporations to expand the intellectual horizons of those employees who were or would be in leadership or managerial positions. Essentially, these efforts, sparked in each instance by a top-level figure in the corporation, had sought to expose employees to theory and knowledge in the social sciences. These programs were soon discontinued because there seemed to be no useful transfer of knowledge from the educational experience to the work setting. As someone said, "Everybody who took advantage of this mini-college experience enjoyed it, but there was no reason to believe that it had anything to do with who was to become a good manager or leader." A third theme, expressed by all but most clearly by representatives of public utilities, labor unions, and public agencies, did not conern liberal arts programs but the failure of public schools to prepare literate people, at least to the point that they could read and fill out an application for employment. A fourth theme, stated by representatives of the private sector, was that many employees had more formal education than their jobs required.

I shall not dwell on the point that your position in society and your exposure to the educational system color your assessment of school personnel and programs. Economic and/or institutional self-interests are potent influences on how you think. Indeed, we would be very surprised if an institution, in either the public or the private sector, took actions that ran counter to its own interests. What we tend to overlook is that institutions vary considerably in how they define self-interest and that variation guarantees that schools will be seen and judged from very different perspectives. Moreover, institution A will be unaware of, indeed uninterested in, the fact that institutions B through X see schools in very different ways. So, for example, if the distinguished college that convened the meeting had invited representatives of prestigious graduate and professional schools, it probably would have been highly praised for the excellence and relevance of its liberal arts program. The same situation obtains with the public schools; for example, colleges view public schools in terms of their own interests, but they are only one type of institution among many with unique interests. And the icing on this cake of variation is that within schools different groups define the self-interests of schools differently. Schools are like societal ink blots: what you (as a representative of a group or institution) see in them and how you evaluate them derive from a perspective peculiar to you. If we have a variety of public schools, a variety of parochial schools, and a variety of private schools, this situation says far less about people's attitude toward diversity than it does about how they define the relationship between self-interest and education.

It has always struck me as odd that critics of schools have seemed unable to confront the fact that their views reflect, among other things, where they are in the social order, as if the substance of their criticisms did not arise from a soil compounded of color, religion (or lack of one), level of education, social class, age, geography, ethnicity, etc. The point here is analogous to one that has been made in regard to the heredity versus environment controversy that erupts periodically. Each side claims to possess a truth independent of social, economic, or other considerations. The evidence suggests otherwise. These controversies do not derive primarily from scientific data but from "truths" that are extrapolations from studies to statements that implicitly or explicitly suggest a societal action or direction. (And, let us not forget, there have been egregious instances in which the so-called truth seemed so obvious and socially important that individuals felt justified in fabricating confirmatory data.)

As soon as we make statements that in any way bear on the nature of our society (what it is or should be) we are, like it or not, reflecting to some degree where we are or have been in the social order. This is not an ad hominem argument. It is not a problem of motivation at all. It is a reminder that our socialization is not a random affair. We are products of a socialization process that shapes us through a host of interrelated influences. It is a process that takes place in a certain part of the social order, and different parts produce different world views. We like to believe that the truths we proclaim about what society is or should be or will become—how that society is ordered and why—derive from cold reason and implacable logic. The fascination of history to me is in its demonstration of how different groups in the past were unable to entertain the possibility that their views of society reflected aspects of a world view of which they were unaware. One can never fully explicate, let alone transcend, the influence of one's world view. But if one cannot fully accomplish those tasks, one nevertheless stands to benefit from recognizing the problem and striving for partial success. I have illustrated these issues in *Psychology Misdirected* (1981). And if that book is unconvincing to the reader, I recommend Dollard's *Criteria for the Life History* (1935), as penetrating an analysis as has ever been written on how culture and the social order place their stamps on each of us.

We can no more stop ourselves from making statements, positive or negative, about schools and school personnel than we can stop the tides. In this discussion it has not been my intention to suggest either that we pay the critics no mind or that critics go on an extended leave of silence. My sole purpose has been to suggest that attempting to reach and adopt a relatively dispassionate view of schools is not a simple matter of will power plus good intentions. There is a prior task: accepting the fact that everyone's perspective on schools is a function in part of who and where one was and is in the social order. This realization can help you to understand the perspective of others. In turn, you may become both more humble and more realistic about the pace and direction of efforts to change schools; in the process of uncovering ordinarily unrecognized aspects of your perspective, you may find yourself questioning the sources of the traditional picture you and others have of what schools look like, where they are, what goes on in them, and how they relate to their surrounds.

Why is it so difficult for us seriously to examine the universe of alternatives to our picture of schools? Why is it that however great the substantive differences in their criticisms, critics share a picture of where schooling should take place and who should participate in the venture? And when I say "picture," I mean a place the architecture of which may vary, the internal spatial and human organization of which may vary, but *within* which all, or almost all, of what we mean by education goes on. If we unreflectively accept that picture, if when challenged we have inordinate difficulty imagining alternative pictures, if we are comfortable with one and only one picture, this situation reveals more about culture, socialization, tradition, and socioeconomic history than it does about the psychology of individuals. Is it possible, as I shall discuss later, that our inability to imagine alternatives and our disappointment with efforts to improve schools are testimony to the role of silent axioms, which if confronted and articulated illuminate the nature of our society and present us with new alternatives, at the same time that the formidable obstacles to implementing these alternatives become clear? I am suggesting that it is profitable to look at what different critics, even critics of apparently diametrically opposed views, have in common. Let us begin with one commonality that has all the characteristics of a glimpse of the obvious: what goes on inside schools should stand in some relationship to what goes on outside schools.

4

EXPERIENCE IN AND OUTSIDE SCHOOL

WHAT STUDENTS LEARN and experience in school should stand in some relationship to what they learn and experience outside school. If that statement seems obvious both as a value and as a goal, it nevertheless has features of the untestable abstraction because when people nod agreement to the statement, it is not clear what is being agreed to. Do we mean, for example, that what a kindergartner learns and experiences in school should stand in some *current* relationship to what is being learned and experienced outside school? Or do we have in mind *future* learning and experience outside school? Similarly, is what a high school student learns in a math or social studies class to stand in relationship to current or future experience outside school? What about the *past*? When a student is in a history or literature class, is what he or she is learning to stand in relation to a "dead" past that was once outside or to one that has continuity with the outside present and future? Some people would argue that they mean all of the above, as if such comprehensiveness either settled the problem or contributed a great deal of meaning. If one were to ask what such a statement means in terms of what one should be able to observe in and out of schools in order to conclude that these statements of goals and values are being appropriately implemented, the answers would not come easily and, if my experience is not atypical, would be generalizations by no means clear in meaning.

When I pose this question, I do not expect the answers to resemble a teacher's daily lesson plan. Rather, I expect concrete examples or detailed descriptions that allow one to compare the answer to what one would observe in a modal classroom or school. More correctly, the answer should permit one to contrast proposed inside-outside relationships with those relationships as we would observe them in our schools. If, as is unlikely, the two pictures are highly similar, we have to look elsewhere for the sources of disappointment with our schools. But if those pictures diverge, especially if they diverge a great deal, we have to pursue the reasons therein, on the assumption that whatever contributes to the divergence may be relevant to our disappointment. It is, of course, possible that faced with obvious divergences, some people would make the judgment, for any number of reasons, that the "theoretical" picture is utterly impractical and that the "actual" picture of these inside-outside relationships is now both more understandable and more acceptable. In that event, we not only have to temper criticism but also have to concede that our social world is not organized to make it practical to implement the theoretical picture to a desired degree. The initial assumption would have to be restated: what students learn and experience in school will, unfortunately, stand in a limited relationship to what they learn and experience outside school. And these limitations, it would be apparent, derive not only from what schools and school personnel are but also from the traditions and attitudes that bulwark our society and its structures. What some people regard as impractical because it may require significant and difficult changes inside and outside schools can be a goad to those for whom the impractical is a welcome challenge.

There are other possible reactions to divergence, but at this point I wish to stress only that the first task is to recognize that the assumption in any of its forms leads us to look at and far beyond schools. How learning and experience in schools should relate to what is learned and experienced outside schools cannot be answered by looking only at schools. However obvious this point may seem, it is remarkable how different critics have examined the assumption primarily by looking at schools. What is even more remarkable to me, taking into account the unanimous acceptance of the assumption of inside-outside relationships, is how unclearly and unsystematically that assumption has been posed and discussed. That lack of clarity has not been helped, indeed it has been aggravated, by the attention that has been given to another and far more circumscribed assumption to which we now turn. Here, too, the assumption has all of the characteristics of a glimpse of the obvious but, unlike the first assumption, it is taken seriously, so seriously that it deflects attention away from the first assumption even though the two revolve around the same issues and principles.

The second assumption is: that which a student learns and experiences at any one point in his or her schooling should stand in some relationship to a later point in schooling. The later point may be tomorrow, next month, next year, or five years in the future but it is a point that is, in terms of time and place, within the school. When a school says, for example, that it has a mathematics curriculum, it means that there is a graded sequence spanning several grades and that there is a rationale justifying that sequence. Likewise, if you ask why kindergartners engage in activities A, B, and C, the answer will be phrased in terms of skills, knowledge, and attitudes that are necessary for the transition to first grade and the mastery of the beginning phases of reading, arithmetic, writing, and other subjects. Every teacher knows that whatever he or she is requiring students to learn is preparation for, and organized in relation to, what the student will be asked to learn and experience the next semester or year. In fact, one of the sources of friction among teachers in adjacent grades is the claim that teachers in the lower grade are not preparing students well for the next grade. And, as the reader undoubtedly knows, colleges blame high schools, which blame middle schools, which blame elementary schools, which blame parents. (This approach has given rise to a flourishing curriculum publishing industry, journals devoted to the theory and evaluation of curricula, and sustained controversies about the substance and adequacy of different curricula — their psychological underpinnings, the demands they place on teachers, and their interest value for students.) If for any one year one were able to list every workshop, lecture, or graduate course designed for school personnel — and the list would run into the thousands — the percentage that would explicitly concern curriculum would be very large. And there would be little or nothing said on those occasions that bears on the relationship between learning and experience inside and outside of schools.

Schooling is seen as a continuous, integrated process in which learning and experience at different points in time become fused in a more complex and differentiated pattern of knowledge, skill, and conception. As a goal that view is unchallengeable. But the question that has to be asked is: what price do we pay when that goal is in practice defined primarily in terms of within-school learning and experience? More concretely, does that definition permit us to understand better not only some major criticisms of schools but also why efforts to change and improve schools have been disappointing both to critics and to the public? Is it not possible that the perceived problematic relationship between what students learn and experience in and outside schools is in part a consequence of the unreflective emphasis on learning and experience within schools? Can the issues surrounding the integration of learning at two different points in time within schools be discussed, let alone resolved, without attention to *concurrent* learning and experience in and out of school?

There is no group more preoccupied with making schools more interesting places than curriculum developers. The "making school interesting" industry received its greatest impetus from the American uproar following the launch of the first sputnik, as I suggested earlier. Our country, the critics said, was behind the Soviet Union in the quality of education and a contributing factor was the inadequacy of curricula. School learning, we were told, could be interesting, enjoyable, and mind expanding. Turned off students could be turned on by better curricula. It is my impression that the new math curricula that were introduced at the time received more play in the mass media than any curricula before or since (with the possible exception of curricula for sex education). What got conjured up in people's minds was a picture of somnolent students waking up to a fairyland of intellectual delights. I am not being facetious or disdainful but rather trying to convey how the assessment that schools were uninteresting places was (and is) a central feature of the diagnosis of the ills of our educational system. And this feature was found at all levels of schooling. The problem was most clear at the high school level because our society was starting to see that it had a problem on its hands: disaffected youth, many in number, varied in their expression and style, and heterogeneous in background. High schools were beginning to be declared disaster areas that could not be ignored. As a high school principal said to me at the time, "We have several types of students. Those who do not come to school. Those who come to school but who hang around, make trouble, and don't go to classes. Those who come to class but whose minds are elsewhere. And then there are those, a minority to be sure, who come to class and their minds are there."

(A digression: as I was writing these words in March 1982 I received a call from the head of staff development at a modest-sized school system in a nearby state. The community had, I was told, a per capita expenditure for its schools that put it in the top 2 percent of all school districts in the country. I was asked whether I could recommend resource people who could help the system with some problems: absenteeism in the high schools, drugs, and discipline. This person said that the district's problems were not severe, comparatively speaking, but pressure was mounting from within and without the schools to do something. I relate this telephone conversation because it was less discouraging—not more encouraging—than my contacts with school settings usually are.)

Let us begin to examine these questions by focusing on an observation about which there is a consensus: schools are not very interesting places for most of the people in them. That is indisputably the case for high and middle or junior high schools, especially in our metropolitan areas. In fact, the post-World War II era has spawned a sizable literature on how stultifying schools can be. From the standpoint of eliciting and studying student attitudes toward schooling, the most systematic and comprehensive study is that by Buxton (1973). His report does not, to indulge understatement, lead to reassuring conclusions. But Buxton, a longtime colleague of mine at Yale, is a sober, "hard-nosed" type of psychologist who would not be regarded as a flaming liberal or radical intent on redoing society or its major institutions. He came to his study because of a long-standing interest in adolescents, and he was not bent on criticizing schools. In fact, Buxton was both surprised and perturbed by his findings. I point these things out because so much of the literature sharply critical of high schools has been based on participant-observation by social scientists of reformist or radical leanings. That statement should in no way be taken as a criticism by me because their descriptions of how people in schools feel and act not only have a ring of truth but also do not conflict with the conclusions of Buxton's study.

Two things are noteworthy about our unsuccessful efforts to make schools interesting. The first is the assumption that students are truly interested in the subject matters, e.g., math and social studies—or, more correctly, that the ways in which children normally and spontaneously think about and experience these subject areas are similar in content and form to the ways in which they are or should be presented in the curriculum. It is one thing to say that in the course of development the phenomenology of children contains a good deal of questioning and answering about numbers, human relationships, spatial relationships, the physical world, causality, biological functions, and other matters that Piaget's work did so much to illuminate. It is quite another to say that the characteristics of this questioning and self-generated answering — as well as the characteristics of the occasions in which they emerge — are highly similar to those that the curriculum seeks to re-create or to capitalize on. So, the curriculum developers are correct in assuming that children are interested in these matters, but not necessarily in assuming that they are addressing these matters in ways attuned to the phenomenology of the student. It would be fair to say that curriculum developers spend a lot of time trying to figure out how to interest students in what the curriculum developers believe is the appropriate content and form of the subject matter. It is also fair to say that they have fallen far short of their mark. The second assumption underlying these efforts is that it is possible to engender interest within the confines of a classroom or school (more correctly, within the confines of the classroom and the division of the day into periods, each of which is devoted to a particular subject or activity). That assumption, rarely articulated, has a compelling surface validity despite the fact that students and teachers have long experienced school in ways that should have brought the assumption into serious question. That assumption has been seriously questioned in recent decades in relation to high schools. Critiques have encompassed any or all of the following observations:

1. Schools are very uninteresting places for both students and teachers.
2. Students are capable of, and would be eager to accept, more responsibility for their own learning. This is a matter not of empowerment based on abstract principles but of capitalizing on the motivations of students. Students, sometimes vaguely, sometimes clearly, resent and are bored with the passive role assigned to them.
3. Students have strong interests in and about the world

but that world is not related to the one they experience is school.

4. Students do experience the outside world in ways that are intellectually, educationally, and personally productive.

5. Only to a very limited degree can that outside world be re-created or simulated in a classroom or school.

These critiques do not come from people who overidealize youth. Nor do they come from people who believe that children have the capacity and wisdom to go their own ways, as if the role of adults were to insure that nothing gets in the way of children's self-direction and self-expression. And they do not come from people who downplay the goal of attaining structure and direction in experience. What these critiques have in common is the observation that schools are uninteresting places, the emphasis on learning and experience over time *in* school is misplaced and self-defeating, and we can no longer ignore the importance of integrating concurrent learning in and out of schools. They also have in common the belief that the problem of interest cannot be resolved by curricula riveted on the traditional classroom.

Let me illustrate some of these points with an example that I use less because it is typical and more because it has been described and evaluated in an atypically comprehensive and judicious fashion.* I refer to Project City Science, a program car-

*Paul Longo of Queens College directed the evaluation and report, which is in three volumes. Despite its intimidating size, the report is quite instructive and very readable. Anyone interested in what efforts at educational change are like, how they are formulated and implemented, and what obstacles they encounter in an uncontrollable, unpredictable world will find this report very informative. I am sorry that I was unaware of this document when I wrote the second edition of *The Culture of the Schools and the Problem of Change* (Sarason, 1982) because it beautifully confirms how I conceptualize and judge modal attempts at educational change, attempts that have brought disillusionment with, and criticism of, schools in their wake. These attempts begin by viewing schools as places of salvation and end by scapegoating them. Longo's evaluation is refreshingly far more balanced in this regard.

ried out by New York University in conjunction with several junior high schools in poor New York neighborhoods. Funding came from the National Science Foundation. The purpose of the project was "to help bring about a major, lasting and self-perpetuating improvement, principally in New York City, in the teaching of science in the middle grades between elementary and high school" (Longo, 1979, p. 12). Longo went on to state:

> While the rationale for placing primary emphasis on science rather than on other subjects, such as reading and mathematics, is not clearly stated, it is evident that the proposers of [Project City Science] PCS feel that science is an area in which instruction is particularly ineffective. It is noted that:
>
> science teaching at the middle school level in New York City and many other cities can only be regarded, on the whole, as gravely inadequate. . . . [Furthermore,] science education in the city elementary schools remains woefully weak, when not absent altogether.

Having concluded that, "improving elementary school science in the cities seems to be an intractable problem of massive proportions" project staff apparently decided that the middle school (i.e. grades 6–9) should become the logical focus of their efforts. The reasons offered for this appear to be three-fold. First, a large fraction of inner city youth do not go on to attend high school, and so efforts made at a later stage would be too late. Second, by the time students reach high school, a deep antipathy toward the study of science has already developed, and so they will usually not choose to take courses in science; and, third, even though many educators agree that the junior high school years may be critical for students, very little emphasis has been placed on developing procedures that improve instruction or modernize curriculum at this level—particularly in science.

The proposal goes on to clearly emphasize its junior high school focus.

For many city youngsters, junior high school provides the *only* formal instruction in science they receive in their lives! . . . it constitutes quantitatively the most science they will formally encounter.

Project emphasis was not solely upon the direct improvement of science instruction in the school, but upon the development of a model program for training junior high school science teachers as well. The intent was to both provide science teachers for the New York City middle schools, and to develop a training model with widespread potential. The then Project Director, interviewed for an article about PCS, indicated what the program's major concerns were:

First, we're doing inservice training of teachers who are already in the schools. Second, we're designing a training program for the whole next generation of junior high school teachers. Third, we're working to analyze instructional problems and devise system-wide solutions. . . . Over the long run, [the director] can envision Project City Science helping to effect a new kind of science teaching. . . . If Project City Science succeeds, and if it is duplicated in other cities, in ten years we could replace up to 40 percent with a cadre of science teachers trained for the job. . . . What we want to develop is a design that can be used in city schools throughout the country, something that can be adopted quickly by other universities and other school districts.(Pp. 12–13)

One more quotation is relevant to the major problems the project was created to address:

Assuming, then, that there is an especially urgent need to improve science instruction during the transition years, what are the particular problems that must be solved or at least ameliorated? The 1974 proposal explicitly claimed, and Project experience has subsequently supported, *that three major problems exist*:

1. *The failure of teacher training*, both preservice, and inservice, to prepare science teachers to deal effectively with the early adolescent child in the inner-city situation.

2. A continuing reliance on *science programs that do not reflect* sufficiently what has been learned in the last decade or so about science curricula and new approaches to teaching science.
3. *A scarcity of systematic* knowledge about the age group and about what conditions and techniques best promote an *interest in a learning of science* at that age and in inner-city circumstances.

Implicit in the proposal and accentuated by Project experience is a fourth problem: *The failure* on all sides to identify, organize, and bring *to bear in a coordinated way* the not inconsiderable *material and human resources* of the state, city, district schools, universities, and community at large. Related to this is the problem of establishing a self-sustaining system for continuing reform rather than merely instituting this or that improvement, regardless of how alluring a given reform seems to be in the short run, or however much desired by one or the other agency or institution. (Longo, 1979, p. 14)

The problems were many but it was recognized that among the most crucial was how to engender in pupils an interest in science. More correctly, how first to oversome *antipathy* and then to engender and sustain interest.

I have gone into detail about this project to make a point that, once made, will seem obvious. Indeed, the point is so obvious that it apparently required no statement or examination by the creators of the project or, for that matter, by the people at the National Science Foundation who decided to fund this and similar efforts. (Let us not scapegoat the project directors. We can assume that the project was scrutinized by a variety of specialists for whom the obvious also was literally unremarkable.) *Insofar as the schools were concerned, the emphasis was exclusively on the classroom—that was where interest was to be engendered and productive learning to take place. It was in the classroom that success would be judged by changes in test scores over time. For all practical purposes, learning and experiencing*

science outside school—utilizing "the not inconsiderable mate-
rial and human resources of the state, city, district schools, uni-
versities, and community at large"—were not in the picture.
We can assume that Project City Science did engender more interest in students but there is nothing in the evaluation to suggest that it was other than a sometime thing.

I am not suggesting that it is impossible for classroom
learning to be interesting. I have seen classrooms, albeit a very
small percentage of the classrooms I have observed, in which
teachers and students experience and sustain interest, even excitement, in learning. Very few of these unusual classrooms are
in high or junior high schools; by far, the majority are in elementary schools. What is common to these classrooms is the
ability of the teacher to create an atmosphere that approxi-
mates that of outside situations that stimulate and elicit a
child's attention and interest—really, anybody's attention and
interest.

Imagine that two criteria could be met. The first is that we
can get agreement about the characteristics of "real—life" situations that elicit children's interest. The second is that we can
reliably rate classrooms for the degree to which they contain
these characteristics. My experience suggests that the more a
classroom contains the characteristics of outside-school situations, the more the people in that classroom will experience and
sustain interest. This very observation has led to the criticism
that there is nothing wrong with schools that better selection of
teachers could not cure. And it is this observation that has powered funding for in-service programs to improve the quality of
teaching. After all, the reasoning goes, if a few teachers can do
it (regardless of what *it* may be), why can't others learn to do it?
That is a legitimate question in the sense that it emerges from
observation and deserves scrutiny. But it has always seemed
strange to me that those who ask this question have inordinate
difficulty recognizing another legitimate question: is there
something about encapsulated classrooms and schools—spaces,
places, and social organizations that are physically and psychologically separate from the outside world—that makes it ex-

traordinarily difficult for them to be interesting? Should not the fact that so few teachers meet our expectations cause us to examine the basis of our expectations? Are we putting students and teachers into a situation that far from engendering and sustaining interest contains, by virtue of its isolation and internal structure, nearly insurmountable obstacles to such interest?

I cannot refrain from relating the following story. I was trotting out these arguments to a friend who had long worked with prison inmates, staff, and administrators. I did not get very far when he stopped me and, much like a father patting a child on the head for trying to think like an adult, he said in essence:

> What you are trying to say is in principle on all fours with the history of attempts to humanize prisons. You can always point to a few prison personnel who truly can relate to prisoners in very helpful, sensitive ways. There are even a few prisons you might be tempted to say are humane. So why can't we select our personnel better and have less junglelike prisons? Why is our track record poor even in those few instances in which bleeding hearts like me had the opportunity, to a modest degree, to make these changes? We did some good and if given new opportunities I would break my neck to do better. But, it took me a long time to recognize that it is the nature of prisons that sets drastic limits to achieving my goals. There is a part of me that still gets angry as hell when I see brutality or insensitivity on the part of prisoners or staff. There is another part of me that says that the problem is as much in what prisons are as in personality makeups. That is a hard fact to which to adjust because there is no way that the public is going to give up its belief that the problem resides primarily in what people *are*. That's the essence of the problem. Plato still lives!

Over the decades I have worked with school personnel in classes, workshops, and in-service training meetings. Whenever possible I request that participants take a few minutes to ponder this question: think of two instances—they could be from any time in your life, they could have occurred anyplace, and they could have lasted from a few minutes to hours, days, or months—during which your interest in something was kindled to a degree and in a way that allows you to say that the episode had an influence on you. I then ask each member of the group briefly to describe the instances in such a way as to highlight their major characteristics. A number of features always come up: the occasion contained an element of novelty; it bore strongly on an existing (sometimes subliminal, sometimes explicit) need or interest; it was not planned or predictable but simply happened; it involved another person, usually older, with mentorlike qualities; it was marked by a sense of excitement, or exploration, or "new meanings"; it stuck in memory, sometimes with few or no apparent sustained behavioral consequences, sometimes with life-changing consequences; it was recalled with pleasure and nostalgia. Now, two other characteristics: the instances tended to occur in adolescence or early adulthood and only a small number occurred in a school setting.

After each person describes his or her instances and the characteristics common to them are recognized by the group, I ask, "How frequently have you had experiences in school as a teacher that were interesting?" The immediate response usually is a subdued ripple of anxious laughter. Three statements can summarize the discussion that typically follows. First, the frequency of interesting experiences is very low. Second, the organization of a school does not make it likely that the characteristics of interesting experiences can occur. Third, within the classroom, school teachers are too isolated from each other and from the world at large; i.e., the social contexts from which interesting experiences might emerge are not likely to be found in schools. In one of these groups, at a point at which the participants were both puzzled and bothered by what was being discussed, one teacher said, "But that does not mean that we do not get satisfaction from what we do." To which another teacher replied, "You're right, but how long can you go without an interesting experience? If it were not for the kicks I get from interesting experiences outside of school, my level of satisfaction would be a lot less than it is now." My impression from these discussions is that high and junior high school teachers, in contrast to those in elementary school, report less satisfaction from their work and more bitterness about the infrequency of interesting experiences.

I sometimes pose a second question: how frequently do you think students have interesting experiences in school? Here one must immediately separate elementary from high or junior high school personnel because the latter typically raise the problem of student uninterest, to which I respond, "Granted that it would be quite unfair to place blame for this exclusively on junior high and high schools, what is it about these places that may be aggravating the problem?" The inevitable answer is: these schools have too many students; the way the school day is organized makes it impossible for teachers to remember the names of all students, let alone get to know other than a handful; teachers are, depending on where the school is, at best monitors and at worst police in training; these places are more like factories than schools. The reader will remember that earlier in this chapter I related that while I was writing I received a telephone call for assistance from a high school in a very affluent town in a nearby state. Discipline, drugs, and absenteeism were the problems with which they were unsuccessfully coping. I was asked to make a visit, I said yes, suggested a date, and was told that I would be contacted in a few days to confirm the appointment. The call came canceling the appointment. The person calling me was embarrassed and even angry because the task of getting a "resource person" had been dumped into his lap and he was told to act quickly. He went on to tell me that he had just found out that the immediate stimulus for the first call had been a stabbing, and that the superintendent had decided that what was needed was a new principal and not an outside consultant. I give this account not to paint high schools as armed camps, which most are not, or to suggest that there are really no differences between schools in ghettos and affluent suburbia, which would be ridiculous, but rather as a way to convey to readers who have no contact with junior high and high schools how bothered, bewildered, and despairing school personnel are about their efforts to understand, stimulate, and manage students. Stabbings are rare—absenteeism, discipline problems, and drugs are not. Junior and high schools can be exciting places but it is the kind of excitement no one wants. That they are uninteresting places for those who populate them—that, too, no one wants but no one seems to know what to change and how to change it.

As I have stressed in this book, schools are uninteresting places. But the word "places" does not capture the core of the problem as seen by school personnel. It is *people*, the students, who are uninterested, and that is to teachers and other staff the important etiological factor. As a superintendent of schools said:

> Kids enter kindergarten and first grade with interests. They are motivated to be and learn in school. As they go through the grades they seem to lose more and more interest and most of them slip over into the uninterested category. So the dropout rate is scandalous, or most who graduate have really learned to dislike learning. If it weren't for that small minority who are really interested, who occasionally brighten your day so that you can come to work the next day, schools would explode. At least the teachers would.

When I asked him whether it is possible that our traditional conception of school as *the* place in which students and teachers can have interesting educational experiences may be getting in the way, he was very puzzled and finally said, "Where else would schooling take place?" The inability to generate other than a very limited universe of alternatives (or any alternatives) in the face of an intractable social-institutional problem is a sign of how effectively tradition and culture function to blind us; but more about that later.

Some readers will find themselves saying to me, "You may be right about *public* schools as uninteresting places. And you may be right that whatever we have done to improve matters is no cause for enthusiasm or encouragement. But how do you account for the fact that *private* schools are more interesting places than public schools, regardless of their use of classrooms?" I do not regard it as a fact that private schools are more interesting for either students or teachers. It may be that students in private schools are more motivated for academic achievement. And it may be that they do better on achievement tests, pose fewer disciplinary problems, and have a lower rate of absenteeism.* But that says nothing about educational experiences being more interesting in private schools. Although my experience in and with private schools is less than that in and with public schools, my observations do not support the conclusion that they differ in terms of being interesting places. In fact, in my talks with private school personnel the usual problem comes up: how, as one teacher put it, can you light an intellectual fire in the bulk of students for whom learning is such a bore?

But why, some readers will wonder, do I stress the notion of schools as interesting places? Is it not the primary goal of schooling to foster the acquisition of knowledge and skills and

*With the publication of Coleman's *High School Achievement* (1982) comparing public and private schools—in which public schools came out a poor second—the critics of public schools were confirmed in their opinions, especially those critics in favor of a voucher system that would allow parents to shop around to find a school appropriate to their children. These critics and the public at large will probably not hear either about what critics of that report have written or about the statistical analyses that suggest that differences between public and private schools may be minuscule or even nonexistent. Rejoinders to, or retractions of, what makes front-page headlines are never published on the front page. However, for my present purposes this controversy is not important because neither the report nor its critics are at all concerned about how interesting schools are, although I would guess that none of the participants in the controversy would rate public or private schools as places that their occupants find interesting.

only secondarily to provide an interesting context for this to happen? Is it the goal of the school to be a happy place? Are schools supposed to be centers for entertainment, suppliers more of what students want than of what they need in this world? Granted that schools should be more interesting places than they are, are you not diverting attention from their deficits in regard to academic achievement? Is not the return to basics in part a reaction to what happened when schools introduced all kinds of gimmicks and frills that catered to students' interests?

Let me begin my answer by noting that I do not use the word "interesting" as a synonym for "happy." When students *and* school personnel complain about schools as uninteresting places, they are complaining not about the absence of happiness but rather about boredom and the lack of the sense of personal challenge and meaning (i.e., the sense that one is engaged in a process that pulls one willingly to a desired future, to a tomorrow that will add to one's knowledge, outlook, worth, and mastery). To be engaged in serious learning—which is tantamount to experiencing change—is to encounter difficulty, frustration, challenge, excitement, questioning, and satisfaction. It is not a happy process, although the feeling of happiness is occasionally there. The complaint of students and teachers is that school learning is not a satisfying experience and, therefore, it is uninteresting. To assume that students and teachers seek happiness is at best a caricature of their complaint and at worst a total misunderstanding of what they seek.

Another part of the answer is that my emphasis on schools as uninteresting places rests on what students and teachers have for decades reported. What their reports demonstrate is that regardless of the substance or content of the curriculum, there is something about schools that does not engage the interest of most students. And that lack of engagement forces one to predict that the current back-to-basics movement will be no more successful than the emphases it presumably seeks to remedy or replace. The problem does not inhere in the curriculum but in the limits that the organization and culture of the school place on engaging the interest of students; as long as we continue to view education as something that should take place in a school building, we drastically restrict the opportunities for students and teachers to experience serious, interesting learning. That conclusion, as we shall see in later chapters, has long been recognized by schools as valid for certain types of students, a small minority, but its applicability to all students has not been noted. For example, that conclusion has long been considered valid for the least and the most educationally talented students for whom what was available in the school was considered to be insufficiently appropriate and interesting. Several times during the year one can count on reading newspaper accounts of so-called gifted students for whom the school (or parents) arranged serious educational experiences in diverse community settings. And one can also count on reading about students, who are clearly not educationally talented, who are engaged in some hands-on experience in the community. Historically, the creation of vocational schools was in part a recognition that for some students the academic aspects of schooling hold no interest; they require an educational setting that will engage what is thought to be their practical interests. I need not belabor the point that school personnel have long been sensitive to the fact that without student interest productive learning does not occur. Someone once said that a teacher's definition of paradise is a classroom with one half the students he or she now has. It would be nearer the truth to say that teachers fantasize paradise as a place with classrooms of students who are interested and eager to learn. One of the delights of fantasy is that it gets us away from the nature and demands of reality. And the reality that the fantasies of school personnel avoid confronting is that the traditional classroom is not, has not been, and cannot be a very interesting place for the bulk of students and school personnel. Whatever schools are or have been, they are not and have not been interesting places.

The final part of the answer is usually given not by me but by those who wonder why I stress the idea of schools as interesting places. The fact is that those who question my emphasis fre-

quently (and quickly) convey in indirect ways that they know
that to argue against the centrality of the concept of interest is
like arguing for sin and against virtue. (One person said to me,
"I feel I am arguing in favor of a motorless car. It looks good,
sounds good, but moves you nowhere."). Usually, those who
question my stance see me as advocating permissiveness and
downplaying the so-called basics, a devotee of process over substance. I am able to convince most of these critics that I am not
doing either of these things but rather emphasizing how central
interest is in learning *anything* one thinks worthwhile. Once
they understand what I am saying, they have less difficulty facing up to two things: school tended to be uninteresting for them
and schools have been resistant to efforts to make them interesting places. So what do we do? Get rid of schools? The second
question, we shall see, is a trap because it suggests a flight into
action that temporarily may dilute the sense of frustration at
the same time that it adds confusion to apathy and despair. It
would also be a trap if advocating such an action could be interpreted as giving school personnel their final comeuppance,
because it suggests that school personnel are to blame if schools
are uninteresting places. That would be an instance of blaming
the victim because school personnel, no less than we and a good
deal more than most of us, have been socialized to define education as that which takes place *in* schools. That such a definition, literally poured into concrete, may be drastically limiting
to efforts to make education interesting is hard for any of us to
seriously consider, not only because it requires us to think in
new ways but also because subliminally we know that the obstacles to society's acceptance of the implications of these ways of
thinking would be many and strong. After all, when we talk
about schools we are talking about institutions that in their size,
structure, stated purposes, internal dynamics, and relation to
the social surround reflect this country's social, intellectual, religious, political, and economic history. That it reflects these
factors is easy to state and document. What is extraordinarily
difficult is to become aware of the degree to which our com-

munities depend on schools being where they are, bounded as they are, and organized as they are. That dependence is not a willed one or the result of a conspiracy—such oversimplifications obscure more than they clarify. For my present purposes it is sufficient to say that it is not until you come to see how self-defeating it is to continue to expect that schools can be truly interesting places (and then come to see the necessity of expanding one's conception of where and how serious learning can occur) that you will begin to glimpse how much of the way our communities are organized and function depend on schools being where they are, set off from the community as they are, and organized internally as they are.

I have argued that if schools are, by and large, uninteresting places, part of the explanation is in the emphasis on learning in the bounded classroom and school. Not only does that emphasis place definite limits on the degree to which schooling can be interesting, but also it permits us to avoid a critical question: can students experience schooling as interesting if their teachers do not? Let me try to throw light on that question by a comparative approach. If you were to ask, as I have, university professors to justify the existence of a university, one of the most frequent answers would be, in one form or another, that a university is a place that creates the conditions in which its faculty can learn, change, and grow. If university faculty are to contribute to knowledge, then the university has to be organized on a basis and structured in a way to support faculty in their investigations, learning, and changing. In fact, as I pointed out earlier, the university assumes that to the degree that it creates the conditions that nurture the development of its faculty, students will experience learning as both interesting and productive. But, some professors will note, you can have a university without students; i.e., the primary justification of a university is its obligation to faculty. That justification arouses ambivalence in many people. On the one hand, they interpret that justification as a form of undeserved (or enviable) indulgence of narcissism, social irresponsibility, or sheer laziness. On the other, they cannot ignore — living as we do in a culture that respects practical knowledge and people with know-how — the fact that university faculty have served society well by these criteria (not all fields represented in the university, of course, but enough to keep the ambivalence in check). The idea that the primary function of a university is to support the development of its faculty receives grudging acceptance on the part of the public. If university faculty justify the existence of the university as they do, and if they are aware that this justification is rare in the bulk of other work settings, they are aware also that the way they justify the university makes it a very vulnerable institution in our society. After all, to be part of an institution whose obligation is to create the conditions that further your development (and make it interesting) produces if not guilt then at least the sense that one is fortunate.

Now, if you ask school personnel to justify the existence of schools, the answer is always that schools are for the pupils: their needs, their development. That justification, of course, is dramatically different from the one given by university faculty. Can teaching be interesting and personally and intellectually productive if school teachers are not provided the conditions that contribute to their own learning and personal and intellectual change and growth? If the needs of pupils and teachers are not co-equal — if meeting the needs of the former is seen as a necessity while those of the latter are either not recognized or viewed as a luxury or indulgence or frill — can teachers sustain those conditions that contribute to an interesting educational experience for pupils?

One of the unverbalized assumptions undergirding the organization and thrust of our schools is that the conditions that make schools interesting places for children can be created and sustained by teachers for whom those conditions exist only minimally, at best. There is nothing in theory, research, or practice that lends credence to that assumption. On the contrary, whatever we have learned about what makes for interesting experiences, about what makes for boredom in and disaffection from learning, about the features of settings that elicit and sustain interest — all of this and more underline the importance of symmetry in making life interesting for teacher and pupil. If schools are uninteresting places, it is in part because we have focused only on what we think pupils are and need, totally ignoring what teachers are and need. I have never met anyone who denied that children are curious about a lot of things, that they strive to achieve a sense of mastery, that they want to feel as propelled from within as stimulated from without, and that they know the difference between learning that is interesting and learning that is stultifying. In short, as they grow older, students increasingly appreciate the difference between labor and work, i.e., between end products that in no way bear the stamp of the producer and end products that do bear such a stamp (if only partially). Put another way, no one asserts that students do or should experience every minute of every day as fascinating; at the same time, however, no one asserts that for most of the school day students should be either bored or passive. And in what way are teachers different from children in terms of needs and expectations? Are teachers people whose curiosity has been satisfied? Are they people who feel no need to deepen their understanding or expand their mastery? Are they by nature devotees of ritual, far more interested in being laborers that workers? Are teachers allergic to change and growth and exploration? (Do not many critics impugn the very motivations and behavior on the part of teachers that the latter attack in their students?)

In this chapter I have discussed several factors that help explain not only why efforts to change and improve schools have been disappointing but also why future efforts are likely to fail. That conclusion derives from a rejection, in toto or in part, of four interrelated assumptions. First, schools are or should be the primary places in which education takes place. Second, it is possible to create within schools the conditions that make for interesting experiences. Third, schools are primarily for students. Fourth, it is possible in school for teachers to create and sustain for students the conditions of productive and interesting learning when those conditions do not exist for teachers.

The conclusion I have come to will be resisted in diverse ways, all of which I have encountered in myself in my efforts over the years to understand why schools have not been amenable to change. What might be some of the basic but unverbalized assumptions without which the organization, thrust, and problems of schools are incomprehensible? It was not until I was able to ask and pursue this question that I began to see how amazingly effective our socialization is — so effective that we are unable to formulate, let alone challenge, these undergirding assumptions. But even if one begins to see and to take faltering steps to overcome what our socialization has made it unnecessary for us to verbalize, our socialization immediately confronts us with a fact that we knew in some abstract way but never understood in terms of what it meant vis-à-vis the way in which society is organized. And that fact is that when you begin to challenge the assumptions on which our schools are based, you begin to see how much our society depends on schools continuing to be what they are and where they are.

The idea that there must be things we can do inside schools that will make them more interesting places and instill in the unformed minds of students a respect for learning, even a hunger for learning, a sense of mastery over self and one's world and a sense of purpose that pulls one to a tomorrow built on the achievements of today and yesterday — put whatever way you wish for students in language flower or mundane, the idea that they can be achieved will die hard, if it dies at all. That is not a gloomy forecast but a recognition that our world views change very slowly. Nor is this prediction gloomy in the sense that it implies a lack of alternatives. Inevitably, as one's world view starts to change, the elements of a new view come to the fore; the consequences and pace of such developments are not predictable expect in barest outlines. As we shall see in later chapters, some of those elements are already on the scene waiting, so to speak, for their general significance to be recognized.

New world views—whether they be literally about the world or about a major institution, and the two are always interrelated—do not appear full-blown, discontinuous with the old ones. It takes future historians to discern that the seeds of a new world view were imperceptibly sprouting in the old. So, for example, today we know that our world view has changed and continues to change in regard to men and women, race, and the family. Our libraries are being enlarged daily by books trying to describe how and why this world view came about, why it took so long to unfold, and what it portends for the future. And if there is any consensus about these matters it is in regard to two facts: the strength of unverbalized assumptions about the way the world is and should be and the extent to which the socioeconomic and political organization of society depends not only on those assumptions but also on their remaining unchallenged.

Our schools have not been exempt from challenges to traditional world views. Since the adoption of compulsory education in the nineteenth century and with ever increasing intensity down to the present, the place and function of our schools in society are issues that have never been off the societal agenda. And when future historians write their accounts of the post–World War II era, they will give a good deal of attention to the dissatisfactions that surfaced about schools, the efforts to transform and improve them, and the malaise and puzzlement that were consequences of the failure of these efforts. It is the malaise and puzzlement that suggest that in regard to schools we are still in the grips of unverbalized assumptions some of which I have presented in these pages. Compared to other changes that are taking place in our world view, changes in our schools have to be regarded as minimal at best. (I hasten to point out that I do not equate change with good and resistance to change with bad; such thoughtless equations seem with some people to take the place of reflective thinking.) That changes in schools have been minimal, on a comparative basis, seems satisfactory to no one. Indeed, there are those who would be delighted with proof that schools have hardly changed because they are convinced that schools have changed a good deal but for the wrong reasons and in the wrong directions.

Before proceeding to an alternative view to our present conception of schools, I shall review some of the changes in world view that have taken place in our society over past decades. This focus puts us in a better position to comprehend not only why our current conceptions of schools are in need of drastic overhaul but also — and no less important — the directions in which alternative conceptions should take us.

SCHOOLS AS UNINTERESTING PLACES

CHANGES IN WORLD VIEW do not begin with an announcement proclaiming the death of the old and the birth of the new, nor are they brought about by predictions that this discovery or that technological innovation will transform our lives. Changes in world view are not willed. Most of the time we are unaware that we have a world view, and when we are forced to recognize that we have one, the realization comes as a surprise because we sense that we are possessed far more by it than we possess it as a way of explaining the world: what the world is, why it is what it is, how it works, how it changes, etc. Some people deny that they have a world view, arguing, "Who am I to have an explanation for what and why the world is what it is?" Such a denial, of course, betrays the presence of a world view in which the individual sees himself or herself as a particle in a social cloud chamber, buffeted by forces neither understandable nor controllable. The process by which we become socialized inevitably provides us with our world view. It is a process intended to create continuity between generations and a sense of community within each generation. The more effective the process, the less occasion there is to be reminded that indeed we do have a world view.

There are three types of occasions that make us aware that we have a world view. The first is when as a member of a group (ethnic, national, racial, religious, cultural) we come into contact with outsiders who obviously and incomprehensibly experience and explain the world in a fashion different from ours. The second is when two generations become aware that they no longer share a certain set of expectations and explanations; i.e., although to an outsider these generations appear to be quite alike, their members perceive an important difference in outlook. The third way we become aware that we have a world view is when we read intellectual or cultural history and realize that past eras and societies experienced and explained the world in ways strangely different from ours. Common to all these occasions, without which similarity they would have no significance for this discussion, is the shock experienced when we recognize that we have a world view about which we did not have to think, that our world view is one of many, and that it is fated to be supplanted over time by a different world view. The shock of recognition is not, of course, accompanied by glee if only because the dynamics of these occasions compel us actively to articulate that which we had previously passively harbored.

To illustrate what I mean by the shock of recognition, I ask my students: is there an assumption, almost always unverbalized, that we accept and without which the structure and substance of what we do today or did yesterday make no sense? On every occasion on which I have posed this question, no student has ever mentioned the assumption that we will be alive tomorrow. Once this answer is articulated, one can literally see a shock of recognition—the realization that how we experience our world is governed by assumptions of which we are not aware; it also becomes clear that any world view is but one of many.

Those of us in midlife or beyond find ourselves saying, certainly we are told in countless ways in the media, that younger people have an outlook different from ours. The explanations are many and complex. Some people maintain that generational differences and conflicts have always been a feature of human society and what is distinctive about the post–World War II era are the dimensions and pace of these generational differences. That is undoubtedly the case, but it is an argument that both concedes that world views do change, in part at least, and avoids coming to grips with what those changes might be and how we might take them into account. There is, of course, a very good reason for this avoidance: trying to fathom a complex present (and the word "complex" is a vast understatement) should strike any reasonable person as an awesome task. Besides, anyone attempting this task has his or her own world view, which at best can be transcended only partially. In approaching this task I do so with a very restricted focus: what features of the world view absorbed by children perhaps represent a change in stance in regard to schooling? Put another way, have changes occurred that not only help explain why schools have become as problematic as they are as institutions but also suggest the direction in which their transformation might go?

We have to remind ourselves that only recently has Western society come to think that young children have very active minds—as question asking, question answering, and mastery seeking suggest. The phrase "to accept as factual" has to be qualified because, as we shall see later, to accept something as factual does not mean that one takes it seriously in action. But in contrast to a century or so ago a remarkable change in world view about the psychological content, structure, and processes of very young children has occurred. And that remarkable change brought in its wake equally remarkable changes in child rearing, educational theories and institutions, and attitudes toward individuals, society, and the future. Schooling—and increasingly that has meant more and more schooling—became both an end in itself and a vehicle through which rising expectations could be realized. Schooling became a right and a necessity as much to meet the needs of society as to accord opportunities for individual talent and expectations. Any discrepancies between rhetoric and reality nevertheless served as goads to reform and not as disconfirmations of our views about children. Basically, the change was very optimistic about schooling and capabilities. It was also a long view, an onward and upward view that had no end point.

From the standpoint of understanding contemporary society, especially our educational institutions, World War II is the obvious benchmark, less because it transformed the world and more because the war unleashed certain pre-World War II tendencies. In regard to education, the immediate momentous consequence of World War II was the passage of the GI Bill of Rights. In simplified terms, a grateful society enthusiastically agreed to underwrite the education of millions of veterans for many of whom (because of economic, cultural, or racial reasons) increased schooling had been and would have been impossible. World War II had been preceded by the Great Depression, and for a large number of veterans the obtaining of a higher education, or some specialized education following high school, was a treasured fantasy that foundered on socioeconomic realities. They were never in doubt that the more education the better, but they were no less in doubt that reality showed no signs of accommodating to an ideal in which they and the larger society believed. The GI Bill of Rights changed all that for millions of veterans. The disjunction between rhetoric and reality would be discernibly reduced.

It is a commentary, in the form of an indictment, that American social science has never focused on the consequences, psychological and social, of the GI bill. I do not say this because of what that legislation meant and did for (and to) higher education. I say it because of the fantastic reinforcement that this legislation provided to several aspects of our world view. First, schooling was an absolute necessity to a long and productive life. Second, schooling was the vehicle through which needed societal (indeed world) transformations would occur; i.e., the new world that needed to be built to prevent new worldwide calamities required a new kind of citizen. Third, the Scientific Age, ushered in by the scientific and technological advances that were a direct outgrowth of the war, required drastic changes in our schools. Fourth, the right to dream about, and to expect to understand and partake in, the new world was not to be restricted to an elite group. What I am suggesting here is that the significance of the GI bill lay not only in the meanings it had for adult veterans but also in what the act meant for the views they would hold in regard to their children, i.e., for the coming population explosion, which was as predictable as the later decline in birth rate. What a world war had made possible for many veterans became their goal for a peaceful world. Elsewhere I have discussed the post–World War II era as the Age of Psychology or the Age of Mental Health and near the center of that heightened self-awareness was a concern about how to rear children so that they would not experience the emotional problems that plagued their elders (Sarason, 1977). In countless ways and through different media, children could not avoid absorbing the belief that schooling was the royal road to success. And not only was schooling an absolute necessity to insure the future good life but also the better one did in school the better one's chances to give substance to dreams. One might well characterize this emphasis as one of great expectations.

It was not only parents who had great expectations for their children but it was the children themselves who were taught to have great expectations. Coming as so many parents did from backgrounds in which great expectations had little foundation in reality, they were bent on insuring that their children would have great expectations that had a better chance of being realized. However, parents were caught on the horns of a dilemma: how to inculcate expectations without interfering with "healthy" development. Benjamin Spock became a household name—his book sold in the millions—in part because parents worried that they would unwittingly visit on their children what had been visited on them. It would be wrong to say that parents pampered or spoiled their chidren. This interpretation does not get at what was central to parental concerns: to give the best to children so that the best would come out of them. Parents were aware — and if they were not aware they were told to accept as fact — that the world in which their children would live would be dramatically different from the world the parents knew. No parents wanted their children to be unprepared for the future. It is no wonder that children of the post–World War II era had great expectations, as it is no wonder that the pressures to achieve did not exist in a pure form but rather were associated with anxiety, doubt, or some form of hesitancy. But great expectations did not exist in the abstract.

By the end of the 1940s, television was upon us. Until then, especially for children, radio had been the major instrument through which the larger world had come into the home. Today people have to be reminded that there is no type of program on television that did not have a counterpart on radio. You *heard* the radio and you *created* in your mind pictures to go with the words you heard. There were, of course, the movies, but that was for most people a once-a-week affair (for those who in the Depression years could afford to go). Radio, like the later TV, was constantly available. That radio required audiences to use their imagination — creating a world they could not test by reality — was recognized by many adults in the early days of television, when radio shows and luminaries emerged on the television screen. Frequently, that experience was disastrous because what we saw on television did not fit with what our minds had conjured up; i.e., it was paler and less interesting. Whereas radio had provided no test of the reality of our imaginative concoctions, to children in the post–World War II era the TV screen *was* reality. I am not interested here in making comparative judgments between radio and television, except to emphasize that TV brought the larger world visually to children. That point is obvious enough, of course, but what is not so obvious is the range of events that children could see with an ease theretofore impossible. Whatever was on television children wanted to see and frequently what they saw was intended for their parents' eyes and not theirs. Children could literally see what was going on in the world via news programs, special educational programs, etc. That they watched cartoons and children's programs goes without saying, but far more was available to them. I well remember what began to appear on television shortly after the 1954 desegregation decision: the scenes of physical violence and racial hatred following the 1954 desegregation decision. And, let us not forget, that earlier the Korean War and atomic explosions had been brought into the home. How and why one should build bomb shelters were questions frequently discussed on TV programs in those years.

If I remember these things, it is because in a fleeting and superficial way I wondered what children were absorbing not only from what they saw on the screen but also from their parents' discussions of these events. I bring these matters up to make the point that children were asking and answering for themselves questions about the world and their place in it. Their curiosity was stimulated and once that happens the internal dynamics take on a life of their own. But grisly scenes of violence, hatred, and destruction were only a part of what was available to children on the screen. They also saw slices of life and the world with little or no dysphoric content that piqued their curiosity. And that is the point: however passive the stance of the watcher-listener, what was seen on the screen stimulated the questioning-answering process we call "curiosity" about a wide range of phenomena that children had no reason to believe were not real. They saw people and situations, ways of living, faraway places, modes of travel — *they saw possibilities for living, working, and behaving that were both countless and compelling.* Some of these possibilities were associated with anxiety, but more of them were not. *Children became consumers of possibilities and there was much, intended or otherwise, in the messages to blur the line between possibility and reality.* They were "learning," they were being shown and told, that there were many fascinating ways in which one could and should experience the world. The theme and rhetoric of great expectations now had a force undreamed of before. And that theme, as I shall emphasize later, had both positive and negative affective components. Compared to this world of possibilities, the school was a world of the irrelevant, the mundane—a desertlike way station on the route to the good life.

We are used to hearing that we are a mobile society, a tendency that was accelerated by World War II and the subsequent emergence of the so-called affluent society. When we say "mobile" we ordinarily refer to the frequent moving of families from one place to another. But, from the standpoint of young children, there was the equally significant postwar increase in travel specifically for the purpose of seeing and experiencing the world. Although this clearly varied with socioeconomic status, it is safe to say that more children saw more of this world than their counterparts in previous generations had done. Many of their parents' curiosity about the world had been stimulated by their war experiences, the age of the automobile was upon us, the transcontinental superhighways were being built, airplanes were flying faster to more places more cheaply, the credit card era had already arrived, families were scattered all over the country (California was on the way to becoming the most populated state), the travel agent became an important person in an evergrowing industry, and the mass media (for children it was TV) were intent on our becoming consumers of the travel experience. To encapsulate the message children were absorbing, I can do no better than the motto of our family's travel agent: "See the world before you leave it."

For children in the post–World War II era this *was* a world of endless possibilities, a view that was reinforced by the parental belief that travel for children was both educational and recreational. Two parental tendencies were frequently operative: the desire for their children to have a variety of experiences that had been denied the parents and the belief that the more of this world of possibilities their children saw and experienced, the better off they would be in the future. If parents tended to underestimate the strength and scope of their children's curiosity, they did not underestimate their obligation to stimulate and buttress that curiosity. To expect and to experience a great deal—this message bombarded children. The world of the school and the world of possibilities were in different experiential orbits. As a high school teacher once said to me in describing the difficulty he had in getting students to be interested in what he was teaching (history): "How can you keep them down on the farm once they have seen Paree?" The glitter, glamor, and excitement that Paris represented to many Americans (World War I veterans included) after the first world war were associated with the entire globe by the generations born in the post–World War II era.

In the late 1950s one began to hear, from parents and others, that children growing up in the post–World War II period were the smartest generation ever. What was being conveyed in this judgment were several things. First, they were and would be the best educated generations the world had ever seen. Second, they knew more about their world than their parents had known about theirs. Third, they had or would have skill and understanding related to science and technology that were beyond the parental ken. Fourth, such skill and understanding were assoicated with a moral outlook that was the basis for optimism about the future. Let us leave aside the error of confusing education with wisdom, although it is important to note that this confusion made many parents either unable or unwilling to play the traditional, directive parental role. They were caught on the horns of a dilemma: the world they knew was and should be superseded; the new world was that of their children. Should they not avoid perpetuating the old in the new? Inevitably, the answer on the level of action was yes and no.

The significance of this parental view was, first, the emphasis that it placed on schooling or, more correctly, on *increased* schooling. Education was salvation for the individual, the society, and the world. What was communicated to children was that there were many things one could be in life but a prerequisite for any of them was schooling—and a lot of it. The other significance of this parental view, quite clear in the ever growing middle classes, was the obligation it placed on parents to provide opportunities outside school to supplement and bulwark what children were learning in school. All of this was oriented to a future point at which the rites of passage would cease and the good life would be experienced. Implicit, and some parents made it explicit, in the message was that schooling, however uninteresting and ritualistic, had to be completed if the promised future pleasures were to be had. Have great expectations; the possibilities in the future are many; and if schooling is long and unstimulating, that is the price you pay to have a lively future. It was a message of evangelism and patience. Parents wanted schooling to be interesting and challenging but, generally speaking, they knew it was not. As I said previously, the movement to make schooling interesting became big business in the post-World War II era. It was an industry that *everyone* wanted to succeed.

I have made much of schools as uninteresting places. It is appropriate, therefore, that I elaborate on this point by describing briefly a relevant study, the latest of only a dozen or so over the course of this century (Susskind, 1969, 1979). From both a theoretical and a practical standpoint—by which I mean theories of child development and intellectual growth, educational and learning theory, and techniques of teaching—the importance of question asking has always been emphasized. It is surprising, therefore, that very few studies have focused on this type of behavior. Susskind did a comprehensive review of the literature. He expressed surprise that a type of behavior considered by everyone to be of great importance had hardly been investigated. However, he pointed out that whatever their level of sophistication, published reports described a remarkably similar state of affairs. Before I summarize the findings, readers may wish to tackle Susskind's (1969) problem:

> Before exploring the research literature we suggest that the reader attempt to estimate the rates of two classroom behav-

iors. Imagine yourself in a fifth grade, social studies classroom in a predominantly white, middle-class school. During a half-hour lesson, in which the teacher and the class talk to each other (there is no silent work), how many questions are asked (a) by the teacher, (b) by the students? How do the two rates correlate? (P. 38)

The first two questions are deceptively simple because, as Susskind made clear, there are different types of questions and there are problems as to how questions (and which questions) are to be counted. For example, if the teacher asks the same question of five children, should it be counted once or five times? Susskind developed a comprehensive set of workable categories, and the interested reader is referred to his work. I will now summarize the answers to the above questions in light of existing studies, including Susskind's research:

1. The rate of teacher questions per half hour ranged from 45 to 150.
2. Educators, as well as other groups, vastly underestimated the rate of teacher questions; estimates ranged from 12 to 20 per half hour.
3. From 67 to 95 percent of all teacher questions required straight recall from students.
4. Children asked fewer than 2 questions per half hour.
5. The greater the tendency for a teacher to ask straight recall questions, the fewer the questions initiated by children.
6. The more a teacher asked personally relevant questions, the higher the rate of questioning on the part of children.
7. The rate of questions by children did not seem to vary with either IQ or social class.

If these findings help us to understand why schools are uninteresting places, they also underline the contrast between what students experience in the world of schooling and that to which they are exposed on the outside. Let us now return to what students in the post-World War II period encountered outside their schools.

The process by which one is socialized does not fully explain how one's world view is formed, especially since part of that world view is not the consequence of conscious thought. Indeed, one could argue that world views cannot be pierced except retrospectively, i.e., by looking back at sequences and concatenations of events and contexts and inferring the silent axioms without which the activities of broad groups of people are inexplicable. As any historian or anthropologist could tell us, it is no easy task to understand a society, particularly when that society actively embraces the ideas of growth, change, and progress. In this chapter I have restricted myself to factors that influenced the world view of children in the post-World War II period in regard to schooling. It has undoubtedly become apparent to the reader that such a restriction may meet the needs of modest ambition but does violence to the coherence of world views by leading one to ignore or gloss over features of the society that may seem distant to issues of schooling but are nevertheless crucial in shaping a world view in its relation to schooling. Thus, the two decades after World War II witnessed four major happenings that inevitably affected the question asking-question answering dynamics of children. I do not feel compelled to pursue the point that children are aware, in ways appropriate to their development, far more than adults realize. More correctly, even though many adults know that children are absorbing more than they can or do put into words, or their direct questions would suggest, their observations and attempts to understand what children are absorbing and thinking about are incomplete. In any event, the four major happenings were racial conflict and violence, women's liberation, the Kinsey report, and the assassination of President Kennedy. There are those who have told us that the fifteen or so years after the end of World War II were relatively quiet years, a view wrapped up in the phrase "silent fifties." These years were far from silent or somnolent and if in comparison to most of the sixties the preceding years lacked sizzle and upheaval, that is no warrant for characterizing those years as some do, especially in regard to what children were hearing and seeing, i.e., the "messages" they were interpreting in their own ways.

It is hard to exaggerate what took place immediately before and after publication of the Kinsey report on male sexual behavior. If that book had contained positive proof that the world would end in a year, it could not have gotten much more play in the media. Far more than Benjamin Spock, Alfred Kinsey became a household name. The report was discussed, criticized, reviled, and applauded; i.e., it had all the ingredients that made adult indifference impossible. In this long scientific, religious, moral, and psychological drama, everybody was both actor and audience. (And, let us not forget, one of the scenes in the drama concerned what adults reported about their heterosexual and homosexual memories, inclinations, and behavior.) To assume that children were spending these days ignorant of, or indifferent to, what was occupying the attention of the adults around them, as if they were living on another planet, is to do violence to what we have learned about child development. (Clinicians tell us that denial is a mechanism of ego defense characteristic of childhood; I have long regarded that assertion as a vast misperception of the role of that mechanism in adults, especially in regard to their actual interactions with children.)

My purpose here is not to draw conclusions about what the furor over the Kinsey report signified for the emerging world view of children but to suggest commonalities between that drama and the civil rights and women's liberation movements. Unlike the Kinsey drama, which was time-limited, these two movements were sustained, gaining momentum and attention, albeit with less Madison Avenue fanfare. What did the Kinsey report and the two movements have in common that would in some way influence the world view of children? One theme was that this society assigned and confined people to narrow roles;

i.e., it denied a universe of possibilities that people could experience. Being black or white, male or female were not fair bases for restricting what people could be or experience. There were several parts to this theme: there was a universe of alternatives; people should not be prevented from experiencing those alternatives; and people should assert their right to pursue these alternatives. A related theme was that the major institutions of this society, not excluding the family and the schools, were obstacles to realizing this world of possibilities.

Implicit in these themes was one I discussed earlier: great expectations. If ours had become a world of great possibilities, one had the right, if not the obligation, to expect much. And a lot of individuals and groups were acting in accord with these interrelated themes. They saw and proclaimed a new world, one in conflict with the old, one that had to overcome the other. These were not themes of permissiveness or indulgence or hedonism but themes of redefinition. As has been pointed out elsewhere, the post–World War II era can be described (within and among nations) as one in which people were either encouraged or felt the need to redefine themselves in ways different from those that society had previously used in regard to them (Sarason, 1977; Sarason & Lorentz, 1979).

I do not pretend to understand the processes by which what was in the societal atmosphere was absorbed by children growing up in the decades after World War II. That they were aware of, and sensitive to, these happenings I cannot doubt. That the turbulent 1960s did not spring like Athena from the head of Zeus should be obvious. With varying degrees of sensitivity and understanding, children of those decades knew what was going on. Our problem is to identify the silent axioms that undergirded their emerging world view. The word "axioms" may give too great an impression of structure or organization. In any event, I suggest that the basis of their emerging world view went something like this: this is an endlessly fascinating world of possibilities; I would like to experience as much of it as possible and I should experience as much of it as possible; however, the world is not set up to accommodate my expectations about these possibilities, so something is wrong somewhere. Like so much that is unconscious in us, this underlying view received affirmation and negation side by side. And that affirmation and negation mirrored the realities of daily life. If, on the level of rhetoric, schooling was to support the affirmative part of the world view, on the level of practice or daily experience, it strengthened the negative part.

I have not discussed one of the four major happenings in the two decades after World War II: the assassination of President Kennedy. That omission was deliberate because that event has to be seen in relation to a phenomenon that occurred at the end of World War II and brought in its wake something new in our thinking: atomic energy and the possibilities it implied for the continuation of human life, i.e., for the ending of human life on earth. To someone of or near my generation, our world view was based on the unformulated but bedrock assumption that civilized man had an endless future on this planet. Depending on one's temperament or point of view, that future may have been rosy or gloomy or somewhere in between, but that there was a future was never in doubt. To children born during the two decades after World War II, doubt about the future became part of their world view. I became aware of this when, in the presence of our seven-year-old daughter, my wife and I were discussing moving from the house in which we lived. At some point in the conversation my daughter said, "Why don't we move to Ireland?" "Why," we asked, "should we move to Ireland?" Her answer was: "My teacher said that when they start to drop atomic bombs, it is unlikely they will drop any on Ireland." We laughed as parents are wont to do in response to their children's view of the world, but over the years I could not get it out of my mind because there was a part of me that said that what her remarks reflected was enormously important. Indeed, several years afterward, in connection with some research I was contemplating, I asked teenagers about their memories of those earlier days. I related what our daughter had said and then asked what they remembered. I was struck by two things in their replies. First, their replies were given immediately. Second, these young people confirmed what my daughter had said, reporting responses ranging from anxiety because their family did not have a bomb shelter to paralyzing nightmares.

A second anecdote. I was supervising the senior thesis of a Yale undergraduate woman. Her thesis concerned the views of the future held by female undergraduates (sophomores to seniors). The student wrote a first draft, which I read several days before the Three Mile Island disaster. When the student came in, two days after that event, to go over her draft, she related how panicky and anxious the students in her residential college were about the immediate and long-term consequences of that event for health and life. "That is all they are talking about," she said. This student saw a discrepancy between what interviewees for her thesis had told her about their view of the future and the views they expressed after Three Mile Island, and she added a section to her thesis on that contrast.

Countless people have commented on the significance of the possibility of atomic destruction (and the Kennedy assassination) for the generations I am discussing. Briefly, young people have incorporated into their world view a recognition of the fragility of life in a somewhat absurd, self-defeating, uncontrollable world. Yes, it is a world of endless possibilities: positive and fascinating, on the one hand, and negative and nightmarish, on the other. If the paradise and Armageddon of traditional religion have no meaning for many of them, the secular version of "rise and fall" does.

There was a more subtle consequence I would like to emphasize because of what it has meant for the experience of schooling, a consequence not well formulated in the emerging postwar world view. Put into words it would go like this: it doesn't make sense to think and plan for a long-term future since there may be no future. Alternatively: why should I deny myself the pleasures of the present for future pleasures that may be denied me anyway? This leads to the conclusion: if I accommodate to the pressures to conform and I play the game of waiting, I am pleasing others at my expense. What I am suggesting is that the emerging world view contained, as never before, a foreshortened view of the future that was the polar opposite of the traditional long view. Both views were present, the old and the new, but now at an unprecedented level of tension and contradiction.

The concept of world view refers to a transactional process by which one shapes and is shaped by experiences that define reality and the nature of the future. The products of that transactional process—a process experienced both actively and passively—are tendencies that vary widely in terms of how they are represented in awareness. The degree of variation is determined largely by the thrust and strength of what one perceives to be happening in one's smaller and larger society. The world view does not wait to be called into play; rather, it is a congeries of tendencies that allows us to assimilate experience in a socially predictable and acceptable fashion until events "out there" intrude to upset the relationships that comprise the core of that world view.

What bearing does the foregoing have for the experience of schooling? Why did schools become more problematic than ever before as places that would be interesting, stimulating, and productive in children of the sense of exploration, mastery, and differentiation? Schools have always been uninteresting places. There is nothing new about that, just as there is nothing new in the fact that life in school bears little resemblance to life outside it. What was different about the post-World War II period was initially the unprecedented effort both to bulwark and to improve the schools, then the recognition that this effort was misfiring, and today the large number of people who are indifferent to the fate of the schools. It is beyond the scope of this book to discuss all the factors that have contributed to this state of affairs. What is relevant to my purpose is to indicate the role played by the emerging world view of postwar children. In several interrelated respects, that view differed markedly from that of earlier generations:

1. Before school and during the school years, more children than ever before literally saw more of the world; i.e., their curiosity about the world was constantly being stimulated. It would be more correct to say that more children from more diverse strata saw more of the world than did the parental generations.

2. The world children saw and heard about seemed to contain endless possibilities that were intriguing, satisfying, and pleasurable. If theirs was a world of possibilities, children wanted to master and possess that world in some way.

3. Children learned to expect that this world of possibilities could become reality for them. Far from conflicting with their view of the world of possibilities, their expectations made that world more attractive. Dreams could become realities. The world was set up to make that possible.

4. For expectations to be realized, one had to go through rites of passage the major purpose of which was not only to acquire skills as means to long-term ends but also to permit exploration of, and increased knowledge about, the world of possibilities. Schools were the place in which the world of possibilities became connected with the need to explore, master, and know. Schools were where you began to *act on* the world.

In a single sentence, children of the post–World War II decades came to school prepared to be active and stimulated in relation to a world of fascinating possibilities, not to a world of schooling that was *obviously* unconnected to a world they saw and heard about elsewhere, not to a setting in which passivity kept the need for exploration and mastery contained within the bounds of fantasy. I am reminded here of what someone said following a visit to the Soviet Union a few years after the Bolshevik revolution: "I have seen the future and it works." This individual, like so many others at that time, wanted dearly to believe that his hopes and expectations about the reformation of man in society in an unseemly world would be realized in the Soviet experiment. Analogously, the generations of children I am talking about came to school having been told and convinced that their years in school would work to fulfill their expectations. They learned, however, that the future was not turning out as planned. Just as revolutions take place *after* a period of rising expectations, the turmoil of the 1960s has to be seen in terms of the expectations inculcated in children of the post-World War II era. Nuclear catastrophe and the Vietnam War — both threatening young people's expectations for a long-term future and vitiating the motivation to conform to a disillusioning present in order to win later satisfaction — were, among other things, a threat to their world view.

It would be an instance of misplaced concreteness to conclude that schools have gotten worse. Such a conclusion may serve the need to blame, but it is an obstacle to recognizing that the plight of schools today represents an extreme exacerbation of a long-standing disjunction between pupils' need to explore, master, and experience, on the one hand, and the impossibility of meeting those needs in the physically and psychologically isolated school, on the other. The assumption that schools as we know them can meet those needs has been so much a part of our world view — so bedrock an assumption that we literally cannot question it and have blank minds when we are forced to consider alternatives — that it has directed us to efforts, that however understandable, were and are doomed to failure. Public versus private school, big versus small school, old versus new curriculum, community versus professional control of schools, back to basics versus indulgent frills, law and order versus misguided permissiveness — common between and among all these polarities is the assumption that schools can be places in which students can experience the sense of being worthwhile, i.e., that there is truly *worth* to what they are learning and experiencing, the sense that one's curiosity about one's world is affirmed and supported. Please note that nothing in what I have said suggests that happiness is or should be a goal of schooling. The curiosity of children about the world is to them a serious matter the measure of which is the degree to which what they are asked to learn and experience makes sense in terms of their world view. As never before, the generations born in the post–World War II era have been telling us that schooling makes far less sense than their elders are prepared to recognize, let alone comprehend. What young people do not understand is that their elders are prisoners of a world view in which schools are places — very discrete, locatable, bounded places — in which productive learning of subject matter and skills could occur. That that element in their world view was wrong (self-defeating) was and has remained unquestioned.

Let me illustrate this point by analogy. Imagine the following situation:

> It is the period, say, between 1930 and 1945. You are a mental health professional. In each of those years you attend every convention of every association devoted to the study and care of mentally ill or mentally retarded individuals. During that period you work both inside and outside institutions that care for these individuals. What are some of the obvious themes that would run through all these experiences? What would be some of the concerns shared by you and your colleagues?

Before answering these questions, you should recognize that mental health professionals are, on average, a serious, highly motivated, socially concerned group adhering to the highest ethical standards of the day. They are not incompetents. They want to serve and protect the afflicted individual and society. And that brings us to the first theme and concern on your list: society has been niggardly both in supporting existing institutions and in building more facilities for those who need them. A second theme, and a very perturbing one to mental health professionals, is that too many of these institutions contain morally scandalous conditions that can be remedied and ultimately eliminated only by introducing new ideas and programs. Of course, there are good institutions and there is no reason why all institutions cannot emulate them: the problem is to get more public funds and better people to implement the latest advances in theory and practice. *But behind all these themes and concerns is the assumption that institutions need to exist, that the people in them need to be there, and that there is no alternative to institutional care. That these institutions exist is testimony that they should exist.* From the vantage point of to-day, we know that this assumption is largely invalid. Within half of a century changes in the larger society were mirrored in a changed world view about where and how these afflicted individuals should be treated. Because these geographically and socially isolated institutions existed was no longer considered evidence that they should exist. This dramatic change did not come about easily and it is far from being taken seriously as it should be in practice. In fact, Kiesler (1983) recently presented compelling data relevant in two respects: the research evidence is unambiguous in demonstrating that alternatives to traditional institutional programs are more beneficial as judged by any criterion; yet these institutions continue to exist and in fact are showing a fantastic increase in readmissions. In short, world views do not change quickly and, when they start to change, actions reflecting the new world view encounter mammoth obstacles rooted in the old.

In the post–World War II era every major institution in our society has been subject to criticism and pressure to change. If schools and their personnel feel beleaguered and fight for their survival, this reaction is natural. But as long as school personnel and their critics continue to accept the assumption that there are no alternatives to schools as we know them—that whatever changes are needed can and should take place inside school buildings—they invite disillusionment and disappointment. As long as they do not recognize and confront the implications of the changing world view of post–World War II generations; as long as they ignore the centrality in that world view of learning by acting in and on the world; as long as they underestimate and thus fail to assuage the hunger for experience; and as long as subject matter is viewed as something that can be learned only in a classroom, we shall continue to witness a drama the title of which is "The More Things Change, the More They Remain the Same."

6

WORK, LABOR, AND SUBJECT MATTER

THE HELIUM AND OXYGEN ATOMS have different structures but that does not mean that in order to understand the differences you need a separate theory for each element. We proceed on the assumption that the differences are explainable in terms of principles applicable to both. Adults and children are also different from each other but that does not mean that we need two psychologies: one for us and one for them. The differences are both obvious and momentous — they *are* differences that make a difference — but so are the principles by which we view and explain their similarities. This is the point I was making when I described my discussions with teachers about the characteristics of interesting experiences. It is beyond the purposes of this book to spell out and contrast conceptions or theories the aim of which is to explain the differences in substance and structure we observe in human behavior. Restricted as my focus is to schooling and concerned as I am that the thrust of my argument not be lost in a sea of competing theories and data, I shall follow the advice of someone who, in another connection, said, "Be relentlessly concrete."* What follows is a passage from *Physical Knowledge in Preschool Education: Implications of Piaget's Theory* (Kamii & DeVries, 1978):

> What we mean by "physical-knowledge activities" can be best explained by contrasting these with activities typically found in "science education." For illustrative purposes we shall present two different ways of teaching an activity on crystals. The first, quoted from a text on preschool education, is an example of the "science education" approach:*
>
> Theme: Crystals
> Behavioral objective: At the end of the experience, the child will be able to
>
> 1. Pick out crystals when shown a variety of things.
> 2. Define what a crystal is.
> 3. Discuss the steps in making crystals at school.
>
> Learning activities:
>
> The teacher will show the children different crystals and rocks. She will explain what a crystal is and what things are crystals (sand, sugar, salt, etc.). Then she will show some crystals she made previously. The children are given materials . . . so they can make crystals to take home. A magnifying glass is used so the children can examine the crystals.
>
> Method 1: Mix ½ cup each of salt, bluing, water, and 1 [tablespoon] ammonia. Pour over crumpled paper towels. In 1 hour crystals begin to form. They reach a peak in about 4 hours and last for a couple of days. . . .
>
> *We are aware of the existence of such innovative programs . . . which warn against the verbalism of traditional science education. We are also aware of the fact that, in reality, most preschool teachers do not teach in such didactic ways. We nevertheless refer to the "science education" approach throughout this book as if it were one uniformly didactic approach for the following rea-

*This was said in a letter that Robert Heilbronner wrote to a friend of mine who had sent him a manuscript he had written. The psychological wisdom implied in that advice is often ignored. Both writers and teachers

sons: Innovators in science education have generally not considered pre-school education, and their work begins at the kindergarten level. Authors of early-education texts, on the other hand, have not been influenced by these recent ideas, and their chapters on science education are invariably filled with verbalistic instruction and "scientific" content. When we refer to the "science education" approach in this book, we thus have in mind this characteristic of published texts in early education.

Maureen Ellis, one of our teacher colleagues, read the above lesson, modified it into a physical-knowledge activity, and wrote the following account of her teaching with crystals:

While looking through an early-education text, I found the "recipe" for making crystals. I decided to try it, but not as a science project because I had no idea why crystals formed. It was as much magic to me as to the kids; so we used it like a cooking activity. I told them that we didn't know why it happened, but they got the idea that when some things mix together, sometimes something extraordinary happens. The activity was such a success that for days individual children were showing others how to make crystals, and some made their "own" to take home.

This experiment inspired other experiments and a whole atmosphere of experimentation. One boy, during cleanup, decided to pour the grease from the popcorn pan into a cup with water and food coloring. He put it on the windowsill until the next day. He was sure "something" would happen and was surprised when nothing much did. Another child said she knew an experiment with salt, soap, and pepper (which she had seen on television). She demonstrated for those who were interested. A third child was inspired by the soap experiment to fill a cup with water and put a bar of soap in. She was astonished by the change in water level and then tested other things in the water — a pair of scissors, chalk, crayon, and her hand to see the change in water level.

---

fail to provide the kind of descriptive detail that permits assimilation and serves as a basis for action, symbolic or overt. I am in no way derogating theorizing but rather emphasizing the importance of the concrete as a goad to curiosity and a stimulus to symbolic or overt action in regard to the concrete; i.e., it continues and reinforces one process with two aspects to which we give the labels "assimilation" and "accommodation." As the reader will see from the passage that follows, this point is central to Piaget's work, as it is to that of John Dewey. To my knowledge, no one has seriously noted and discussed the similarities in the formulations of Piaget and Dewey, a comparison that would be as fascinating as it is overdue.

The next day, one child brought a cup filled with beans, blue water, styrofoam packing materials, and a Q-Tip. "This is my experiment. Cook it," he said. So I asked what he thought would happen to each of the things in the cup. He made a few predictions, and I told him we could cook it the next day. (I wanted to experiment first to see if there might be anything dangerous involved.) At group time, he told everyone about his experiment, and the group made predictions which I wrote on the blackboard. Among these were: "The whole thing will get hot," "The water will change color," "The beans will get cooked, and you can eat them," and "The beans will grow." When I asked, "Will anything melt?" the children predicted that the styrofoam would not melt, but that the Q-Tip would. The next day, the child did his cooking experiment, and wrote down the results with my help. Many of his predictions were found to be true, but there were some surprises: It smelled terrible, the Q-Tip did not melt, and the whole thing bubbled.

In the "science education" approach above, the teacher's objective is for the children to learn about crystals. More specifically, the objectives are to get children to become able to recognize and define crystals, and to describe how they can be made. In this content-centered approach, children listen to explanations, look at what the teacher shows, and do what he or she planned.

In the "physical-knowledge" approach, by contrast, the teacher's objective is for the children to pursue the problems and questions they come up with. The purpose of making crystals is thus not to teach about crystals per se, but to stimulate various ideas within a total atmosphere of experimentation. In the situation reported above, the making of crystals inspired four children in different ways—to make "something" with grease from the popcorn pan, to make specks of pepper "swim" in water, to watch what happens to the water level when various objects are dropped into a container, and to cook a variety of objects. It also stimulated other children to think about many possible outcomes, and encourage decentering through exchange of ideas about what might happen. The physical-knowledge approach, thus, emphasizes children's initiative, their actions on objects, and their observation of the feedback from objects.

All babies and young children are naturally interested in examining objects, acting on them, and observing the objects' reactions. Our aim in physical-knowledge activities is to use this spontaneous interest by encouraging children to structure their knowledge in ways that are natural extensions of the knowledge they already have. Thus, learning in the physical-knowledge approach is always rooted in the child's natural development. As we saw in the lesson on crystals, "science education" basically unloads adult-organized content on children.

The child's action on objects and his observation of the object's reaction are both important in all activities involving physical knowledge. However, we see two kinds of activities based on the relative importance of action and observation. In the first type, activities involving the movement of objects (or mechanics), the role of the child's action is primary and that of observation is secondary. Aiming a ball down an incline toward a container is an example of this kind of activity. The role of action is primary here because there is a direct and immediately observable correspondence between where the child positions the ball and where it rolls down. If he varies his action by moving the ball six inches to the right, the ball rolls down about six inches to the right of the previous fall line, parallel to it.

The second kind of activity involves the changes in objects. Making crystals is an example of this kind of activity. In activities involving the movement of objects, the objects only move—they do not change. In making crystals, however, the object itself changes. The role of observation thus becomes primary and that of the child's action becomes secondary. The role of action is secondary because the reaction of the object is neither direct nor immediate; that is, the outcome is due not to the child's action as such, but to the properties of the objects. Action is secondary also because, for example, mixing grease, water, and food color involves basically the same action as mixing salt, bluing, water, and ammonia. Yet the reaction of the second set of substances is very different, which leads to the conclusion that only under certain circumstances do crystals begin to form. Of primary importance, therefore, is the role of observation—the structuring of what is observable. (Pp. 1-3)

Several things are noteworthy in this excerpt. The first is the rejection of the practice of according to the pupil the passive role of listener and observer. The second is the recognition that when curiosity is aroused about something, the desire to act on that thing in some way—to change or control it in some way, to be part of it in some way—is also created. The third is that the process of question asking and acting on it has or can have a self-sustaining quality that may take unpredictable but desirable directions in regard to the child's understanding of the nature of his or her world; i.e., it is not, and certainly need not be, a self-limiting process. Fourth, what to an adult may not look like subject matter (e.g., science) is quintessentially that for a child: the experiential building blocks that sustain curiosity and give direction to action literally at the same time that internal thinking becomes more differentiated. Fifth, what we traditionally call "subject matter"—a set of facts and skills interconnected by concepts, all of which have been singled out by adults—attains its intended meaning for the child only through a process that takes account of the child's curiosity, interests, conceptual level, and need to act on the world.

There is another way one can put the differences in conceptualization and approach that Kamii and DeVries illustrated. It is an alternative that adults will readily comprehend because it involves a distinction that not only is central to their lives but also lies at the heart of a major social problem. I refer to the distinction between *labor* and *work*. When we say that a person labors we refer to an activity the end product of which in no way bears the doer's personal stamp. It is an activity so structured, ordinarily so predetermined, that there is no room for the product to reflect something distinctive about its maker. So, when we say someone is a laborer or occupies a certain place on an assembly line, what gets conjured up in our minds is an impersonal relationship between person and product; i.e., the product is independent of its maker. One maker can substitute for another but one would never know by looking at the product. The activity, of course, has meaning for the person but whatever that meaning may be, it is supposed to remain internal and not to affect the product. It is, so to speak, a mindless activity. The individual is active, he or she "acts on," but with the aim of further predetermined actions from which personal meanings are divorced. We know when we labor and why we dislike or abhor it. The concept of work, in contrast, refers to an activity that in some way bears the personal stamp of its performer; the product or consequence has a signature that can be recognized by the maker and others. How clear that signature is, how large the area in which labor and work overlap, is not the issue. To the extent that a person's acting on the world is part of a continuing process in which what is acted on changes, in turn producing changes in the person that alter subsequent actions, we say that the individual is working rather than laboring. A Supreme Court justice said that although he had trouble defining pornography, he knew pornography when he saw it. Similarly, we may not be satisfied with our definitions of work and labor, but we know when we are either laboring or working.

This distinction between work and labor is precisely that between the two approaches to science education that Kamii and DeVries contrasted. In one approach the structure of the activity is so predetermined as to leave little room for active assimilation and accommodation; i.e., it does not capitalize on the child's curiosity and desire to explore and change what is out there, to digest and master a relationship between what is internal and what is external—a relationship that by its nature contains unpredictable features. The other approach is not a learning by doing, as if doing in and of itself has productive consequences. It is an approach, as Dewey and Piaget *continually* noted, in which activity (overt or symbolic) contains, expresses, and alters the relationships between internal schemas and external contexts. This kind of activity goes on willy-nilly, as Piaget amply documented. No one has disputed Piaget on that score. The educational task is to take that activity seriously, to transform the education process so that it maximizes the experience of working and minimizes the experience of laboring. If children say schooling is uninteresting, they are saying in their own way that they know the difference between work and labor. Boredom is one of the hallmarks of laboring.

It is noteworthy that in his preface to Kamii and DeVries's 1978 volume Piaget criticized, as he always has done, the efforts of educators to trasform into standardized texts the "operatory tasks" used by him and his colleagues as the basis for asking questions in "free conversation" with children. However, he noted with approval that Kamii and DeVries

> centered their effort on inventing activities to permit children to act on objects and observe the reactions or transformations of these objects (which is the essence of physical knowledge, where the role of the subject's actions is indispensable for understanding the nature of the phenomena involved). The importance of errors is not neglected, as an error corrected is often more instructive than an immediate success. (P. vii)

The developmental principles on which the demonstrations of Kamii and DeVries with preschoolers were based are applicable at all levels of education and with any subject matter. That these principles are distinguished by their absence in our schools needs no documentation. It is true that here and there one finds that these principles are recognized and an effort is being made to act appropriately on them, but such instances are rare indeed as one moves from elementary to high school. High schools pay unwitting tribute to these principles. On the one hand, they are agonizingly aware of how difficult it is to engender and sustain in students an interest in subject matter (e.g., math, history, or science). On the other, in the past two decades many high schools have initiated programs that provide opportunities *outside school* for students to experience,

explore, and act on some ongoing community effort. I am referring here to the upsurge of what has been called "experiential education," an upsurge (a cyclical phenomenon in American education) that explicitly reflects one fact and one
assumption. The fact is that attempts to harness and direct the
energies and interests of students in the classroom have failed.
That is not to deny that students can be kept in the classroom
and that many will learn something about what others think
they should learn but rather to assert that this is achieved at
very high cost: student boredom and loss of interest in learning
and teacher burnout. The assumption on which experiential
education rests is that students have both a need for and a desire to *work*: to be part of an environment on which they can
act and from which they can assimilate knowledge and acquire
skills that expand the range of their potential actions. Although
the conceptual rationales put forth to justify experiential education never mention Piaget and his developmental findings
and formulations, the assumption underlying experiential education obviously is consistent with what Piaget has given us. I
have to add that if we view what Piaget has given us as a theoretical framework for mental development, then it is grossly un-
justified to say that experiential education is based on an en-
compassing framework.

There is an irony here. To the extent that experiential education achieves its goals, it sharpens the contrast between what
students experience in and outside school, with the classroom
coming out a very poor second. This contrast is further sharpened because the thrust of experiential education very frequently is unrelated to subject matter. That is to say, it is an
add-on to the curriculum or a substitute for traditional courses.
Furthermore, far more often than not, experiential education is
aimed largely at students for whom traditional courses are not
deemed appropriate. At its worst, experiential education has to
be put in the category of busy work, or make-work (the word
"labor" would be more appropriate in these terms), mirroring
what goes on in classrooms. At its best, experiential education

provides a sustained out-of-classroom experience that requires observation, acting on, more observation, more acting on, all of this supervised in a way and to a degree so as to give structure, substance, and direction to the student's experience, knowledge, and outlook; i.e., this effort has all of the characteristics of productive work.

The most successful experiential programs from the standpoint of integrating outside experience with classroom subject matter have focused on the physical or social environment. Projects testing and monitoring water and air quality, providing public agencies and community groups with this information, and analyzing relevant legislation and programs can teach geography, chemistry, mathematics, and social studies—aspects of these subjects arise and are dealt with in the course of a sustained out-of-classroom activity. In a middle school of six hundred children, half the youngsters voluntarily spend several hours of school time each week in some helping relationship with handicapped people in community settings, e.g., senior citizens, mentally retarded individuals, or people with cerebral palsy. Each week these experiences are discussed and analyzed not only from the standpoint of the nature of the helping relationship but also in terms of biology, human development, social organization, and social history. What speaks volumes about what these middle school youngsters do is the fact that the settings in which they *work* have requested more students and more of their time. The principal who started this program was crystal clear about his rationale: children were curious about their community, they wanted to engage in what to them would be valued work, they could be useful, the work experience could be educationally and intellectually justified by traditional criteria, teachers would find their supervisory relationships to these students and the community settings both stimulating and educationally challenging, and the benefits of this program were unachievable in the classroom.

Most of what I have observed or read about "experiential education" I find far from encouraging. The term "experiential education" has become a slogan, a rallying cry, that at the same time that it stands for the recognition of the limitations of classroom learning and of the frustrations they pose for the needs and the curiosities of students tends, in practice at least, to justify experience for the sake of experience, as if experience in and of itself has educational and intellectual value. The impression is also conveyed that if students are permitted to do something they want to do, it will have desirable educational and intellectual consequences. In no way am I suggesting that if someone does something he or she wants to do, the activity will be devoid of value. Nor am I suggesting that if a student participates in a project in which he or she has expressed no interest, the effort inevitably will prove counterproductive (although that is clearly the case with much classroom learning). What I am suggesting is that the term "experiential education" too frequently centers on experience and not on education. Put another way, when what the student experiences is not for the purpose of mastering the knowledge and acquiring the skills we associate with traditional subject matters, then the term "education" loses meaning; i.e., it is a term that refers to everything and, therefore, to nothing. What we call "subject matter" is not an encapsulated body of knowledge and skills that exists for its own sake outside of time, something to be learned because of its intrinsic value. Traditional subject matters reflect our society's longtime, systematic efforts to describe and understand the world in terms of numbers, history, chemistry, physics, literature, social process, etc. At any one time a subject matter is the history of how people tried to understand, to explore, and to act on the world from a particular but everchanging perspective. A subject matter is a record of our transactions with the world. Subject matter never existed, and does not now exist, independent of that kind of transaction. Directly relevant here is Dewey's *Interest and Effort in Education* (1975) a monograph that is rarely cited. From the standpoint of my argument, Dewey's small volume provides one of the most powerful arguments against the school as a site in which interest, effort, and subject matter can coalesce to serve productive thinking and doing. May I note in passing that it is in this 1913 publication that Dewey says: "The school of so-called 'free expression' . . . fails to note that one thing that is urgent for expression in the spontaneous activity of the child is *intellectual* in character. Since this factor is primarily the *educative* one, as far as instruction is concerned, other aspects of activity should be made means to its effective operation."(p.83)

We are all aware of the demise of the classics as subject matter in schools. How do we explain why for more than a century Thomas Bulfinch's *Age of Fable* was such a popular book in and out of schools? Part of the answer has been provided by Cleary (1982) in a dissertation both fascinating and instructive. She demonstrated that already in the first half of the nineteenth century Bulfinch's views of the relationship between interest and subject matter contained the core of Dewey's conceptions. The demise of the classics was in large part the result of ignoring Bulfinch's pedagogical aim and method, and the current signs of its rebirth described by Cleary are the result of taking his aim and method seriously.

Few people would disagree with the assertion that the major purpose of education is to encourage students to explore, understand, adapt to, and even change the world; to accomplish that purpose requires experiencing the world through the medium of different subject matters. For an experience to be educational it cannot be separate from the medium of subject matter, which itself derives from transactions between people and their world, past and present. Subject matter can be written about, aspects of it can be memorized, and certain skills can be learned, but the relationship between these accomplishments and the structure and evolution of subject matter is akin to that between a word and the thing it signifies. There is a difference between talking about subject matter and experiencing it.

You do not learn by doing. You learn by thinking→acting →thinking→acting, etc., in the way so well illustrated by Kamii and DeVries. In and of itself, doing, like experiencing, can be a mindless affair. To glorify experience independent of the direction and structure it gives to, and gets from, transactions is worse than missing the point: it is to devalue subject matter and to shortchange the individual in terms of understanding and coping with the world. If I do not glorify experience, I also do not glorify subject matter when it is presented as independent of the student's world as he or she experiences and knows it.

In the *New York Times* of April 6, 1982, there was an interview with the dean for science in the College of Liberal Arts and Science of the City University of New York. Dean Harry Lustig described the severity of the shortage of math and science teachers: in the previous year, Connecticut had graduated *no one* certified to teach high school science; Minnesota had graduated one person; in Chicago there was only one licensed physics teacher for every two high schools; throughout the country 22 percent of high school mathematics teaching posts were vacant and 26 percent of posts were filled either by noncertified or by temporarily certified teachers. Lustig offered two reasons for this serious shortage. First, anyone with a science or mathematics background can make more money in industry than in teaching. Second:

> If you haven't been motivated, haven't had the foundation for science in junior high school, it may very well be too late. Let's face it, the sciences are hard and we're living in a very soft world. Students are allowed to take electives instead of hard courses. We've had a fantastic decrease in the number of students signing up for the hard sciences. They'd rather take easy subjects and get higher grades.

I sympathize with the dean's concerns but not with his diagnosis. He was seeing the problem from the perspective of the subject matter of science as if that subject existed outside time and history. The fact is that in the past there was both no shortage of science and math teachers (in fact, there was an oversupply) *and* no evidence that the quality of teaching was better or that students found these courses more interesting than they do today. Indeed, the orbiting by Russia of the first sputnik in 1957 catalyzed a national uproar about the outmoded and stultifying math and science curricula to which students were exposed. It may well be that in past decades math and science teachers "knew" their subject matter far better than teachers today but there is no reason to believe that this knowledge made science more interesting for students. During the decade of the fifties I spent a good deal of time in junior high and high schools and one had to be especially dense not to be aware of the plight of science teachers and their students. I take no satisfaction in having predicted that the new math and science curricula that began to be introduced in the late fifties and early sixties would confirm the maxim that the more things change the more they remain the same. That prediction may have been wrong: the situation has not remained the same, it has gotten worse. Here, again, we see the fallacy that knowledge of subject matter—knowledge independent of how the structure and skills of that subject matter arose from transactions between thinking and action, between the reciprocal influences of the internal processes of investigators and external phenomena—can be assimilated in a meaningful way by passive students in a classroom. (Parenthetically, in the interview Lustig expresses the opinion that the teaching of science in private schools is as poor and motivation extinguishing as it is in public schools.)

Let me now present the major reason I find the interview significant. Asked about the possibility of colleges dealing directly with students in secondary schools, Lustig replied:

> We've had pilot programs like this and they have worked very well at City College. In cooperation with the New York Academy of Science we have a summer research program for junior high school students.
>
> They come in very scared. These are all minority kids from the South Bronx and they are on grade level, but they are

not selected for being particularly outstanding in science. We put them into research labs and they really learn something about science. They change, many of them completely—they become confident of themselves in science.

How do we account for these results, which are by no means unusual, as anecdote upon anecdote would attest? The fact that these junior high school students had a sustained experience outside school is not in itself educationally significant. What is significant are two features of the experience: they could observe adults *working* at science and, we can assume, they participated in activities that at their level were in principle similar to those in which their mentors were engaged. That is to say, the thrust and structure of the experience contained the psychological and situational features described by Kamii and DeVries for "physical-knowledge activities." For these junior high school students, science was not an abstraction or a set of principles, laws, and procedures to be learned by rote or in a sociophysical context in which what one does seems to be unconnected to the real world and to be important only in terms of a grade.

Let me state what I am *not* suggesting. I am not suggesting that one should find out what students are interested in and then help them pursue their interests. Of course, when it comes to expressed interests, you do not look a gift horse in the mouth. But I have yet to see an instance in which such an interest was not or could not easily be related to organized bodies of knowledge and skills (subject matters) that represent man's way of comprehending his world. I emphasize subject matter not because I view it as a good in itself, as if it were an intellectual vitamin that had beneficial effects regardless of whatever else one was or was not ingesting. Rather, I think subject matter allows an experience to attain meanings in a wider context of human endeavors. No teacher would deny the validity of the maxim that you teach students, not subject matter, i.e., you use your knowledge of a person to structure experience in which features of the subject matter are naturally contained and exemplified, i.e., the experience is an activity that possesses a concreteness (the "stuff" of experience) that is the basis for comprehending abstractions applicable to what on the surface are very diverse experiences or phenomena.

I have spent years training clinical psychologists, especially in relation to their psychotherapeutic functions. To be a psychotherapist is a very serious matter and those who are responsible for selecting and supervising doctoral students in this field approach their task with a good deal of concern. That concern manifests itself in many ways one of which takes the form of a question: what should a clinical trainee *know* before being permitted to deal with the personal problems of others? I have italicized the word "know" because despite widely differing opinions of what the content of that knowing should be, there is agreement that one should not permit a student to conduct therapy who has insufficient knowledge of subject matter — theories and research on personality, psychopathology, and human development. So, if you are a partisan of the psychoanalytic orientation, you require your students to take seminars in which they read Freud, Jung, Adler, Sullivan, Horney, Hartman, and many others. The curriculum will differ if you favor the Skinnerian, Rogerian, or Perlsian perspectives. It is quite a smorgasbord but the student is required to eat from it, however restricted the diet the particular teacher imposes. The student needs that nourishment in subject matter before experiencing the psychotherapeutic role. But whatever the emphasis of clinical training programs, they apparently consider it both educationally unsound and ethically questionable to permit a student to be in the psychotherapeutic role before attaining some mastery of subject matter. So, like elementary, junior high, and high school students, the clinical students learn subject matter. In earlier decades the clinical student learned a lot of subjects and it was by no means unusual for the doctoral student to see his or her first patient in the third year of a four- or five-year program.

It says a lot about the weight of absorbed tradition that it took me years to become aware of the obvious: despite knowledge of subject matter, when clinical students encountered their first client, knowledge of subject matter was of no help to them. Far from being available and applicable, that knowledge frequently was an interference to observation of, and appropriate response to, what was going on. In many instances their knowledge was awesome in range and organization. They had read widely and deeply, could define the major concepts, and "knew" a great deal about interpersonal dynamics that predictably occur in the helping interaction. However, once in the therapeutic relationship, these students were, generally speaking, inadequate to the task. And by inadequate I mean they felt inadequate — puzzled and overwhelmed by the discrepancy between what they thought they knew and the realities they were experiencing.* With time and close supervision, they would begin to understand how theory and abstractions not grounded in active experience can be at best impractical and at worst dangerous.

Why not put the clinical student into the therapeutic role as soon as he or she enters the program, before or concomitant with the presentation of subject matter? Why not provide an out-of-school experience that would serve as a concrete basis for comprehending in-school subject matter? I resisted that approach for some time on the ground that it was ethically dubious, but I never found this argument persuasive and for three reasons. First, the traditional way also presented me with an ethical problem: how does one justify exposing a client to a therapist with only book knowledge? The answer, of course, is

---

*In fairness, I have to report that long before faculty realized that something was wrong, students complained about the hiatus between what they learned in seminars and exposure to the therapeutic role itself, with the result that they were put in that role earlier but always after taking some formal seminars. Indeed, in the post–World War II era this kind of change began to take place in many areas of professional education. For example, if you examine medical education before and after World War II, you find dramatic changes in the timing of students' exposure to clinical situations.

that experience with clients has to start sometime and no one has come up with a way otherwise to produce a full-blown professional. Aside from inertia, the capacity to rationalize bulwarks the status quo. The second reason I did not find the argument persuasive was that it vastly underestimated (indeed, ignored) the student's past experiences in helping roles other than the psychotherapeutic. Of course, the therapeutic relationship has features ordinarily not found in other helping relationships, but that does not mean they do not have features in common, features the student (and supervisor) can capitalize on in understanding particular interactions and arriving at generalizations. Third, these students were a highly self-selected group; i.e., they had come to graduate school precisely because they had clinical interests and sought a clinical career. If there was anything you could capitalize on, it was their interest and motivation.

I was emboldened to change the accustomed practice in direct response to my experience with public schools. I realized that the separation of subject matter from concrete experience, classroom from the rest of the student's world, was a disservice to students, teachers, and the intellectual merits of subject matter. So, I put students in the therapeutic role very quickly. What happened? Obviously, any conclusions I present are subject to the criticism that I had a vested interest in certain outcomes. The one unassailable fact is that Esther Sarason and I did not give more supervisory time than we had given students before (one supervisory session for each therapeutic hour). The most cautious conclusion is that there was no difference in performance with clients between these students and former students. For students who had no formal exposure to subject matter, this initial experience in the role of therapist was highly instructive on several grounds: their expectations were both challenged and changed, the complexity of the endeavor was impressed on them, and the readings assigned to them could be assimilated into their concrete experience. They now had a tentative foundation for dealing with the mysteries and myths surrounding psychotherapy, with which almost everyone in our society is familiar through the mass media and even some of the professional literature. From the standpoint of the supervisors, it was relieving not to have to deal to a discouraging degree with students who had learned jargon and theories only to have them interfere with the therapist-client situation. This is not to say that what we did was without the problems one encounters with novices, or that we had hit upon a way to smooth the course of complex learning. Nor do I assert that the accustomed way of doing things is devoid of merit. What our experience does permit me to assert is that what we did, far from presenting any special problems, was more stimulating and more productive both for students and for us.

The existence of schools as bounded, isolated entities is the single most effective barrier to wedding subject matter and experience in ways that are sustaining, enlivening, and broadening. The fact that schools exist as they do has the effect of separating rather than integrating subject matter and active experience, of separating the concrete from the abstract, of perpetuating the enormous gulf between received and experienced knowledge. I said earlier that in the post–World War II era a major industry has grown up centering on the following questions. How do we make schools more interesting places? How can we help students overcome boredom in regard to subject matter? How can we get students to see that subject matter can be both interesting and important? The diversity of answers has been enormous, and quite costly, but with very few exceptions we have assumed that the questions could be successfully answered by making changes *within* the school. As I have emphasized, we have failed to recognize the possibility that the school building is a very large part of the problem and that changes in the world view of post–World War II generations have made the traditional conception of school and schooling more problematic than ever before. Indeed, this era has experienced a nostalgic yearning for that Golden Age in which students did what they were supposed to do, learned what they were supposed to learn, and forever enjoyed the fruits of their schooling; that schools have never been interesting places for the bulk of students has been glossed over with the justification that the end justifies the means, even though the ends are vaguely defined (if they are defined at all).

It is far beyond the scope of this book to trace the development of the idea that schools are places where students in classrooms learn subject matters that sometime, somewhere, are applicable to and necessary for adapting to and comprehending the world. It is a history extremely long and complex. One aspect of that history is directly relevant to my argument that the very existence of the school building is inimical to a productive encounter with subject matter. I refer to an intellectual tradition most clearly formulated by Plato twenty-five hundred years ago, a tradition that stamped theory with more value than practice, that in fact derogated practice and exalted ideas and theory. In this scheme, the real world is the world of ideas and their essence, i.e., the truths inevitably obscured by, corrupted by, and distorted in the world of appearances. Plato was being quite consistent when he outlined an educational curriculum for the philosopher-king who would lead and administer a just society, a curriculum that would keep the ruler occupied in the world of ideas until he was almost fifty years of age. What most of us today call the "real world" was precisely the one against which Plato's students needed protection until they had mastered the world of essences. Today's school is a descendant of Plato's; in both, subject matter and daily experience are kept apart. In *The Quest for Certainty* (1960), which I regard as one of the great books of this century, Dewey beautifully and incisively analyzed and exposed the insidious consequences of Plato's devaluation of practice and reverence for theory. That Dewey wrote the book is, of course, not surprising to anyone familiar with his earlier thinking and writings as well as with the fact that Dewey resorted to practice when he created his lab school at the University of Chicago in 1896.

I indicated earlier that one of the major developments in schools in the postwar decades has been recognition of the need to direct students into activities, for the most part outside school, that speak to their interests, require their participation in planning and implementation, and seem justified on educational grounds. Helping the elderly, cleaning up neighborhoods, working with preschool children and the disabled, counseling and tutoring peers, manning health outreach services—these are only a few examples of youth participation programs. The National Commission on Resources for Youth, a nonprofit agency started by Mary Kohler, a former juvenile court judge, has played a pioneering role in creating some of these programs. The commission has also reviewed more than fifteen hundred such projects on the basis of explicit criteria for the degree and quality of students' role as well as for the presence of a seminar the purpose of which is to help the student put experience into some organized conceptual context. Documentation was based on, among other things, an on-site visit. Anyone who has doubts or qualms about the personal and educational value of these activities should consult the files and literature of that agency. Just as the dean I quoted on an earlier page was mightily impressed with what minority junior high school students learned and experienced in a summer research program in a college laboratory, the reader of files of the commission's reports will be impressed. There is no mystery here to be explained because there is no special mystery to understanding the conditions for and the characteristics of interesting, sustaining work *regardless of what age the person is: six, twelve, thirty, or eighty years of age.* My disquiet with these programs, many of which I have personally observed, has nothing to do with their intrinsic value, separating as I do these programs from those that make a fetish of experience as a good in itself, as if soaking up self-initiated experience, one does not run the risk of becoming drowned in it. My disquiet has been on other grounds, the most important of which is that the rationale for these activities has not, with very few exceptions, been rooted in traditional subject matters. At best these activities have been viewed by school personnel and the community at large as valuable additions to the curriculum and at worst as frills or sops for unmotivated or difficult students for whom the "core curriculum" (the traditional subject matters) hold no attraction, i.e., a price one pays for containing the energies of otherwise unmanageable youth. It is wholly understandable if the perceived benefits of these programs have stimulated efforts to introduce such programs for more students at all levels in more schools. What is less understandable is the failure to recognize that one of the reasons these programs were initiated (with increasing frequency in the post–World War II era) was the inability to engender sufficient student interest in the traditional subject matter. Ironically, that very point was one explicitly recognized by those people in the late 1950s and early 1960s who were developing the new math, biology, physics, and social studies curricula. They made much of the fact that experiencing and learning these subject matters could and should be not only interesting but enjoyable and they "sold" (literally and figuratively) their curricula on that basis. To say that they failed is to be charitable. They started with the traditional conception of subject matter, and they ended up with traditionally discouraging results. The analogy to old wine in new bottles is inappropriate because in new or old bottles wine is tasty and enjoyable. In the new as well as the old curricula subject matter has been unpalatable.

A second source of disquiet with experiential education is more difficult for me to discuss because it puts me in the role of seer. More specifically, it involves a prediction I made in the 1960s that today is being confirmed in the mass media. The prediction had several parts:

1. The efforts to improve education in classrooms and schools through new curricula would fail.

2. The movement to provide community experiences for students would gain momentum.

3. Eventually, the interaction between failure of the new curricula to achieve their purposes and changes in the larger society would produce another clamor to do *something* about the

inadequate educational performance of the bulk of students; i.e., there would be another back-to-basics movement.

4. One of the first casualties (and even scapegoats) of this clamor would be programs and activities that were not considered basic.

5. In the uproar, the history of similar clamors and their consequences would be ignored, another example of Santayana's law that those who ignore history are doomed to repeat it.

There is no need for me to repeat the litany of findings about the unhealthy state of our schools. At the very least, this state of affairs insures that those who administer our mass media will not be wanting of material to use. Predictably, this litany has lacked an organizing core that could compel interest that might lead to action. That core, again predictably, was provided in a speech by President Reagan to a conference convened by the National Science Foundation. As reported in the *New York Times* of May 13, 1982: "President Reagan said today that the education of American school children in science and mathematics had reached such a deplorable state that *it threatened the nation's military and economic security*" (italics added). Nothing magnetizes attention as much or as swiftly as the belief that a set of problems imperils national security and ecnomic stability. The article went on to say:

> The Secretary of Education, T. H. Bell, attributed the problem in part to the concern for educational equality in recent years, which, he said, has led to a sacrifice of quality and excellence. "There has been a certain element of mediocrity creeping in and general muddling of our objects," he said. . . .
>
> Among possible remedies suggested by Mr. Bell were expansion of schools that specialize in mathematics and science; establishment of more academically and professionally oriented high schools like the Bronx High School of Science, and encouragement of state and local school authorities to increase science requirements.

He asked the states to consider dual pay scales under which science teachers, who are in short supply, would get higher pay than others. . . .

Frank Press, the Academy's president, said the country was in danger of "raising a new generation of Americans that is scientifically illiterate."

According to Paul DeHart Hurd, emeritus professor at Stanford University, the typical grade school gets only one hour of science and four hours of arithmetic every week. Only a third of high school students are graduated with three years of mathematics, he said.

Citing a growing shortage of math and science teachers, he said that half the people teaching those subjects in high schools this year were unqualified and were teaching only with emergency certificates.

The prospect of a growing shortage of scientists and engineers was of deep concern to the military, Secretary of Defense Caspar W. Weinberger told the conference.

The National Science Board, the policy-making body of the National Science Foundation, recently established a Commission on Precollege Education in Mathematics, Science and Technology to examine the problem.

To those with short memories, these concerns and recommendations may seem both reasonable and realistic. In fact, the president, the Secretary of education, the secretary of defense, and science educators are repeating what their counterparts were saying after the Soviets launched the first sputnik. The dates are different but everything else is the same. There is another trivial difference: following sputnik, Washington allocated billions to improve education, whereas the Reagan administration has no such intention. The content of today's diagnosis and treatment is a rerun of an earlier failure, and it is hard to avoid the conclusion that what truly imperils society is an ahistorical stance.

The back-to-basics, let's not be distracted by frills, movement — blaming schools, their personnel, students, and concern with educational equality — has the dubious virtue of exhibiting clarity of purpose and the fatal, inherent defect of being a repetition compulsion. It is an example of doing what we know how to do despite the evidence that what we will do derives from ignorance. It's like the joke about the patient who goes to his physician because he has a cold. The physician examines him and tells him to go home and open up all the windows in his house, get undressed, and then stand in front of a window and breathe deeply for a half hour. The patient says, "But it's winter. If I do that, I'll get pneumonia." To which the physician replies, "*That* I know how to treat." The back-to-basics movement stems from both despair and ignorance, a combination that apparently precludes examination of the axioms that have narrowed the universe of explanations for the problems at hand. What we are witness to today are recommendations that would give greater force to the idea that classrooms in school buildings are the only places in which subject matter can be made interesting for, and productively assimilated by, students isolated from the phenomena of daily living.

As long as efforts to improve education begin with the imagery of classrooms and school buildings; as long as that imagery bifurcates student experience into an inside and outside world; as long as that imagery pictures teachers as the major fount of intellectual knowledge and stimulation; as long as subject matters are presented as contents and skills to be learned independently of their experienced manifestation and importance in individual and social living — in the world as we know it; as long as the structure and organization of subject matter is presented without reference to intellectual history — as long as we remain imprisoned in a world view in which education has these features, we set ouselves up for disappointment.

It may be helpful to the reader, as it has been to me, to approach the problem in terms of a piece of imaginary legislation: For example, in the course of two years when I spent two days a week working with teachers in an inner city elementary school

the most troubling problem to the teachers was how ill prepared the children were for learning the "basics"—reading,
arithmetic, and writing. I spent most of my time in the kindergarten and the first two grades and it was indeed upsetting to
witness the struggles of teachers and pupils in these "lessons." It
had not taken me long to get past the point of assigning blame:
primers that were uninteresting, teachers locked into the rigidities of lesson plans, and students for the most part dutiful but
far from inspired. I should add that it was a pressured atmosphere if only because teachers in the upper grades complained
loudly about the difficulties posed for them in teaching students
poorly grounded in the basics. At one of my meetings with first
and second grade teachers I asked the teachers what they
thought about Sarason's law: to make it illegal to teach the basics in the first two grades. I made this proposal to a group of
elementary school teachers in an inner-city school, and their
first reaction was very positive. By traditional standards these
were good teachers: motivated, devoted to the curriculum, but
experiencing their work as an uphill struggle in which the outcome in regard to most of the children would be poor. They did
not approach the school day with anything resembling eager-
ness, and neither did the children. So, if the teachers were initially positive, this response was understandable. However,
there was no disposition to take my proposal seriously. I then
asked, "What adverse consequences would there be for children
and society if the legislation were enacted?" The teachers were
puzzled. Here was a proposal that appeared to be drastic in its
implications and yet they could not come up with compelling
arguments (compelling to them) about adverse consequences.
No proposal for change is without its problems and no proposal
is exempt from Murray Levine's maxim, "problem creation
through problem solution." Yet, no one could come up with the
argument that the fabric of society and of childrens' lives would
come apart if the legislation went into effect. Finally, one
teacher asked, as much to herself as to the group, "What would
we *do* with the children if we were prevented from teaching
them the basics in the early grades?" (With all other groups of

educators, this question has come up and led to similar, if not identical, remarks.)

Two things emerged from our ensuing discussion. The first was that teachers accept, without reflection, a conception of curriculum that puts them in an active role and students in a comparatively passive one in a classroom. Without a curriculum that gives direction, organization, and meaning to his or her days, weeks, and year, the teacher would be at a loss. It is worthy of emphasis that this traditional conception of curriculum gives far more direction and purpose to teachers than it does to students. The second point is more subtle and fateful: the traditional conception of curriculum rests on the unchallenged assumption that this approach is the best means to capitalize on the needs, interests, and capabilities of children; i.e., it is the best way to stimulate and enlarge the intellectual horizons and curiosity of children. If we had no curriculum that emphasized reading, writing, and arithmetic, the minds of these young children would lack nourishment and they would presumably be scarred for life. What would we *do* with the children? The answer, of course, is that there is a staggeringly large universe of possibilities from which one could draw in order to capitalize on the interests and curiosity of children, possibilities that derive from their question asking about a world they are trying to understand.* It is in the process of exploring that world that the basics can begin to have instrumental value, not in the world of teacher and curriculum. What is basic is not subject matter but those matters in which the child is interested.

Once when I presented my imaginary legislation, I was accused by an academic of being anti-intellectual. That was a surprising accusation on several grounds. For one thing, the ac-

---

*If you consult Kamii and DeVries (1978) on preschoolers—a book deriving from the work of Piaget on cognitive development—you get a good idea of the range of possibilities that can be capitalized on by teachers of first and second graders, especially if you unburden yourself of the practice of regarding the classroom as the only place in which schooling should go on.

cusation came from a person who had long been concerned about the failure of schools to spark the interests of pupils in subject matter. For another, he knew well that his own field had benefited greatly from the efforts of people, going back a long way, to observe and act on phenomena that puzzled and interested them, to pursue questions not in the abstract but in the context of transactions between what was inside and outside them, using subject matter as means and not ends. Finally, far from being regarded as anti-intellectual, I had most frequently been accused of putting too much emphasis on traditional subject matters. The fact is that I do regard these subject matters as important, far too important not to be productively assimilated by students in their efforts to understand and act on the world as they experience it outside the bounded, isolated classroom.

What is happening today as the inadequacies of schooling are coming back to the national agenda is a renewed focus on high schools. I am aware of several ongoing projects and commissions each of which will undoubtedly describe in detail past mistakes, the current malaise, the illiteracy of students in matters scientific, the gulf that exists between the worlds of school and work, and the woefully poor preparation of teachers. There is no reason to believe that when these reports are published, they will not be greeted as much needed answers, as solutions to be acted on in the same way that Conant's 1963 report was. Unfortunately, there is also no reason to believe that these reports will verbalize and challenge the assumption that subject matter should be taught in the usual classroom in the usual school.

As long as that view maintains its hold, as long as our conception of schooling is put into that truly procustean bed, we are incapable of even recognizing the possibility that there are more productive ways in which students can be exposed to subject matter—ways that start with the interests and questions of students and seek to place them in sites in which they can experience the multifaceted significance of subject matter, ways

that take seriously the obvious fact that subject matter has derived from, has influenced, and continues to influence the
world as it has been known in the past and is known in the
present.

To entertain alternatives to traditional practice is never
easy. The process usually begins with the recognition that what
you are doing simply is not having its intended consequences.
But that recognition, more often than not, leads to a resolve to
try to improve what you are doing, making changes here and
there that allow you to continue doing what you have been doing but with the hope of better results. If these efforts are inef-
fective, a variety of explanations can be offered that direct
blame away from what you are doing. As we have seen, that has
been happening in the case of schooling, especially in the
post–World War II era, in regard to diverse groups that for one
assigned reason or another do not succeed in school and are
considered unable to do so. Indeed, such students at the middle
and high school level have been channeled into programs that
either do not require them to be in school very much or expose
them on only the most superficial level to traditional subject
matters. These instances of "blaming the victim" (although
more than that is involved) are justified on the basis of the fiction that the intended consequences of schooling are being obtained by the bulk of students. In short, if you get rid of those
youngsters unable or unwilling to do well, the school will be
able to provide what society has always expected it to do. As I
have noted, this so-called solution fails to recognize that for
most students "making it" in school, schooling is a bore; that
getting a passing grade (overlooking grade inflation in the process) says little or nothing about interest or fruitful assimilation
of subject matter; and that functional illiteracy, scientific or
other, seems to be on the increase. One comes to expect descriptions about a ray of hope here and a ray of hope there; and
a slight increase in test scores, or the arrest in decline of certain
test scores, are greeted as indications that the worst was over
and the corner turned. Here is a desperate effort to justify con-

tinuing to do what has always been done. There was and is no disposition to examine the basic assumption that schools are places where subject matter can be productively experienced and assimilated.

As I asked previously: *if it were illegal to teach math, science, or any other subject matter in a classroom or school, how and where would we teach it?* That is far less of a radical question than it would appear. The evidence is overwhelming that middle and high school students can be engaged in structured and supervised experiences outside school that maintain their interest and have obviously beneficial intellectual and educational consequences. But, with some notable exceptions, the core subject matters have not been touched in these contexts and, therefore, the student spends most of his or her school day inside the classroom. We are so used to thinking of subject matter in terms of a particular physical site that is organized in a particular way—and for which there is a particular curriculum—that our minds go blank when we are asked seriously to come up with alternatives. As I have emphasized, that inability or unwillingness to come up with alternatives is testimony to how well we have been socialized to accept and to think within a particular world view.

Let me give an example that has the additional virtue of emphasizing the insidious consequences of the ahistorical stance. As recently as thirty years ago, a college student, for example, a sophomore or junior, who requested a year off to gain experience through travel or some kind of work appropriate to his or her interests was looked upon as deviant and therefore suspect. You were expected to go to college for four uninterrupted years, take a curriculum for the most part required, and then enter the larger society or go right on to graduate or professional school. You could absent yourself from the sequence for medical reasons or you might fail. Few students would have dared to state directly that they wanted to further their education in ways not possible in the college program. From the standpoint of the college, such a student would have been viewed as arrogant or unmotivated or irresponsible or dilettant-ish or all of these. Likewise, graduate and professional schools would have viewed as suspect any student who did not seek ad-mission immediately after college. The situation is different to-day. In fact, many colleges now encourage, organize and super-vise a year of experience away from the college, justifying this option on intellectual or educational grounds. These programs, of course, are not of a piece, varying from being aimless, con-tent-free, and poorly supervised to tightly integrating subject matter and out-of-school experience. The important point is that one no longer needs to defend the principle that there are places and ways of learning outside the classroom that foster in-tellectual or educational growth. But at the college level, as on preceding levels, that principle is not invoked in the case of the so-called core curriculum. The principle is admitted for certain subject matters; that it may be no less applicable for most, if not all, other subject matters cannot even be entertained as a possibility.

In developing my argument in this chapter I have empha-sized subject matter, the practical, adaptive, and developmen-tal significance of which hardly surfaces when subject matter must be learned as an arid mental exercise in a classroom. That emphasis was deliberate because we are at the beginning of a new era in which the back-to-basics movement insures that sub-ject matter will again be center stage and in which, given our ahistorical stance, every past mistake stands a good chance of being repeated. To reinvent the wheel is a tremendous intellec-tual feat, however redundant it may be. To reinvent a poorly functioning wheel is no basis for commendation. Today, that malfunctioning wheel is being reinvented around the country. No place is the reinvention proceeding as quickly and self-defeatingly as in Washington, where empty administration speeches express pious commitments to excellence and fear about the nation's military and industrial leadership but cannot hide the fact that not one new idea has surfaced and that a seri-ous effort to explain past failures emanating from Washington apparently has been ruled off limits. Let me be clear that what is emanating from Washington is not peculiar to the Reagan administration; it was no different under Carter, Nixon, Johnson, or Kennedy. If Reagan were to spend the money for education his critics are recommending, there literally would be no difference between what he would do and what his predecessors did. Each president presents a new wrinkle, e.g., Nixon's experimental schools program, which could not have been more of a failure than it was despite its enormous cost (Sarason, 1982). They are wrinkles in the same fabric.

I believe that the mastery of subject matter is essential on a number of grounds. Indeed, my firm belief that such mastery is crucial for adaptation over one's lifetime drove me to the conclusion that far from facilitating mastery over subject matter, the classroom extinguishes interest. The school is not the solution. The problem inheres in the school's existence, more correctly, in the narrow limits that our conventional imagery of schools imposes on our imagination.

Although in this chapter I have focused on subject matter, it should be clear from earlier chapters that my critique rests on two assumptions. The first is less an assumption than a well-validated fact: an educational activity that does not derive from or spark a person's curiosity and interest *and* take place in a context that is personally meaningful, permitting actions that affect and in turn are affected by that context, stands little chance of being productively integrated into that person's knowledge and orientation. The second is the assumption that the world view of people born in the post-World War II era, profoundly altered by changes that have occurred in this society and the world, makes it extremely unlikely that our schools will be able to contain these students, or hold their interest, or help them to understand their world for the purposes of adaptation and mastery. When one starts with these assumptions, the crucial significance of subject matter, far from being devalued, becomes critical at the same time that the fate of subject matter in the lives of students is unfortunately gloomy.

I assume that no reader of this book is satisfied with our schools. I also assume that readers do not need to be convinced that what our schools do or do not accomplish has had and will continue to have serious consequences for our society. I am also safe in assuming that most readers are puzzled and troubled by the failure of past efforts to improve schooling. What I cannot assume is that the reader has been able to avoid assigning blame to this group or that. However understandable the assignment of blame may be, when one is faced with a serious problem with which one must deal, this stance will prove counterproductive. A final assumption I make is that most readers have responded to my arguments with their own questions. If you are saying that we should not be teaching what we teach in classrooms in our schools, what should we *do*? Granted that your argument has merit, does it not lead to wildly impractical conclusions? Are not your recommendations another example of the road to hell being paved with good intentions? Have we not had a surfeit of utopian schemes and panaceas of which your argument is a version? These are fair questions but let us in the following chapters examine the possibility that the answers envisioned divert us from the purpose these questions serve. That the response to the challenge of change in individuals, institutions, and society engenders obstacles of diversion is among the best documented facts in human history.

WHAT SHOULD
WE DO?

THE QUESTION POSED in the chapter title is phrased in a way to suggest that what is being asked for is a detailed blueprint for action; i.e., let's substitute one way of doing things for another. This reading ignores two interrelated factors. The first is the assumption that we have worked through an analysis of things as they are now being done to the point that we can seriously entertain alternatives. And by "seriously" I mean being prepared to think differently, or to consider new doings in a very altered context of ideas and directions. The second factor derives from the fact that neither individuals nor organizations respond without resistance to the need for, or the challenge to, change. The latter factor deserves a closer look.

Among psychotherapists there is a maxim that an individual's decision to seek help, to start the process of change, is half the struggle. The remaining half of the struggle centers around the ever present resistance to giving up long-standing styles of thinking and acting. This is no less the case with organizations and social institutions (Mason & Mitroff, 1981). In *Challenging Strategic Planning and Assumptions* (1981), Mason and Mitroff describe well how the process of formulating and accepting a new organizational policy encounters two obstacles: inertia and unwillingness or inability to become aware of new alternatives. No less important, however, is the authors' development of a process that not only forces people to become aware that the universe of alternatives is greater than they customarily think but also facilitates one's coming to grips with the substance and implications of this expanded universe of alternatives. It is one thing to become aware of alternatives; it is another to examine them seriously.

I am not offering, at least in the narrow sense, a psychological explanation for wariness in response to the question: what should we *do*? In the case of schooling it is not a matter of people's motivations or the intrapsychic perversities and paradoxes of the human mind. If that were the case, the problem would be far less thorny than it is. What makes the question so problematic in its formulation and the universe of answers it suggests is that it is about an institution that for centuries has been embedded in society in particular ways and associated with imagery that gives schools a reality no less substantial and enduring than that of Mount Everest. Implicit in the question of what we should do is the question of what we should do about the places we call schools, whereas the thrust of my argument is that one should not begin with our customary imagery of a school building and its physical and organizational structure but rather with this question: in what activities can students engage that will capture their interest; expand and stimulate their knowledge of, and experience with, the social and physical world; serve to illuminate and develop skills and concepts that have broadened and transformed human experience; and sustain the sense of purpose, mastery, and continuity? I do not put the question this way to establish that I am for virtue and against sin but rather to indicate that the question in no way assumes that the answer requires schools as we have known them. The traditional way of viewing schools *requires* the assumption that it is impossible both in principle and in practice to achieve the goals implied by the way I have posed the question except through schools as we know them. As I have repeatedly noted, this is never verbalized and yet, as soon as it is verbalized, many people sense its inappropriateness.

I once asked a physicist with a long-standing interest in our schools and in the increasing dimensions and implications of scientific illiteracy, "If it were illegal to teach physics in classrooms in our schools, how would you do it?" Far from being nonplussed, as I had expected, he described a summer research program he had set up for high school students in the course of which they had learned calculus without the word "calculus" having ever been uttered. This, of course, did not take place in a classroom with Dr. Vinson as teacher but emerged in relation to questions deriving from the tasks on which the students and their mentors were working. Vinson is dean of arts and sciences at the University of Hartford, in a city that is the insurance capital of the world. As consultant to, and university liaison with, insurance companies, Vinson has become very knowledgeable about what these companies are and do. If we thought of these companies as potential schools for middle and high school students, how could they be used and for what subjects? Suffice it to say that by the end of an hour we had far from exhausted the potential of these sites as places relevant to learning not only about biology and health, statistics and mathematics, and meteorology but also about the economic and social organization of our society, past and present. Our thinking was geared not to the goal of teaching about insurance but rather to that of stimulating and illuminating the acquisition of knowledge and skills in various subjects. Just as the usual imagery of schools constricts our thinking about students and learning, so the labels we apply to out-of-school sites—and the imagery those labels conjure up—curb our imagination.

I have suggested that the question about what we should do will be fruitful to the extent that it follows a process of reexamination that has required you seriously to consider alternatives to traditional conceptions of schooling. But, once you begin to pursue seriously the kind of alternative Vinson and I were pursuing, you begin to glimpse the objections that people will understandably raise. For example, as soon as one admits that many community sites could serve the purposes of education, intimidating questions arise—intimidating precisely because of the changes that such an admission brings in its wake. What would we do with school personnel educated and trained to work with traditional curricula in traditional classrooms in traditional school buildings? Would it not be necessary drastically to alter teacher training programs? What would be the role of educational personnel in selecting and working with community sites? How, when, and where would these personnel meet with students? Would it be necessary to abandon school buildings? Given the number of students, is it not wildly unrealistic to expect to find enough sites with educational potential? These and other questions really speak to two points that are not logically related but are presented as if they were so related. The first point is that institutional change, not only in schools but in colleges and universities as well, is necessary. To conclude that efforts to improve schools have been spectacularly unsuccessful, that prospects for future improvement are gloomy, that schools as they now exist are incapable of achieving their goals, that alternatives have to be seriously considered—to come to these conclusions *and* to expect that any serious alternative will not (should not) require substantial institutional changes is remarkably unrealistic. Here we come to the second point: many people suggest that it is better to stay with familiar and manageable setups than to grapple with the problems of institutional change, which inevitably will create turmoil. These points derive from an even more fundamental misconception, which I will leave for the moment. I wish to turn next to an objection that is intended to deliver the coup de grace to my argument.

The objection can be put in the form of a question: granted that the situation is as intractable as you say as long as we stay within the confines of our usual ways of thinking about schooling, and granted even that the changes you suggest have merit in principle and in another kind of world ought to be acted on, is it not wishful thinking to assume that community organizations (public and private, formal and informal, profit and nonprofit) will agree to become schooling sites? Will organizations that justify their existence on noneducational grounds, whose survival depends on performing functions (e.g., making a profit) unrelated to public schooling, cooperate in such a venture? These questions betray ignorance of two related facts. First, cooperative arrangements between schools and noneducational organizations have dramatically increased in number in the post–World War II period. In saying this I am not passing judgment on the direction and efficacy of these arrangements but only emphasizing their prevalence. Every school system with which I have had direct contact over the past twenty years, and the number is not minuscule, not only has had these relationships but also has sought to expand them. Second, noneducational organizations in the community have, more often than not, been receptive, rather than resistant, to overtures from schools. In an earlier chapter I noted that whatever merits programs of experiential education may have, they too frequently lack an intellectual-educational direction that would make subject matter meaningful, useful, and heuristic. One could argue that it is one thing for noneducational organizations to provide students with experiences that fit organizational purposes and quite another to expect them to become truly educational sites. That objection misses the point that the two purposes are not antithetical: the domains of theory and practice are separate only in an artificial way. But, the argument could continue, what would be the relationship between teachers and those in the organization with whom the students would apprentice? And, assuming that the preceding question could be answered satisfactorily, would not the effort cave in

under the weight of the number of students involved? Moreover, would not the problems that my suggestion would entail
create an administrative nightmare, a cure worse than the disease?

In light of all of these objections, let me elaborate further
on my reluctance to answer the question of what we should do.
The reader will recall that this question presupposes, at a minimum, that one has concluded that alternatives to present
thinking and practice have to be seriously considered. However,
whether one is dealing with an individual or an organization,
the pressure to change, to consider unfamiliar alternatives, is
on a collision course with the quest for certainty: the desire,
quite understandable, to judge any alternative by the criterion
of certainty or predictability, i.e., the degree to which it provides a blueprint or a road map that clearly tells one how things
will look and how one will be able to go from here to there.
When one has come to the understanding that customary imagery, ideas, and practices have to be given up—and the adjective
"customary" hardly conveys the hold that our imagery of
schools has on our thinking and, therefore, on our attempts to
free ourselves from its hold—it requires no special insight to realize that we will want to feel certain that the new direction is
the answer. Convinced of the inadequacies of the present, pressured to move in new directions, bewildered by alternatives that
are both unfamiliar and upsetting in their implications, it
should occasion no surprise if we resort to the quest for certainty as a way of avoiding the implications of the initial conclusion that we must move in new ways. We can never overestimate two processes (in the case of either individuals or
organizations): the effectiveness with which we have been socialized to view the world in particular ways and, not surprisingly, the extraordinary difficulty of taking distance from (let
alone gaining control over) the consequences of our socialization.

The sources of the objections are not understandable in
terms of our extant psychologies of the individual organism—

psychologies that focus on the individual independent of time, place, and social history (Sarason, 1981). The objections to Copernican theory, Darwinian theory, and psychoanalytic theory are not understandable in terms of the workings of individual minds isolated from all of the factors that shape and give direction to a world view. And it was (and still is) no different in principle in the case of objections to alternative views of women, racial and ethnic minorities, the handicapped, etc. Whenever some aspect of a world view is challenged — like the proper locus of schooling — objections to the challenge, precisely because they are voiced by so many people, say far less about these people as individuals than they do about the formation of their shared world view. To expect, therefore, that a proposal that clearly challenges centuries-old conceptions about how and where schooling can occur will be responded to dispassionately is to ignore how much a product of a long history we are. This, of course, does not automatically confer merit on a proposal or invalidate any or all objections to it. But it should alert us to the ease with which our treasured world view can defeat the goal of recognizing, confronting, and acting in accord with alternatives to what is perceived as an intractable state of affairs.

The question about what we should do has another source that should make one wary about a direct answer. Associated with that question are imagery and conceptions about how social change comes about, more specifically, that ideas should be formulated into a policy statement, which will lead to actions aimed at solving the problem at hand. And when we say "solving" we are unaware that we are using the word in its natural science sense, i.e., in the sense that four divided by two gives the solution "two." We dearly want to believe that the problems of schools have solutions in that sense; consequently, we dismiss alternatives that do not appear to be solutions — a variant of the quest for certainty. The fact is that the problems with which we are dealing do not have clear-cut, sure-fire solutions. But there is more to this difficulty than that because in practice — and nowhere is this more demonstrable than in the educational arena—new ideas embedded in new policies are produced by a few top-level staff members, who frequently are insensitive to the needs of those who will be affected by the new policy, those who will have to implement it, to understand, to work through, and to act fully in accord with the new policy. The belief that good ideas will survive and win out, Darwinian style, in the realm of implementation has contributed more than its share to the current malaise. Regardless of the new policy's merits, its fate turns on the extent to which the people most closely involved in its implementation agree about its substance, appropriateness, and consequences for action. If anything is clear in the history of educational innovations and improvements, it has been the failure of policymakers to put ideas into currency before putting them into action. Telling people what they should do before they have had the opportunity to examine and work through the significance of a new approach is inherently unproductive, especially if in doing so one is reinforcing the tendency to be satisfied with answers which do not prepare you for what is ahead, answers given as "solutions" that are not digested and to which something akin to an allergic reaction develops.

It should be clear that my proposal about schooling is not intended either as a policy or a course of action. If I had the power to put the proposal into action, I would not do so. The proposal is not, initially at least, a problem in social engineering, conjuring up, as that phrase does, how-to-do-it, blueprint imagery. The proposal is intended to achieve several purposes. The first is to ask consideration of the possibility that our schools have been, are, and will continue to be uninteresting places that are inimical to the assimilation and utilization of areas of knowledge that help one understand the social and physical world and that give direction to one's life. The second is to gain recognition of the fact that schools are what they are in part because they reflect a world view that says that schooling should take place, best takes place, in a school building. The third purpose is to suggest that there are alternatives against which we struggle precisely because they require us to alter our world view. Finally, if these three purposes are achieved, if we can seriously "play with" alternatives, we are starting a process in which our imaginativeness and creativity will render the unfamiliar less troublesome and more realistic. I put quotation marks around "play with" to indicate a feature of numerous conversations I have had with people about how subject matter can be learned in sites other than classrooms. A few people are literally unable to think of subject matter as other than *something* you learn in a classroom. However, most people with whom I have talked (and these were not brief encounters several minutes in length) began to enjoy "playing around" with the idea and had little or no difficulty in describing ways that subject matter could be learned outside of a classroom. Here I must add the fact that with few exceptions the two dozen or so people with whom I talked were from the hard sciences: physicists, chemists, mathematicians, biologists, and earth-environmental scientists. This was not happenstance. For one thing, I chose these people because of the current (and recurrent) concern about the role of schools in producing scientific illiterates. More personally, my own public school education came perilously close to extinguishing any interest I might have had in the sciences, a result that was hardly remedied in my university education but somewhat more remedied in subsequent decades. I felt comfortable playing around with my proposal in relation to history, social studies, and literature, but not with the sciences. If I had to summarize the most frequent reactions of these people to the conversations, it would go like this: "*Of course* you can learn some of the basic concepts in my field outside of the classroom in a context where these concepts are being applied; it was in the field, not a classroom, where *I* learned the most; your proposal in theory makes sense, but is it *practical?*"

A fascinating issue about schools surfaced in the post–World War II period to challenge our world view and, up to a point, to alter that view. However, this issue—who owns the schools?—takes on a different cast when viewed in relation to my proposal. In a legal sense this question is easy to answer, but its import is broad: who has or should have responsibility for our schools? Put in that way, the issue is political; people who directly or indirectly are affected by educational policies (i.e., parents, teachers, and others with a vested interest in what happens in school) have sought to have some voice in their formulation. In terms of political principle this view of responsibility and participation requires no defense (Sarason, 1982). However, the emergence of this principle as a source of controversy and pressure for change reflected the assumption that to the extent that the principle was accepted, schools would improve: education would be more relevant to societal realities and the academic performance of pupils would improve. It has not worked out that way and there was no good reason why it should have because "community participation" advocates of every description implicitly believed that schools are the primary site at which education should take place. Indeed, in many instances, those who sought a voice in educational decisionmaking were critical of schools because they were not achieving their academic goals in traditional ways. Whatever clarity was attained about the political principle and whatever alterations were achieved in the allocation of power and responsibility, no one reexamined the basic assumption that schools are the best place for instruction to proceed.

Just as war is too important to be left to the generals, education is too important to be left to the professionals—that is another way to describe the position of those who adhered to the political principle of community control. There is an irony here bordering on the unfair. Although there is no doubt that in practice the professional educators "owned" the schools, arrogating to themselves the dominant role in formulating and implementing school policies, the community nevertheless complied with what was happening. We have always both revered and mistrusted experts and the history of America contains many periods in which that ambivalence became manifest. In the main, however, we have been content to let professionals like educators, physicians, lawyers, and city planners exercise leadership and power until changes in the larger society have evoked and helped coalesce opposition to their practices. Anyone familiar with the education of professionals is never surprised at their resistance to the idea of shared responsibility. Just as Winston Churchill said (in relation to the movement for the independence of India) that he had not been chosen prime minister to preside over the dissolution of the British empire, so the professional does not see himself or herself as properly sharing decisionmaking with lay people. Accordingly, when the issue of community participation in educational decisionmaking appeared on the national agenda in the 1960s, especially in our urban areas, there was a serious power struggle. In reality, it was a struggle between parents and educators, with the rest of the community on the sidelines. And that is the point: the way in which educational issues were posed (when they were posed at all) restricted the issue of responsibility to these two groups. How and why other groups in the community should assume responsibility for schooling were questions that could not arise. As long as education was a process that took place in a school building, only parents and teachers had a vested interest in assigning responsibility for schools.

It is obvious that my proposal requires groups other than educators and parents to assume responsibility for education. After all, if education is to take place (can take place) in a variety of community sites, if these sites are to make accommodations to the educational needs of students, it will only be because they have been given and accepted a responsible role in the formulation and implementation of educational policy. In some vague, abstract, civic sense, community groups other than parents and teachers feel responsibility for the performance of schools. But isolated as that feeling is from any relationship to schools, it is no wonder that their opinions are, at best, superficial and, at worst, ill founded and prejudiced. I have argued, as have many others, that separating education *in* schools from education *outside* schools defeats the purpose of education by maintaining a gulf between the two worlds of learning. Here I am similarly arguing that to the extent that most community members are kept apart from the educational process, have no role in that process, their learning and understanding about the two worlds will be next to nil. I must emphasize that my proposal derives not from any political principle but rather from a conception about the characteristics of settings that make learning interesting, adaptive, and sustaining, i.e., that maximize the chance that students will see a close relationship between subject matter and the world in which *they* live. If to do this requires changing our views about where and how education should take place, if it requires looking at our communities in terms of the sites that can accommodate to educational goals, then we are confronted with the implications of the principle that those who are affected by educational policies should have a role in determining those policies. I use the word "confront" advisedly because the implications of the political principle are for most of us unfamiliar and upsetting.

Several people have responded to my argument by calling it "an idea whose time has come." That response troubles me for several reasons. For one thing, it suggests that ideas have a power and persuasiveness before which tradition crumbles, a version of the belief that truth and justice ultimately win in the marketplace of living. No less troubling is the failure to recognize that any idea worth its salt is an expression of time and place: it is a challenge to, or a criticism of, conventional wisdom embedded in the features of society, features that do not change easily. That optimistic view is not the case even in the relatively narrow confines of science, about which most people mistakenly believe that good ideas are irresistible even if they require scientists to change their thinking and *doings*.* It is far less the case in the social arena when the idea requires the con-

---

*For fascinating and instructive examples one should read Mitroff's *Subjective Side of Science: An Inquiry into the Psychology of the Apollo Moon Scientists* (1974).

struction of novel relationships among individuals and institutions. In the field of education, the graveyard of ideas is strewn with good ideas that died because their makers were enamored more with the idea's truth than with its institutional consequences. Separating an idea from the institutional arrangements to which that idea is a reaction, as well as from the predictable social dynamics the idea sets in motion, is unrivaled as a formula for failure, another example of the separation of theory and practice, of treating ideas as asocial products of the human mind.

Let us return to a question that has undoubtedly troubled the reader: why should community sites accommodate to the educational needs of students? This question has to be seen in light of the answer to another question: how does one explain why in the post–World War II period there has been an apparently very significant increase in the frequency and variety of relationships between schools and other organizations (both public and private) in the community? I touched on this subject earlier; here I want to add that these organizations have come to see that it is in their self-interest to provide life and work experiences to students. And by self-interest I refer to several things: the perception that, like it or not, they should cooperate with schools in regard to programs directed at youth who need career guidance or who might otherwise get into trouble; and concern that many people entering the labor force from school are ill equipped to handle available jobs, thus contributing to inefficiency and rising costs. I could summarize these and related points by paraphrasing what a company executive once said to me:

> We are caught in a bind. On the one hand, we are here to make a profit, not to be distracted by having to "make work" or be teachers. On the other, we are in this community and it has a lot of problems and sometimes we feel we are sitting on a powder keg. We have to appear as if we were concerned and wanted to be helpful, and the fact is that we *are* concerned not

only for our particular company but for what is happening throughout our society. Sure, the bottom line is green, but that does not mean that we do not have a conscience. Some of these kids are a delight; others are not. Some of our employees really get a kick from helping and teaching these kids; others do not. I feel sorry for a lot of these kids, and there are days I feel sorry for myself. But the day is past when we can blithely say no to a school request and not have to worry about consequences. We can no longer go it alone and, I suppose, neither can the schools.

This passage suggests a change in attitude about the responsibility of community organizations for education. I do not want to overestimate the depth and scope of this change but neither do I want to underestimate the profound puzzlement of these organizations about how and what they can do to improve education. They feel they are in a bind but that fact alone represents a change from earlier times.

In my talks with people in public and private organizations providing some kind of experience to students, I come up against two familiar beliefs the contradictions between which go unnoticed. The first belief is that learning is productive, meaningful, and quick when it occurs in a context in which it is directly relevant. As one company supervisor said, "You can lecture to kids about work habits, skills, punctuality, and a lot of other desirable things, but it is not until they are on the job observing and working with others that they stand a chance of learning what it is all about and with what consequences." The second belief is in the form of a criticism: the schools are not adequately educating students, especially in regard to the basics. The two beliefs rest on very different and even contradictory conceptions of learners, learning, and the contexts they require.

If the present relationships between schools and community organizations are fragile, problematic, and narrow in scope, it is asking too much to expect that my proposal will be viewed as credible. For it to be credible, let alone to be acted on, requires that more general recognition be accorded the possibility that the real problem is our age-old belief that education best takes place in school buildings. It is only when we are able seriously to entertain alternatives that our imaginations are liberated and what heretofore appeared impractical and utopian begins to look otherwise. As I asked earlier: how and where would one teach subject matter if it were illegal to do so in a school building? The answer is that there are diverse ways in diverse sites in which one could proceed. Not one way in one site. The possibilities, however, cannot be glimpsed until you take alternatives to present thinking and practices seriously. It may come as a surprise that when I have pressed the point with subject matter specialists, they have had far less difficulty coming up with possibilities than other people. And the specialists who had the least difficulty came from the sciences.

Liberating our imaginations (changing our world view) is no warrant for sounding the tocsin and manning the barricades to carry out a revolution. There are three kinds of revolution. The first is sociopolitical (e.g., the French, American, and Russian revolutions). In a relatively short period of violent conflict, clear expression is given to long-standing ideas and social forces. One might say that what we call "the revolution" is an outcropping and, in a sense, a legitimation of long-standing ideas and forces, accepted by some and rejected by others. The second type is exemplified by what we ordinarily call the "scientific-technological revolution": the discovery, also after a long period of latency, of new knowledge and techniques the application of which will considerably change patterns of living. Unlike the sociopolitical type of revolution, which is resisted by significant segments of the society (and sometimes by a majority), the scientific-technological revolution is enthusiastically envisioned and its presumed future delights constitute a source of pleasurable fantasy. In large part this is because over the centuries opposition to science was overcome and we are heirs to a world view in which science and technology are deemed to serve the public welfare. The third type of revolution—in terms of time it is a variant of the second—is most relevant here because it concerns a social problem that has proven intractable, is seen as having adverse consequences for society, seems to cry out for radically new ideas and approaches, but reflects unverbalized assumptions whose hold on our minds is so strong that they cause us to oppose ideas the implications of which are both clear and upsetting. It is a problem that calls for revolutionary thinking but the revolution has hardly begun.

It would be surprising if the situation were otherwise in the case of education: the past century and a half established the idea that *everyone* should be educated *inside* schools. These battles—however justified on political and moral grounds, and without implying that no educational benefits were achieved— were conceptually flawed and with the passage of time the results of these battles have been increasingly counterproductive. It would be unrealistic for me to hope for other than a hearing as prologue to a debate.

The present is not pregnant with *a* future but with many different futures and my argument is not based on a concept of inevitability. If you are a betting person, you would be wise to act as if the traditional concept of education and schools is not endangered. As I pointed out earlier, it appears today that education is being put back on the national agenda because its inadequacies are seen as contributing adversely to national security and economic stability. How long it will stay on the agenda is impossible to predict, but there is no doubt that the issues are being posed in the most traditional terms with almost complete amnesia insofar as previous formulations and debates are concerned. I do not expect our elected policy makers to be knowledgeable about the substance and history of the issues. They depend on advisors to come up with recommendations presumably based on considerations of practicality derived from a searching examination of alternatives and history. What we are witness to today is neither practical nor based on principles that explain past failures.

The current discussion differs from past ones (in degree at least) in several respects. First, more people than ever before—professional educators, the scientific community, and informed citizens—find themselves concluding in some vague way that the problem is not one for which money is the answer. This is disconcerting to the political liberal, predisposed to believe that education is a form of salvation that society should provide to its young regardless of their ethnic, racial, or class backgrounds. It is disconcerting not because they are calling their goals of education into question but because they have become far less sure that increased budgets will have the desired effect. Paradoxically, this conclusion is no less disconcerting to the political conservative, who sees the specter of youth educationally and vocationally unprepared to play an independent and productive role in society. If money is not the answer for the political conservative, what does he or she recommend? (However bothered, the liberal holds on to the belief that increasing or decreasing expenditures for education makes a difference.) I find it a source of irony that it is among conservatives that one tends to get acceptance of radical proposals that challenge the structure and perhaps even the existence of schools as we have known them.* In a rather explicit way, these proposals (e.g., vouchers or tax credits) are based on an indictment of public schools and educators, another example of blaming the victim although the stone throwers cannot see that they, too, are victims of unverbalized assumptions.

What those who are participating in the current discussion (it is far from a debate) have in common, and this reflects something of a difference from earlier discussions, is the sense that we may have reached (and, perhaps, gone beyond) the point at which the gulf between what our youth learn in schools and what they need to know in a society increasingly altered by

---

*Over the decades there has been a surfeit of proposals based on the assumption that by changing the structure of schools one in some way affects or alters the substance of schooling. As in the case of the arts, here the separation of form and content also leads to nonsense.

the dynamics of scientific-technological developments may be unbridgeable. In the late 1950s and in the 1960s, the debates about education contained this perception but it was far overshadowed by matters racial, economic, and moral. Those matters, of course, are still with us and they continue to contribute to that ever growing underclass that no society can long ignore without penalty. However, my experience suggests that more people now see the gulf as affecting more than that underclass.

While I do not expect our elected policymakers to be knowledgeable about the substance and history of efforts to improve education, I do expect somewhat more from those in the scientific community upset by the dimensions and implications of scientific illiteracy. That they are concerned with the problem; that they are beginning to see its implications for individuals, institutions, and the larger society; that they see the problem as getting worse rather than better are all cause for both satisfaction and despair — satisfaction because they may succeed in keeping education on the national agenda and despair because their concern is ahistorical, unimaginative, and astoundingly parochial, bordering on unforgivable arrogance. One expects the sophisticated scientist to know, at least in the abstract, that when a problem appears to be intractable one should flush out and examine the assumptions that have been taken for granted. It may be too much to expect that the scientist who understands this point in relation to his or her field will be able to apply the principle to the arena of society. A good case could be made for the thesis that there is another form of illiteracy, far older than the scientific, that has had enormously adverse consequences for most people of widely differing background and status. I refer to economic illiteracy. Two years ago I asked a group of high school students this question: In terms of selling, what are similarities and differences between a bank and a shoe store? Not one student noted the fact that a bank rents money. That these students spend a fair part of their day thinking about, practicing, and are affected by economic questions and issues is a conclusion that we can accept without waiting for the outcome of research studies. And yet we do next to nothing in capitalizing on this student interest for the purpose of furthering their understanding of the economic dynamics and organization of our society and the international order.

At its root science is a moral enterprise based on and protecting certain rules for behavior: that asking and testing questions about self and the world are both desirable and necessary; that the pursuit of knowledge should be carried out in as dispassionate a way as possible; that one is obliged to make public what one does in an honest fashion; and that a "good" society is one that protects the morality of science from corrupting "outside influences," i.e., just as the institution of science is based on moral rules to police itself, so should the combination of morality and self-interest of the larger society police and serve itself by protecting science. What so many scientists fail to understand is that at its root education is a moral enterprise and that by glossing over that fact we sustain fruitless controversy and continued failure. The scientist has a vision, a world view, of science a crucial feature of which is its self-correcting nature deriving from the morality on which science is based. What is there in the moral basis of schooling that makes self-correction one of its most elusive features?

8

THE MORAL BASIS OF EDUCATION

THE MORALITY OF AN ENDEAVOR, in science and elsewhere, is ordinarily not called into question by either its practitioners or
the larger society. It is called into question when sea-swell
changes in society, reflecting some alteration in world view,
start a process of redefining the rights of individuals and the obligations of society to legitimate those rights. The process is always marked by tension and conflict, the practitioners resenting the implication that the basis for their activities is now seen
as immoral and resisting the consequences of changing their
morality. So, for example, up until two decades ago scientists
using human beings as subjects in their studies employed techniques and research designs that entailed deception and the
withholding of information; they justified their procedures as
means to the end of discovering new knowledge. This was especially the case in medical and social science research. That subjects were no less human than researchers; that they had rights;

that their welfare as individuals was at least co-equal with the need of researchers for new knowledge; that morality taken for granted can lead to a self-serving sense of superiority and worth—few scientists thought about, or agonized over, these considerations.

I can never forget what I observed as a novice in clinical psychology in a mental hospital in 1941–1942. Patients stood in line waiting for their shock treatment: to be strapped to a contraption, wired to sources of electrical power, or given an injection of insulin and then for massive convulsions to begin and to be maintained for what seemed an eternity. Back at the university I also observed some of my friends following the same procedures with cats and dogs, whose situation struck me as more pathetic since the animals were not there because anything was wrong with them; i.e., there was no intent to help them and they were seen as absolutely expendable. Except in the most vague way, my discomfort—indeed, my inability to observe these activities more than once—did not stem from moral revulsion. I knew I could not engage in such activities but not because I was morally superior to those who did. True, I felt something was wrong somewhere, but I also believed that a greater good was being served. *I even envied the aplomb of those who carried out these activities.* And that is the point: there was no disposition whatever to recognize that *perhaps, maybe, conceivably* the moral basis for these activities should be scrutinized. It all seemed so self-evidently justifiable not only to the scientists but also to the major foundation supporting their research. The larger society was not raising any questions of morality. Once the complexity of the issues began to be sensed, we realized that science owed society more than knowledge. And society could no longer be grateful for knowledge however it had been attained. What was most bedeviling to science and society was that the issues did not lend themselves to a once-and-for-all solution.

The post–World War II era raised questions in diverse spheres of society. Whether it was urban renewal or neighborhood destruction, the building of a new factory or a shopping mall, the construction of a new highway, the quality of the physical environment, the labels on food and clothing — in each of these and other instances the right of individuals and organizations to do what they had long been accustomed to doing without interference was being questioned. If the questioning led to battles, symbolic and actual, it was because different moralities were pitted against each other. The shoulds and the oughts of one side, and their consequences for action, were different from those of the other.

The schools, of course, were not exempt. The 1954 desegregation decision reflected, among other things, an altered morality about who can be educated in what schools in what communities. Just as individuals, groups, legislatures, and courts said to scientists that they could no longer ignore the effects of their actions on human beings (and animals) — that in its role as articulator and guardian of morality, society, in the form of its agencies, could not be indifferent to possible infringements on that morality even if they represented the good intentions of high-status groups — so communities were told that they now had to be governed by the morality of the larger society. The 1954 decision gave rise to other morality dramas. If segregating black and white children in schools was immoral and, by our new standards, deleterious to their lives and, therefore, to society, could we continue to justify segregating handicapped children in speical classes or institutions and, in some instances, refusing them entry into neighborhood schools?

This question received a federal legislative answer in 1975 with the passage of Public Law 94-142, the Education of All Handicapped Children Act. By virtue of its intention to affect and transform all schools, this legislation represented the third revolution in American education. The first two were compulsory education and the 1954 desegregation decision. What they all have in common is the bedrock assumption that society owes its young an education. There are two parts to this obligation. The first is that it is in society's interest to educate youth: its myriad institutions need individuals able to sustain them according to the traditions, morality, and laws of the society. There have been, are, and, one hopes, will always be critics who question how society is defining its interests and the consequences, intended or not, of the ways in which it discharges its obligations to young people. But that it is in the interest of a society to seek continuity is not in question, not even by the most orthodox Marxist critic of education in a capitalist society or the most orthodox capitalist critic of a Marxist society. The center of controversy for each is the moral basis on which self-interest is defined and the moral consequences for citizens who are socialized in the institutions built on that basis. The other part of society's obligation is more obviously moral: the child has self-interests in the sense that he or she seeks knowledge and skills to achieve a sense of mastery and self-worth, and this seeking should be both encouraged by and protected through schooling. This belief contains a conception both of what children are and of what society must do on their behalf. I have never met anyone who asserted that denying a child the opportunity to seek mastery and self-worth was good. To take this position is to be on the side of sin and against virtue. If everybody is in favor of virtue, how do we explain why schooling does not appear to do well in discharging the moral imperative? Why do so many children lack a sense of mastery and self-worth? Race, poverty, prejudice, family disorganization, teacher inadequacy, educational bureaucracy, capitalist society, the production ethic, genetics, permissiveness—the explanations are legion but all either locate the problem within individuals, families, or groups or trace it to a basic conflict between the nature of our social order and the needs (rights) of children (a third camp sees an interaction between the first two sources of failure).

One of my favorite jokes is relevant here. It is about a person who decides to see a psychotherapist. He spends most of his first visit describing in detail the nature and origin of his problems. The therapist listens silently, sympathetically, and attentively. Finally, shortly before the end of the hour, the therapist says, "I have heard everything you've said, but the *real* problem, which you did not mention, is that you hate your mother." It is not my intention to deny the appropriateness of the many explanations for the failure of children to develop a sense of mastery and self-worth. Nor is it my intention to convey the impression that if and when actions based on my argument begin to occur, all past problems and their explanations will evaporate. I do not take the position of the therapist who suggested that if the patient only understood that he hated his mother, this insight would dissolve all of his other problems. However, I am like a therapist who suggests that there may be a problem of which the individual is understandably unaware. And that problem resides in taking for granted the axiom that education best takes place in school.

It has been apparent throughout this book that high on my list of values is society's obligation to provide children with opportunities to explore and master their environment and thereby to feel self-worth. That value is easy to state but, like all other statements of what is desirable, its statement does not contain the criteria by which one can judge whether the value is being realized in action. Moreover, the perceived consequences of actions derived from one value are found to conflict with those of the actions derived from other values. Because we do not live in a world of limitless resources and because the connections we make between values and actions are not a matter of an inexorable logic that says that this and only this action is consistent with a particular value, we are always in a situation of ambiguity and trade-offs. It is precisely in the face of inevitable trade-offs that the order of one's values becomes crucial. It is one thing to confront the necessity for compromise, and *in fact* to compromise, but it is quite another to do this in a way that has the effect of reordering one's values. So, when I say that at the top of my list is our obligation to provide children with opportunities that foster a sense of self-worth, I am aware that we live in a complicated world that is not and probably will not be organized around that value. But it is a world that accepts this obligation: witness the efforts made and the resources mustered to give life to that value and the sincere concern of many people with the failure of these efforts. That concern, however, extends beyond children to the fate of our society in a changing international order in which we are effect as well as cause. If education and schooling return to the societal agenda, it will not be because of academic controversy about what children are and need or because of dissatisfaction with the quality of schooling but because of a perceived threat to the world view that embraces our picture of what our society is or should be. Put another way, the perception of threat to traditional values will have forced education back to center stage. There are those who would prefer it otherwise but, ironically, it is the emphasis their values place on social continuity and stability that seem to be forcing them, albeit reluctantly, to do something about schooling. They come to the problem with established values about what the social order is and should be — and what schooling should accomplish in this regard — about these kinds of moral issues they have clarity. But they seem utterly devoid of any sensitivity to the fact that schooling raises moral issues that if skirted will defeat their purposes.

Those who oppose the movement to return to fundamentals come to the problem from the stance that society has an obligation to foster in children their need and desire to explore and master their environment and establish self-worth. That obligation, they argue, is paramount and ultimately in society's best interest. They are clear about the moral basis for schooling and indict society for honoring that basis in rhetoric but not in action. They accept the label "child centered" and vigorously oppose the tendency for schools to put children in a procrustean mold. Individuality, autonomy, self-actualization, differentiated growth, self-worth — these are the ends of schooling and it is immoral to downplay them by casting them in opposition to mastery of the basics. Our society is in trouble, they contend, for failing to take seriously the obligation to nurture the needs, desires, and capabilities of children—a failure both moral and material.

I have argued in this book that this failure at its root is neither moral nor material but rather conceptual—unreflective acceptance of the axiom that education best takes place in school. I have made it clear that I am not opposed to the basics or to the value placed on the nurturing of a child's need to explore and master their environment and establish self-worth. Indeed, I place an emphasis on subject matter far beyond that given by either of these opposing camps. To expect that one can even partially understand and master one's social and physical world without the assimilation of subject matter is nonsensical. To expect that such understanding and mastery can be achieved outside contexts in which subject matter has demonstrated salience and utility is an expectation that traditional schooling has unfortunately invalidated. The traditional view of where education should take place has defeated and will continue to defeat the goals of those in favor of the basics, as well as of those who emphasize society's moral obligation to children. If I have come to this conclusion it is because of the value I place on these goals and of my need to understand why schooling has always fallen so far short of the mark in achieving such goals. No less than a lot of other people, I long believed four things about schools: society is niggardly in support of schools; schools are changeable institutions; schools can be more interesting places than they are; and schooling can be a vehicle for social change. I have had to change my mind. I had to change my mind and conclude that money is a distracting issue; that schools are changeable within very narrow limits; that schools cannot be interesting places; and that whatever changes occur, for good or for bad, will derive from changes in the world view of the larger society.

These conclusions were not easy for me to accept, let alone write about, because of the hopelessness to which they can lead and the ammunition they provide for the two major camps of criticism discussed in Chapter 2. I could not accept hopelessness, and all the evidence seemed to me to make a mockery of the claims of the two camps of criticism. Was it possible that proposed cures sustained the disease? What were we all taking for granted that should be questioned? By asking these questions, I uncovered the axiom that education best takes place in classrooms in schools. What was wrong with that axiom? I had difficulty staying with that question because I could not see a practical alternative, i.e., was questioning the axiom a fruitless indulgence of fantasy or was it not an unnecessary provocation of dysphoria in a world seemingly organized for such provocations? But I was hoist by my own petard and finally was forced to conclude that the unquestioned status of this axiom was the root of the problem. What heretofore seemed unpractical now took on the features of a necessity.

We have learned to distinguish between education and schooling. A child's education begins long before he or she enters school, and after the individual enters school, informal education occurs in hallways, on playgrounds, at home, and around the neighborhood. The emphasis in recent years on the distinction between education and schooling derives almost exclusively from an obvious but overlooked point (especially in regard to ethnic and racial minorities): not only do children learn a great deal at a fast rate before they begin school and not only does that informal education continue during their schooling, but also children are far more curious, active, and eager to achieve mastery in these spheres than they are in classrooms. These out-of-school experiences are productive precisely because they are directed at understanding the nature of self, society, and the physical world. The differences between the behavior of children in formal and informal education settings are stark and to judge the former as superior to the latter is tantamount to denying the value of the need to explore, master, and establish self-worth. That is the position one takes when one unreflectively acts on the axiom that education best takes place in classrooms and schools.

Let me relate some experiences and observations that illustrate how long it can take for the obvious to be recognized or, if

recognized, how difficult it can be to discern the general implications of one's discovery. My first professional job was in a
state training school for mentally retarded individuals. I ad-
ministered psychological tests. It did not take me long to note
that there was, fairly frequently, a discrepancy between problem-solving behavior in and outside the testing situation. For
example, the Porteus Mazes, a paper-and-pencil test, requires
the person to start at a beginning point and draw a continuous
line to the exit; the mazes are graduated in difficulty. One of
the first individuals I tested with this instrument failed misera-
bly. A few days later, this individual, who had an IQ in the for-
ties, ran away from the institution (which was in the middle of
nowhere) and could not be located in a distant city for several
days. How could someone who had exhibited practically no
planning ability on the mazes manage to plan a successful run-
away? Another example: a young woman who obtained a low
IQ score. Her behavior in the testing situation was anxiously
cautious and I concluded on that and other bases that her potential level of performance was probably higher than her score
indicated. She was assigned to work in the hospital laboratory,
and a year later I wrote an article about her: the school's medical director considered this woman's level of performance a legitimate basis for her certification by the state as a laboratory
assistant. I could write a book about such cases, each of which
illustrates a dramatic discrepancy between problem-solving behavior in test and nontest situations.* Indeed, Ginzberg and
Bray's *The Uneducated* (1953) is a comprehensive analysis of
how low test-scoring individuals performed in the armed services during World War II. Their book not only describes discrepancies more dramatic than any I have reported, but contains descriptions and results of an army program in which over
a period of weeks many illiterate adults learned to read and
write to a level adequate to the requirements of army living and

---

*I regret that I have not written such a book, but elsewhere I have dis-
cussed the issues and some cases in some detail (Sarason, 1982; Sarason &
Doris, 1969).

performance. The appendix of that book contains the later reactions of these soldiers to this program, poignant in their ex-
pressiveness and in the contrast between their experience in
that program and when they had been in a regular school.

The significance of these examples resides in what they im-
ply about formal situations conducted by our rules for our purposes but either mystifying or uninteresting to the people we
put in them. These situations do not capitalize on what a person wants to know and learn, on what a person has come to feel
he or she needs to know. The example of the student who decided to run away says something both about motivation and
about the extent to which motivation sensitizes one to features
of the environment and serves to reorder facts in a new cognitive map. The summer research program for minority students
from a junior high school in the South Bronx is another case in
point. When people voluntarily engage in an activity in a prob-
lem-oriented context requiring the active assimilation of knowledge and skills—a process of assimilation and accommodation
involving the concrete and the abstract, the active and the reflective—we should not be surprised to observe excitement and
change.

We live in perilous times that pressure us to explain how
we got where we are and to come up with new approaches to
old problems; at the same time, a pervasive sense of crisis and
futility impoverishes our ability to articulate and reexamine
ideas that we have taken for granted. It becomes too easy to
conclude that we simply have to continue doing what we have
done except to do it better. But that conclusion is an empty,
verbal bromide because there is little or no agreement about
what better means for action or how to justify allocating limited
resources. And in regard to schooling, there is the additional
problem that we have competing diagnoses. Society scapegoats
the schools, school personnel scapegoat society, and both scapegoat groups whom they consider unable or unwilling to learn.

Earlier I mentioned Dewey's 1899 presidential address to
the American Psychological Association (Chapter 3; see also

Sarason, 1981). Here I wish to note certain features of that speech. The first has to do with his description of the modal classroom, a description that bespeaks his indignation about how the child's need and desire to explore and master his or her environment and establish self-worth are dulled or extinguished by educational "commanders." Schools should not be army camps into which come young recruits to be molded into automatons. It is to Dewey's eternal credit that he not only had a clear conception of what children are — a conception in every respect confirmed by research and observations in subsequent decades — but also recognized that conceptions cannot be kept apart from a moral basis, without which they would have no life. No one understood better than Dewey both the history and moral basis of science and the history of education and its problematic moral basis. And he well understood that custom and tradition, in education, as well as in science, at some point become barriers to a new morality that will cast conceptions in a new light:

> So long as custom reigns, as tradition prevails, so long as social values are determined by instinct and habit, there is no conscious question as to the method of their achievement, and hence no need of psychology. Social institutions work of their own inertia, they take the individual up into themselves and carry him along in their own sweep. The individual is dominated by the mass life of his group. Institutions and the customs attaching to them take care of society both as to its ideals and its methods. But when once the values come to consciousness, when once a Socrates insists upon the organic relation of a reflective life and morality, then the means, the machinery by which ethical ideals are projected and manifested, comes to consciousness also. Psychology must needs be born as soon as morality becomes reflective. (Dewey, 1963, p. 313)

More than anyone else in the past century, Dewey contributed to making morality reflective in regard to education. And if he became a towering figure in education, it was because so many people, in and outside of education, had *already* concluded that custom and tradition were no longer adequate for the problems at hand. He had articulated chords and discords about education and schooling that were congruent with what many people observed and felt.

Dewey did not question the axiom that education best takes place in classrooms and schools. He criticized the isolation of schools from their surrounding communities and his statement that school is not a preparation for life but life itself led him to suggest that isolation had to be diluted. Dewey was understandably an optimist in a nation that was optimistic, presumably boundless in opportunities and resources, and that viewed schools as the preeminent source of salvation for its citizens and its future. At that point in Dewey's long life, universal compulsory education was a recent achievement, testimony to the importance placed on schooling; yet what Dewey described still holds true. If it is understandable that Dewey did not question the axiom, it is less understandable that we do not do so today. We are far less of an optimistic nation. We still want to believe that education is society's best vehicle both for continuity and change. We are puzzled at the failure of schools as that kind of vehicle. We do not want to believe that schools are intractable to our social purposes. We sense that custom and tradition are no longer serving as an adequate basis for schooling but we are at sea about what new reflective morality we should consider.

My major theme in this book has been that at its root the problem of our schools is not moral, political, economic, or technical. Rather, the problem flows from the hold that custom and tradition have on our thinking, a hold that prevents us from recognizing that the axiom that education best takes place in schools may be invalid. That schools have performed certain functions for society and that some individuals have derived benefits from schooling are claims I do not deny. But I do deny that schools have ever been able to nurture the need and desire of children to explore and master their environment and establish self-worth. If such nurturing is not high on your list of priorities—if your moral justification for schooling powers other purposes—you will not feel the need to reexamine this axiom. But if such nurturing is high on your list, such a reexamination is in order because the evidence of the past century disconfirms the axiom.

I must repeat what I said earlier: to conclude that the axiom is invalid and that one must seriously pursue alternatives to it is but a necessary and liberating first step. This insight leads to a new universe of alternatives, in Dewey's words, "the means, the machinery by which ethical ideals are projected and manifested." I said earlier that the root of the problem is not moral, political, economic, or technical, but that is in no way to suggest that if you pursue alternatives, these features of social living will go away or be diluted in strength. Quite the opposite. If you pursue this insight, it will then become crystal clear why different groups, wittingly or unwittingly, have the stake they do in keeping schools as they are. I do not subscribe to any theory that explains schools in terms of a conspiracy by some groups and classes against other groups and classes. If such theories had validity, one would have a basis for hoping that someday the conspiracy will be unmasked, that there will be a redistribution of power, and that our schools will then be what we always have wanted them to be. I am very unimpressed with what has happened to schools in those societies in which a revolution has occurred. I am passing no judgment here on the justification for their social upheavals, but I think, their propaganda to the contrary notwithstanding, that their schools have all of the factorylike features of ours—and perhaps more because of a millennarian zeal that makes obedience and conformity to proclaimed goals desirable and necessary.

We have become so unhappy about the inadequacy of our schools and what that portends for the future that we look enviously at foreign countries whose schools seem comparatively tranquil and whose students do better on achievement tests than ours do. In fact, such envy is playing a role in today's concern about scientific illiteracy. Let us not make mindless comparisons between apples and oranges. Let us be concerned about the relationship between results, on the one hand, and the conception of what children are and the moral force that supports this view, on the other. From the standpoint of nurturing a child's need and desire to explore and master his or her environment and establish self-worth, the differences between our schools and those of foreign countries are minuscule and probably nil. One of the great psychologists of this century, Max Wertheimer, observed and reported on the teaching of math in a classroom (Wertheimer, 1945). He demonstrated to the children a solution different from the one they had been taught; they responded by saying that Wertheimer was wrong, i.e, the problem could be solved in only one way. That is the kind of response we should worry about and that is the kind of response I predict one would find in countries whose schools we envy. That prediction should not be taken to mean that if we act on alternatives to the axiom, the shackles on the minds of children will fall away and every child will start to manifest unprecedented creativity and flexibility. But that prediction does reflect my belief that if we were to begin to act on alternatives to the axiom, a larger percentage of children would become the kind of people they want to become and what we want them to become.

We did not get to the moon simply because we knew how to get there. If getting to the moon had depended only on extant theory, research, and technology, we could have gotten there earlier. It was long known what problems had to be worked out if that feat were to be accomplished with minimal danger to those involved. We got to the moon when we did because that abstraction we call "society" had come to see such a feat as congruent with its interests. What heretofore had been seen as either a fantasy or a luxury came to be seen as a realizable possibility, a societal necessity, and a practical affirmation of how science and technology could, would, and should transform our world. Theory and research about man and outer space have a very long history and until the post–World War II era that history was largely about what generations of individuals thought and did. It changed dramatically when international military and political considerations "forced" society to view the scientific and technological possibilities of outer space exploration. To explain why we got to outer space when we did without including the role of perceived threats to this country's military and political power and leadership is excusable only in those who come from outer space. Societal decisions or policies, like those made by individuals, are powered by diverse considerations and, in this particular instance, the sense of threat to our political and military status was such a consideration.

The inadequacies of our schools are seen as threats to societal stability and, as I pointed out earlier, neither the military, nor the political, nor the industrial, nor the professional community (e.g., educational, scientific, technological) is indifferent to this problem. These communities know that the quality of education provided our young is vital to their own interests. Unlike space exploration, however, the history of efforts to improve education through schooling leaves them bewildered about what to do. It is a history that provides no basis for the hope that what has already been tried should inform what we do now. What is so remarkable about the history of science is the fruitfulness of a morality that encourages and protects the ability. indeed the necessity, to stand ideas on their head, to entertain new visions, to enlarge the universe of alternative explanations. Yet even with that morality, it is a history replete with examples of rigid thinking rooted in custom and tradition.

Ideas, for good or for bad, have transformed the world but only after they have gained a currency that makes them seem consonant with the self-interests of that world. It is with that aim that I have written this book. We have had a surfeit of blueprints each based on the axiom that education best takes place in classrooms and schools. However well intentioned, such plans will not work. The consequences of the alternative way of thinking that I have proposed will not work in the scientific sense: achieving solutions to problems that, therefore, do not have to be solved again and again. In the social realm, such problem-solving does not occur. But it is not illusory to claim that taking alternatives seriously will have more desirable consequences for more segments of our society than we now derive from our schools. We did not get to the moon without making technical mistakes, losing lives, and making economic miscalculations on a vast scale. The blueprints were far from perfect, they underwent continual change, and they were preceded by blueprints concerned with problems and possibilities far more modest than putting a person on the moon. Alternatives to the axiom about schooling will run an analogous course.

BIBLIOGRAPHY

BUXTON, C. *Adolescents in Schools*. New Haven: Yale University Press, 1973.

CHERNISS, C. "New Settings in the University: Their Creation, Problems, and Early Development." Ph.D. dissertation, Yale University, 1972.

CLEARY, M. "Thomas Bulfinch, the Age of the Fable, and the Continuity of the Classics in American Education." Ph.D. dissertation, University of Massachusetts, 1982.

COLEMAN, J. S., HOFFER, T., AND KILGORE, S. *High School Achievement*. New York: Basic Books, 1982.

CONANT, J. B. *The Education of Teachers*. New York: McGraw-Hill, 1963.

CREMIN, L. *Transformation of the School*. New York: Knopf, 1961.

DAICHES, D., ed. *The Idea of a New University: An Experiment in Sussex*. Cambridge: MIT Press, 1964.

DEWEY, J. *The Quest for Certainty*. New York: Putnam, 1960 (paperback).

_____. "Psychology and Social Practice." In J. Dewey, *Philosophy, Psychology, and Social Practice*, ed. J. Ratner. New York: Capricorn, 1963 (paperback).

_____. *Interest and Effort in Education*. 1913. Reprint. Carbondale: Southern Illinois University Press, 1975.

DOLLARD, J. *Criteria for the Life History*. New Haven: Yale University Press, 1935.

FORD, B. "School of Education and Social Work." In D. Daiches, ed., *The Idea of a New University: An Experiment in Sussex*. Cambridge: MIT Press, 1964.

GINZBERG, E., AND BRAY, D. *The Uneducated*. New York: Columbia University Press, 1953.

JAMES, W. *Talks to Teachers on Psychology and to Students on Some of Life's Ideals*. New York: Holt, 1902.

KAMII, C., AND DEVRIES, R. D. *Physical Knowledge in Preschool Education: Implications of Piaget's Theory*. Englewood Cliffs: Prentice-Hall, 1978.

KIESLER, C. A. "Mental Hospitals and Alternative Care." *American Psychologist* 37 (1983) 349–360.

LANE H. *The Wild Boy of Aveyron*. Cambridge: Harvard University Press, 1976.

LONGO, P. "Program Evaluation: Project City Science Final Report." Queens College, Department of Education, 1979.

MASON, R. O., AND MITROFF, I. I. *Challenging Strategic Planning Assumptions*. New York: Wiley, 1981.

MITROFF, I. I. *The Subjective Side of Science: An Inquiry into the Psychology of the Apollo Moon Scientists*. New York: Elsevier, 1974.

PAULY, E. W. Manuscript, Institute for Social and Policy Studies, 1982, Yale University.

SARASON, E. K., AND SARASON, S. B. "Some observations on the Teaching of the New Math." In Yale Psycho-educational Clinic, *Collected Papers and Studies*, ed. S. B. Sarason and F. Kaplan. Boston: Massachusetts State Department of Mental Health, 1969.

SARASON, S. B. *Work, Aging, and Social Change: Professionals and the One Life–One Career Imperative*. New York: Free Press, 1977.

_____. "The Nature of Problem Solving in Social Action." *American Psychologist 33* (1978): 370–380.

_____. *Psychology Misdirected*. New York: Free Press, 1981.

_____. *The Culture of the School and the Problem of Change*. 2d ed. Boston: Allyn & Bacon, 1982.(a)

_____. *Psychology and Social Action*. New York: Praeger, 1982. (b)

SARASON, S. B., AND DORIS, J. *Psychological Problems in Mental Deficiency*. New York: Harper & Row, 1969. 4th ed.

_____. *Educational Handicap, Public Policy, and Social Change: A Broadened Perspective on Mental Retardation*. New York: Free Press, 1979.

SARASON, S. B., AND LORENTZ, E. *The Challenge of the Resource Exchange Network*. San Francisco: Jossey-Bass, 1979.

SUSSKIND, D. "Questioning and Curiosity in the Elementary School Classroom." Ph.D. dissertation, Yale University, 1969.

_____. "Encouraging Teachers to Encourage Children's Curiosity." *Journal of Clinical Child Psychology* (1979): 101–103.

WERTHEIMER, M. *Productive Thinking*. New York: Harper, 1945.

WOLF, T. *Alfred Binet*. Chicago: University of Chicago Press, 1973.